A DECADE OF SECTIONAL
CONTROVERSY

A Decade of

Sectional Controversy

1851–1861

By HENRY H. SIMMS

Associate Professor of History
Ohio State University

GREENWOOD PRESS, PUBLISHERS
WESTPORT, CONNECTICUT

Library of Congress Cataloging in Publication Data

Simms, Henry Harrison, 1896-
    A decade of sectional controversy, 1851-1861.

    Reprint of the ed. published by the University of
North Carolina Press, Chapel Hill.
    Bibliography: p.
    Includes index.
    1. United States--Politics and government--1849-
1861. 2. United States--History--Civil War, 1861-
1865--Causes. 3. Slavery in the United States--
Anti-slavery movements. I. Title.
E415.7.S6 1978   973.7'11   77-26208
ISBN 0-313-20061-0

Reprinted with the permission of University of North
Carolina Press

Reprinted in 1978 by Greenwood Press, Inc.
51 Riverside Avenue, Westport, CT 06880

Printed in the United States of America

To My Mother

Preface

FASCINATING and perplexing in its implications, even if tragic in its consequences, the decade prior to 1861 is one of undying interest to students of American history. Since it is the most controversial period in the history of the United States, it seems to the author that any adequate treatment of the era consists in the portrayal of the many and varied factors in the sectional pattern. The development of such a pattern does not preclude the possibility of emphasis upon some factors, but it does afford the reader an opportunity, which he might not otherwise have, to pass judgment upon the validity of the views emphasized.

In developing the theme of sectionalism, the author has devoted some attention to the social characteristics of both the slave and free states. If the South has received more attention than the North, the explanation is to be found in the fact that more controversy ensues in respect to the former than to the latter. Was the South as aristocratic in its political leadership as is generally supposed? To what extent was the section dependent economically upon the North? What was the economic status of the non-slaveholding whites? When did the South come generally to a defense of slavery and why? The above are pertinent questions in any portrayal of the Old South.

If it be granted that slavery was the main bone of contention between the sections during the fifties, there still remains the all-important question as to the factors that made that subject so controversial. The evidence seems convincing enough that slavery had run its course in the territories, yet its status there was hotly debated until secession was an accomplished fact. The controversy over the return of fugitive slaves was all out of proportion to the number that actually escaped. It seems that sound statesmanship might have found some solution for questions of such little practical significance. Instead, those questions, along with irritating incidents, became the means whereby the more radical groups secured control in both North and South. For many, exaggeration and violent abuse became the order of the day. The 350,000 slaveholders were represented as an aristocracy controlling the Federal Government, oppressing the non-slaveholders of the South and attempting to spread slavery over all the free states. On the other hand, the Republicans were termed abolitionists grasping for control of the Federal Government so that they might then use their power to exterminate slavery in the states where it existed. Psychological, political, constitutional, moral and economic factors were all involved in the spirited slavery controversy of this emotional decade. They were all intertwined to some extent, and it goes without saying that one cannot, with any degree of mathematical precision, estimate the influence of each. The bitter verbal assault originating with the abolitionists in the 1830's had led Southerners to reciprocate in similar vein, and that psychological factor became more intense as the sectional dispute was complicated to a greater extent by political, racial and economic forces. Despite the admitted complexity of the situation, the author feels that political factors more than any other produced that hostile feeling which resulted in the separation of the sections. Considerations of party advantage are strongly evident in the exaggerated utterances of party leaders, and in connection with Kansas difficulties, the Dred Scott decision and the fight over compromise in 1860–61.

In the preparation of this volume, original sources were used to a considerable extent. A popular touch has been supplied by the use of leading newspapers from all sections of the country. However, acknowledgment must be made to the numerous scholars who have written valuable monographs and articles on phases of sectional history. No study of the decade could be adequate without such works. The author is especially indebted to Professor Joseph C. Robert of Duke University and Professor Fletcher M. Green of the University of North Carolina for a careful reading of the manuscript, and for many valuable suggestions offered. However, for the conclusions and the defects in the book, the writer accepts full responsibility.

H. H. S.

Contents

A DECADE OF SECTIONAL
CONTROVERSY

I

The Old South

IN THAT vast stretch of territory, extending from the
Mason and Dixon line to the Rio Grande River, there
existed on the eve of the War Between the States a so
cial order which was characterized more by complexity
than by simplicity. The people in that area were largely
of Anglo-Saxon origin, and their economic interests
were predominantly agricultural. Life in the new frontier areas was more democratic, and more boisterous,
than in the older communities; and in the section as a
whole there was a complex social structure which included people of various economic hues and tints.

At the top of the pyramid in this structure were the
slaveholders. They numbered, in 1860, 384,884, and the
diversity in slaves owned ranged all the way from one
to, in a few cases, one thousand or more. Only 2,292
holders owned more than one hundred slaves, 43,990
had from twenty to less than one hundred, 61,710 had
ten to less than twenty, and approximately 200,000
ranged in ownership from two to nine. Slightly less than
one-fifth possessed only one slave.[1] It is apparent from

1. *Agriculture of the United States in 1860; Compiled from
the Original Returns of the Eighth Census* (Washington, 1864),
247. The classification as to ownership is as follows:

        77,333 had one slave
       110,023 had   2 and under   5
        90,556 had   5 and under   10
        61,710 had 10 and under   20
        35,623 had 20 and under   50
         8,367 had 50 and under 100
         2,292 had over 100
         Only one had over 1000.

these figures that a considerable majority of the people in the South was not directly interested in slavery; yet, with some exceptions, slaveholders were heads of families, and these dependents must be considered when one estimates the number directly connected with the "peculiar institution." Of course some who were not engaged in agriculture owned slaves, usually household servants, and this fact helps to explain the considerable number with only one slave.

The great diversity in slaveholding suggests a gradually widening gap between the large planter at the top and the small farmer with few slaves at the bottom. Two of the most significant distinctions were in respect to slave supervision and to personal labor. The large planters, much of whose time was occupied in political and intellectual pursuits and in social diversions, usually placed the control of their laborers in the hands of overseers, but the smaller planters and farmers not only supervised personally the work of their slaves, but frequently worked with them. The philosophical arguments of Harper, Dew and others to the effect that some must labor with their hands in order that others might have time to develop their superior intellectual powers, and that the existence of Negro slavery made the attainment of this goal more practicable than ever, seemed to give a substantial basis to the often repeated claim that labor in the South was considered degrading. This theory, however, was rejected by some and certainly did not correspond altogether to fact. David R. Hundley, a keen observer of social relations during Ante-Bellum days, declared that "No man can travel a day through any thickly-settled portion of the South, but he will come up with some sturdy yeoman and his sons working in company of their negroes; sometimes their own property, at other times hirelings whom they have employed by the month or year." Similar observations are recorded by other contemporary Southerners and by travellers.[2]

Socially, the merchants and professional men ranked somewhat lower than the large planters, but had much in common with planters of moderate means. Lower in the social scale than any of the above groups were the non-slaveholding farmers. Yet it should be emphasized that many in the latter group were not far inferior in the economic scale to the small slaveholding farmers, and lived similarly to them. According to the Census of 1860, more than 60 per cent of the farms in the United States ranged in size from twenty to one hundred acres, and the number listed in that category from the eleven states that were soon to secede was approximately 55 per cent. Slightly more than two-thirds of the farms in the Northwestern states of Ohio, Indiana, Illinois, Michigan and Wisconsin were in the above classification.

2. David R. Hundley, *Social Relations in our Southern States* (New York, 1860), 120–122, 193–197; Basil Hall, *Travels in North America in the Years 1827 and 1828*, 3 vols. (Edinburgh, 1829), vol. III, 279; Frederick L. Olmsted, *A Journey in the Back Country*, 2 vols. (New York, 1860), vol. I, 231, vol. II, 27, 60; also John S. Bassett, *Slavery in the State of North Carolina* (Baltimore, 1899), 8. See remarks of John C. Calhoun in *Appendix to the Congressional Globe*, 30 Cong., 1 sess., June 27, 1848, 872, and of Thomas H. Bayly, a member of the House of Representatives from Virginia, in *Ibid.*, May 16, 1848, 579. They both stated that whites worked in the fields with their own slaves, or those hired, that they were treated with equality and respect when they did, and that the only kind of labor to which whites seriously objected was menial tasks such as bootblacking and carriage-driving. Distinctions in respect to equality, they claimed, were not between rich and poor, but between black and white. For further light on Southern attitude toward labor, see Guion Griffis Johnson, *Ante-Bellum North Carolina* (Chapel Hill, 1937), 77–78.

There were in those eleven Southern states 306,273 slaveholders, but nearly 500,000 farms. When allowance is made, on the one hand, for duplication in farm ownership, and on the other for the fact that some slaveholders were not farmers, it is obvious that there were many small non-slaveholding farmers who lived comfortably at least, and in a fashion strikingly similar to that of large groups of farmers elsewhere.[3] Frank L. Owsley and Harriet C. Owsley, in a recent cross-section study of Alabama, based on unpublished Federal census reports and on county tax lists, have presented convincing evidence that landholdings were more widely distributed in the Old South than has been commonly supposed. They have shown that, due partly to the existence of large tracts of public land, it was not difficult to secure such property, and that non-slaveholders were securing it at a greater rate of increase, 1850 to 1860, than were slaveholders. Approximately 80 per cent of all agricultural families owned the farms they cultivated (except in the pine belt, where the number was 73 per cent). Of the non-slaveholding families, 75 per cent owned their land, four-fifths of them in tracts up to 200 acres, something less than one-fourth in tracts

3. For number of slaveholders see *Agriculture, Eighth Census,* 247. The following tables are based on *Ibid.,* 221.

					United States	North-western States	Southern States
Farms containing 3 acres and under 10					52,642	11,416	14,029
"	"	10	"	"	"	20	157,810	42,747	44,005
"	"	20	"	"	"	50	612,245	196,358	145,700
"	"	50	"	"	"	100	607,668	194,955	123,883
"	"	100	"	"	"	500	486,239	127,044	147,925
"	"	500	"	"	"	1000	20,289	1,876	15,069
"	"	1000	"	"	"	over	5,348	394	4,275

The groupings of Northwestern and Southern states, respectively, refer to those mentioned in the narrative.

from 200 to 1000 acres. These holdings were not confined to the least desirable sections of the South, but were frequently found in the most fertile areas.[4]

People may be poor without being "poor whites," at least in the sense in which that term is used in the South; and if the large class of sturdy, independent farmers described above is not included in that classification, it is evident that the "poor whites" constituted only a small minority of the Southern population. It is not difficult to describe the bottom rail of the white social order. It was composed of people ignorant and illiterate, who lived in filthy cabins, who often had as their only worldly possessions a pig and a cow, and depended upon hunting and fishing to work out their existence. The most depraved of them were called "clay-eaters," a term derived from their practice of appeasing the appetite by eating clay. Other terms applied to the whole group were "hill-billies" and "piney-woods trash," because many lived in the pine woods, or the remote mountains.[5]

The free Negro was a factor not to be overlooked in

4. Frank L. Owsley and Harriet C. Owsley, "The Economic Basis of Society in the Late Ante-Bellum South," in *Journal of Southern History*, vol. VI, No. 1, Feb., 1940 (University, Louisiana), 24–45. They point out that the largest single group of non-slaveholding farmers owned from fifty to one hundred acres, the largest single group of slaveholding farmers, from one hundred to two hundred acres. See also Frank L. Owsley, "Origins of the American Civil War," in *The Southern Review*, vol. V, No. 4, 1940 (University, Louisiana), 609–626.

5. Interesting descriptions of the "poor whites" may be found in William E. Dodd, *The Cotton Kingdom* (New Haven, Yale University Press, 1919), 94–95, and in Paul Buck's article, "The Poor Whites of the Ante-Bellum South," in *The American Historical Review*, vol. XXXI, No. 5 (New York, 1925), 41–55. See also J. E. Cairnes, *The Slave Power* (London and Cambridge, 1863), 358–376.

the social structure of the Old South. As the result of manumissions, which were more practicable before 1830 than after, and of such natural increase as took place, there were in all the slave states in 1860 251,000 free Negroes, something less than 60 per cent of whom were in Maryland and Virginia. Since the total free Negro population was only 487,970 in 1860, it will thus be seen that there were more of that class in the slave than in the free states.[6] Some of the Southern Negroes owned slaves, partly for the purpose of assuring relatives freedom and partly for economic reasons,[7] but on the whole the life of that group was very restricted both by law and by social practices. The restrictions may be explained in terms of the prevalence of race feeling and of the belief that the free Negro was a potential menace to the institution of slavery. An idea of the nature of the restrictions, as they existed in greater or lesser degree, may be obtained by reference to the legislation of three states. In Virginia attempts were made by law to guarantee to free blacks some fundamental property rights and the technical liberty they had; but their movements, as well as assembly for religious worship and for educational instruction were carefully regulated, especially after abolition agitation attracted considerable attention. In Mississippi, which had only 773 free Negroes in 1860, those of that status were considered slaves unless they could prove their freedom, and were considered vagrants unless they remained in the county in which they lived. With their life circum-

6. For figures see *Preliminary Report on the Eighth Census* (Washington, 1862), 5, 133.
7. Ulrich B. Phillips, *American Negro Slavery* (D. Appleton and Company, New York and London, 1929), 433–436.

scribed in still other ways, they were yet often treated kindly as individuals. In both Virginia and Mississippi there were laws before 1860 which made it possible for free Negroes to become slaves, and at least a few took advantage of the law in both states. In Arkansas a very severe anti-Negro law was passed in 1859, to take effect on January 1, 1860. All free blacks were required to leave the state under penalty of ultimately becoming slaves. County courts were to make provision for the aged and the infirm, since the act did not apply to them.[8]

There were approximately 700,000 slaves in the United States in 1790, when the institution was already on the way to extinction in the Northern states, 1,000,-000 when the foreign slave trade was legally forbidden in 1808, and, according to the Census of 1860, 3,953,760 in that year.[9] The codes establishing and maintaining the institution of slavery were very severe, generally more so after 1830 than before. Slaves had usually no standing in court, unless they were suing for freedom, travel and assemblage on their part were much restricted, and they might not be taught to read and write. The owner was given an unusual degree of control over them, but could not take their lives, and was

8. See John H. Russell, *The Free Negro in Virginia, 1619–1865* (Johns Hopkins University Studies in Historical and Political Science, vol. XXXI. The Johns Hopkins Press, Baltimore, 1913), 88–109, 143–145; Charles S. Sydnor, "The Free Negro in Mississippi before the Civil War," in *The American Historical Review,* vol. XXXII, 769–788; John C. Hurd, *The Law of Bondage and Freedom,* vol. II (New York, 1862), 174.

9. *Eighth Census, Preliminary Report,* 133. Under a system of gradual emancipation, slavery lingered on in some of the Northern states until well into the nineteenth century, but came to be confined, of course, to fifteen Southern and border states.

required to furnish them the necessities of life. In various states, his control was restricted in other ways.[10] It seemed necessary to have severe codes, so that they might be applied in case of insurrection, real or threatening, or in the event that abolition materials were being circulated. However, under normal conditions the codes were frequently not enforced. Slaves travelled in groups when they were not accompanied by whites, went individually from place to place without passes, were often taught to read, and frequently received some compensation when they were hired, though legal enactments forbade all such practices.[11]

One has to be careful in regard to generalizations concerning most aspects of slavery, and this caution is as necessary in viewing it as a labor system as it is in other respects. The dividing line between large planters and small planters, between small planters and farmers, is not easy to ascertain. As stated above, many slaveholders gave a great deal of personal supervision to their laborers, and frequently worked with them in the fields. The larger planters, however, because they were frequently absent from the plantation, or because they owned several plantations, usually assigned to the overseer the main functions of slave management and discipline. The overseers were a source of trouble for

10. Phillips, *op. cit.*, 492–502. Professor Phillips of course mentions other restrictions on slaves not included in the above narrative. See also Albert Bushnell Hart, *Slavery and Abolition* (New York and London, 1906), 109–110.

11. Ulrich B. Phillips, *Life and Labor in the Old South* (Boston, 1929), 161–165; Ralph B. Flanders, *Plantation Slavery in Georgia* (Chapel Hill, 1933), 201–203. Frederic Bancroft, *Slave-Trading in the Old South* (Baltimore, 1931), 162–163, writes, in regard to violations of laws forbidding slaves to receive pay when hired, that "Prosecutions for violations of the laws were so rare as to be almost curiosities."

several reasons. They usually belonged to a much lower social order than the planter for whom they worked, and they did not have the same motives as the planters for personal interest in the slaves. They were sometimes reckless and cruel toward those under their control.[12] John Taylor, the prominent Virginia planter and publicist, complained that overseers, when given a share of the crop, impoverished the soil for a few years to enrich themselves, and then secured a position on some other plantation.[13] As has been pointed out by a recent student of the old Southern system, the responsibilities of the overseers were considerable, yet they often showed many shortcomings, among them ignorance and cruelty.[14] James Barbour, Virginia political leader and planter, claimed that the reasons there were so many changes from place to place by those employees were because they were paid low salaries, and accorded harsh treatment by their employers. He had retained the same overseer for more than twenty years.[15]

The hiring of slaves was a common practice on the part of owners. Apart from the fact that such a practice widened the connections and probably the influence of the "peculiar institution," there are some particular points of interest connected with it. In some cases, at least, the hired slave had a greater measure of freedom than otherwise. He was frequently allowed to seek and choose his own master. In some cases it was permissible for him to provide himself with board and lodging by

12. J. C. Ballagh, *History of Slavery in Virginia* (Baltimore, 1902), 102, 104.
13. John Taylor, *The Arator* (Richmond), 57.
14. Flanders, *op. cit.*, 133–143.
15. James Barbour, "Address before the Agricultural Society of Albemarle," November, 1825, in *American Farmer*, vol. VI, 289–291.

means, of course, of money given him for that purpose. As has been stated before, he frequently received a bonus in the form of cash for his services.[16]

Food, clothing, shelter and medical service were absolute essentials to the maintenance of slaves. Their physical well-being was naturally a matter of deep concern to the owners; and, if one may judge from the careful works of recent scholars, the laborers lived in a reasonably comfortable way. Bread, meat, and molasses, often vegetables which frequently came from their own gardens, sometimes supplemented by game and fish, constituted the main elements in the slaves' diet.[17] Sydnor concludes that the "Raiment [of slaves] would probably compare favorably with that of the agricultural laborer of the same region in more recent times," [18] and Phillips concludes that, in regard to food, clothing and shelter, "crude comfort was the rule." [19] Numerous and varied were the means provided for the health of the slaves. Sometimes the master or the mistress administered the products of the medicine chest, at other times planters provided hospitals where medical attention was given; at others they employed a physician by the year, and in many cases employed him only at such times as the slave needed service.[20]

There was considerable diversity in the economic life

16. For an excellent account of slave hiring in tobacco factories, see Joseph C. Robert, *The Tobacco Kingdom* (Durham, North Carolina, 1938), 197–208. For a more general account, see Bancroft, *op. cit.*, 145–163.

17. Phillips, *American Negro Slavery*, 276–279, 296–297; Charles S. Sydnor, *Slavery in Mississippi* (New York and London, 1933), 30–39; Flanders, *op. cit.*, 156–159.

18. Sydnor, *op. cit.*, 30.

19. Phillips, *op. cit.*, 296.

20. Flanders, *op. cit.*, 163–171; Phillips, *op. cit.*, 256, 263, 289, 387; Sydnor, *op. cit.*, 45–53.

of the slaves on the plantations or farms. There were house slaves and field slaves. Butlers and carriage-drivers constituted a kind of "aristocracy" in this lowest social order. Included in it also were carpenters, blacksmiths, millers, seamstresses, tanners and shoe-makers, the latter of whom helped to supply a much needed article. A good illustration of the normal routine in regard to farm work may be found in the following information elicited by John Skinner, editor of the *American Farmer*, from a Virginia farmer, when Skinner was on a tour of that state in 1820:

"My negroes go forth about sun-rise in the morning. Those who plough seldom commence until the sun is an hour high; they breakfast about eight or nine o'clock; dine about one, when they rest their horses an hour or two, and all cease to labor at sunset; when they repair to their quarters, sup, after which some give themselves up to domestic indulgence and social pleasures, while others, the more industrious, give themselves to various employments for their own benefit." [21]

The matter of the physical treatment of slaves cannot be disposed of by any sweeping generalization. It is true that some fled from bondage, but the flight was not always a sure sign of bad treatment, any more than the seeming contentment of the great mass of blacks was a sure sign of good treatment. Laws were not an index as to treatment, because the institution was largely what men made it, not what laws made possible. The most usual form of punishment, though not the most severe, consisted of whipping. A student of this period of history has pointed out, however, that this type of discipline was necessary, if the system were to be maintained at all; and he has further suggested that

21. *American Farmer*, vol. II, 401–402.

whipping was not unusual, before 1860, as a means of punishment.[22] However, special privileges given slaves, not punishment, often achieved desired results. Rewards for good behavior consisted, among others, of gifts of money, special permission to leave the plantation and time off from work.

The observations of a number of travellers may throw some light on this phase of the subject. Travellers usually came with a prejudice against slavery; but the hospitable treatment generally accorded them in the South may have tempered their hostility. Harriet Martineau, a woman of prominence in England, wrote that she "saw endless manifestations of mercy, as well as of its opposite." The masters and mistresses were very thoughtful concerning the comforts of the slaves and in attempting to satisfy their "whims and fancies" by giving them money, and in patience toward them "They probably surpass the whole Christian world." But she was shocked at the complacency with which punishments were regarded, the oppressiveness of the laws upholding slavery, and a licentiousness so general that she concluded that "Some few examples of domestic fidelity may be found." [23] The Hon. Amelia M. Murray, another English woman, saw "kindness, patience and consideration" shown by men and women toward the slaves, and wrote also that she had "seen more of comfort, cheerfulness, contentment, and religious principle among negroes of the Southern States than among any other working population of the same amount,

22. Hart, *Slavery and Abolition*, 114. Whipping, he points out was still the normal method of punishment in the navy and the merchant marine, and was legally permissible as applied to apprentices and, in some communities, to wives.

23. Harriet Martineau, *Society in America*, vol. II (New York and London, 1837), 107–136.

either here, or in England." [24] Another British subject, James Stirling, was glad to leave the "despotism and desolation" of the South,[25] but Nehemiah Adams, a New England minister who went South to improve his health, had expected to find only those fearful aspects of the slave system he had heard described in the North, and instead found cheerfulness and contentment to a marked degree.[26]

Thus far slavery has been considered as a manorial system, but there was a commercial aspect to it that should not be overlooked. Reference is made, of course, to the buying and selling of slaves. Slave-trading was no new phenomenon, for both North and South had participated legally in the foreign slave trade for years before that trade was prohibited in 1808. But the expansion of the cotton area of the lower South during the nineteenth century, and a proportionally decreasing need of slaves in the upper part of the section led to a lively domestic trade from the northern tier of Southern states to those farther south. The trade was also in part intrastate in character. Bancroft, in his standard work on this subject, claims that estimates as to the extent of the trade were often exaggerated, but that it did involve annual transactions, 1850 to 1860, of something less than 80,000. In that figure, both interstate and intrastate sales are included. He estimates also that 60,000 slaves annually were hired during that decade.[27] The transfer of slaves from one area to an-

24. Hon. Amelia M. Murray, *Letters from the United States, Cuba and Canada,* vol. II (London, 1856), 25, 238.

25. James Stirling, *Letters from the Slave States* (London, 1857), 353.

26. Nehemiah Adams, *A Southside View of Slavery* (1854, First Edition), 7–19.

27. Bancroft, *Slave-Trading in the Old South,* 382–406.

other need not in itself have worked any hardship upon them; but the separation of families (if such entities could be said to exist among slaves), which did occur when economic pressure was sufficiently strong, gave rise to probably the most vulnerable point of practical criticism of the slavery regime. There were, however, some efforts made to prevent such separations.[28]

The Southern argument in defense of slavery, particularly that of a philosophical nature, did not become pronounced until after the rise of militant Northern abolitionists during the 1830's, though it is discernible to some extent after the fight over the admission of Missouri, 1819–1821.[29] It was held that the Negro lived a degraded and barbarous life in Africa, and that his condition was infinitely better in his new home than in his old one. In Africa he had been a heathen, but in the United States he was being trained in the precepts of Christianity. There were thousands of slaves who were members of Southern churches, often organized for worship with the whites, sometimes with separate organizations. It should be pointed out, however, that their religious exercises were carefully circumscribed, because such activities could present a good opportunity for insurrectionary schemes to develop. While the churches were emphasizing in the presence of the slave the idea of obedience of servants to masters, they did not hesi-

Wendell H. Stephenson, *Isaac Franklin, Slave Trader and Planter of the Old South* (University, Louisiana, 1938) is a significant contribution to the history of the domestic slave trade in the Southwest.

28. *Ibid.*, 197–221. Bancroft discusses both the motivation behind separations, and such efforts as were made to prevent them. See Adams, *op. cit.*, 79–81, on efforts to prevent separations.

29. The relationship between Southern defense and Northern attack will be discussed in a succeeding chapter.

tate to proclaim widely the responsibilities of masters to servants.[30]

The slave, it was said, was given food, clothing, shelter, medical service, and security in old age. The system lessened the possibility of clashes between capital and labor. Indeed, he was not as much a slave, the argument ran, as were many laborers in the free states, who were alleged not to receive the bare necessities of life. His condition was generally better than that of the free Negro (a point difficult to dispute), and it would be impossible for the two races, the one superior and the other inferior, to harmonize, if emancipation took place. In that case the Negro would feel that he was entitled to civil, political and social equality, and this the white would be unwilling to give him. Only the black could stand the heat of the Southern sun, and, if freed, he would cease to perform that labor which, under slavery, made possible products essential to both Northern and Southern prosperity.

On the philosophical side, it was claimed that slavery was sanctioned by the Bible, that it had strong and substantial historical antecedents and that it permitted those of superior intellectual attainments to develop

30. Albert H. Newman in his *History of the Baptist Churches in the United States* (New York, 1915), 449, 459, states that 200,000 of the 450,000 members of the Southern Baptist Church were colored when that church split in the 1840's. Paul H. Buck, *The Road to Reunion* (Boston, 1937), 64, states that the Southern Methodist Church had 207,776 colored members in 1860. For church tendencies in respect to slavery, see William S. Jenkins, *Pro-Slavery Thought in the Old South* (Chapel Hill, 1935), 207–218, and Sydnor, *op. cit.*, 55–61. A contemporary of the slave era, Bishop Holland McTyeire, throws some interesting light on Methodist Church work among the slaves. See Holland N. McTyeire, *A History of Methodism* (Nashville, 1884), especially 383–389, 584–590.

them, since they did not have to perform the drudgery and menial tasks for which the slaves were so well fitted. The presence of the black slave gave the white racial pride, and was the best guarantee of equality among the whites.[31]

Some phases of slavery defense, particularly those of a theoretical nature, were weak and strained; but viewed from a practical angle, there is much to be said for the defense. Slave labor was not only linked closely with the production of the Southern staples, but slaves were often the subject of wills, deeds of trust and mortgages. Even if some scheme of compensated emancipation could have come to fruition, those who owned the property would no doubt have had to bear a part of the burden in abolishing it. The racial factor was inseparably connected with slavery, and it was no idle talk to raise the question as to the possible relationship between the races, if emancipation came. Questions as to *how* to work out that relationship have been arising ever since emancipation. Professor Phillips, after years of study of Southern history, concluded that the main bond of unity in the South found expression in the resolve "That it shall be and remain a white man's country." [32] Jefferson, though anti-slavery in sentiment, never felt that the two races, with the Negroes free, could live peaceably side by side, and looked to colonization as

31. All phases of the pro-slavery argument may be found in George Fitzhugh, *Sociology for the South, or the Failure of Free Society* and *Cannibals All! or Slaves Without Masters* (Richmond, 1854 and 1857), and in *The Pro-Slavery Argument* by Chancellor Harper, Governor Hammond, Dr. Simms and Professor Dew (Charleston, 1853).

32. Ulrich B. Phillips, "The Central Theme of Southern History," in *American Historical Review*, vol. XXXIV (1929), 31. The whole theme is developed, 30–43.

the only safe means of escape from slavery.[33] William
Harper, pro-slavery in sentiment, could not conceive of
harmony after emancipation.[34] Frederick L. Olmsted,
during his travels in the South in the 1850's, found that
the non-slaveholding whites would be glad to see slavery go, but felt that it would be impossible for society
to survive with the Negro free. He heard such views
frequently, in one interior community so often that the
sentiment seemed to him "to be universal."[35] If slavery   _ South
went, said some, colonization must be the next step.[35]

Writing in 1861, J. D. B. De Bow, who had just re-
cently ceased to be a non-slaveholder himself, explained
in terms of both social and economic factors the attitude of the white without slaves toward the "peculiar
institution." As society existed, civil and political equality of the black did not constitute a threat, and all the
whites were equal; but, if freedom came, many of the
slaveholders could sell enough property to leave the section, and the non-slaveholders would have to remain to
confront the question of equality with the Negro. Economically, he contended, the merchant and the lawyer
depended upon the plantation for their prosperity, and
so did the man without slaves, since he generally raised
products not grown on plantations.[36] Southerners often
differed over matters of policy in respect to slavery, but
it appears that all classes were conscious of the grave

33. Matthew T. Mellon, *Early American Views on Negro
Slavery* (Boston, 1934), 105–109.

34. *Pro-Slavery Argument*, 88–90.

35. Frederick L. Olmsted, *A Journey in the Back Country,
in the Winter of 1853–54*, 2 vols. (New York and London, 1907,
first published in 1860), vol. I, 225–226, 267, 268, vol. II, 24,
also *A Journey in the Seaboard Slave States*, 2 vols. (New York
and London, 1907, originally 1856), vol. II, 218–219.

36. De Bow's *Review of the Southern and Western States*,
vol. XXX (New Orleans), 67–77.

problem in their midst. Some have explained the generally sympathetic attitude of the non-slaveholding white toward slavery on the ground that he hoped some day to be a planter himself, and that factor may be regarded, to some extent, as an influencing factor. Still others have found in the ideal of the simple agricultural life an explanation, no doubt valid to some extent, of such tendencies toward Southern unity as did exist.

The economic interests of the old South were, of course, predominantly agricultural. Cotton, sugar, rice, tobacco, hemp, and indigo to some extent, were the main staples. Beginning at the modest figure of 85,000,-000 pounds in 1810, the cotton crop doubled, or slightly more than doubled, every decade, with the exception of 1840–1850, until by 1860 it had reached a total of 2,-300,000,000 pounds.[37] This phenomenal expansion was made possible by the invention of the cotton gin, for with that instrument it was easy to extract the seed from the fiber of short staple cotton, and hence the product could be profitably raised in the upland areas. That staple was by far the biggest factor in the export trade of the United States; but the growth of the cotton factory system of the North, stimulated as it was by the commercial restrictions of the Jefferson and Madison era and by a protective tariff, was also a stimulant to the production of cotton. It is apparent that the trends mentioned were creating a greater degree of interdependence between the North and the South, but that, as a result of the tariff, they were also creating friction.

While Louisiana was the great sugar-raising state, some sugar was produced in seven other Southern states. The people of Louisiana refined nearly two and

37. Phillips, *American Negro Slavery*, 211.

one-half times as much in 1860 as in 1840.[38] The tobacco crop in the United States in 1849 was approximately 200,000,000 pounds, somewhat less than it had
been ten years before; but by 1859 it had reached the
much larger figure of 434,209,461 pounds. Maryland
and Virginia at the latter date were not raising as large
a proportion of the tobacco of the country as they had
twenty years before, and that fact may be understood
in terms of the expansion of the tobacco area westward.[39] It is interesting to note, that Maryland and Virginia, as was true of the remaining Southern states,
were experiencing noticeable economic changes between 1840 and 1860. Improvements were exemplified
in more diversified farming, in the use of better imple-
ments of husbandry, and in successful experimentation
with fertilizers. Edmund Ruffin and John Skinner were
prominent leaders in this agricultural reform movement.
Small farmers were on the increase, the economic influence of slavery was somewhat lessened, and as a result
those states were being drawn more strongly northward
than southward.[40] A student of economic phases of
United States history has suggested that the assumption
that the South confined itself to cotton raising and depended upon the section north of the Ohio River for
food supplies needs "much modification." [41] It is evident
that there was considerable trade between the South
and the Northwest, involving an exchange of the citrus
fruits, sugar, molasses and cotton of the one section for

38. Isaac Lippincott, *Internal Trade of the United States,
1700–1860* (St. Louis, 1916), 128.
39. Robert, *The Tobacco Kingdom,* 146–157.
40. Avery Craven, *Soil Exhaustion as a Factor in the History
of Virginia and Maryland, 1606–1860* (University of Illinois,
1926), 122, *et seq.*
41. Lippincott, *op. cit.,* 130–132.

the grain, pork, hay and horses of the other.[42] The
Southern states in 1860 were very deficient in wheat,
actually below the middle states in their production per
inhabitant and far surpassed by the Western ones. However, in the production of corn they far surpassed the
middle states, and compared with the Western section
in the ratio of two to three. The Southern group produced more hogs and cattle (other than milch cows)
for each inhabitant than did the Northwest. More than
80 per cent of the sweet potatoes of the country were
raised in the South, but the section was far behind in
the production of Irish potatoes.[43] In the production of
livestock and grain, there was undoubtedly much varia-
tion within the sections, especially in the South, and
that fact helps to explain the direction of the currents
of trade.

Railroad building in the South proceeded at a rapid
pace during the decade before 1860. If Missouri, Kentucky and Maryland be included with the states of the
secession, the increase was from slightly more than
2,000 miles in 1850 to 10,386 in 1860, while that for the
entire country was from 9,021 to 30,635 during the same

42. Henry C. Hubbart, *The Older Middle West, 1840–1880*
(New York and London, 1936), 74–87; E. M. Coulter, "Effects
of Secession upon the Commerce of the Mississippi Valley,"
Mississippi Valley Historical Review, vol. III (1916), 275–278.

43. *Eighth Census, Agriculture* (Introduction), 50–51, 63,
80–82, 117–118, 124–125. For each inhabitant, the eleven
states that seceded produced 3.50 bushels of wheat, 30.83
bushels of corn; the middle states 3.69 bushels of wheat, 9.04
bushels of corn; the Western states, 10 bushels of wheat, 45.27
bushels of corn. The Southern states produced 175 hogs to each
one hundred inhabitants, and 75 head of cattle to same; the
Western states produced 149 hogs to each one hundred inhabitants, and 45 head of cattle to same.

period.[44] The growth of the railway system Northwest to Northeast as well as in the South affected adversely the fortunes of New Orleans. It is true that her population was 168,175 in 1860 as compared with 102,193 in 1840, and that the value of her produce from the interior increased from $96,897,873 in 1850 to $185,211,-254 in 1860. This increase, however, was due largely to heavy cotton receipts, for much of the Northwestern trade, and some of the Southern, that once went by way of New Orleans, was now carried on by rail.[45]

The pre-war South did not make substantial progress in textile manufacturing, though there were indications during the decade or more before 1860 that the section was becoming more interested in that type of economic life. William Gregg, of South Carolina, and Daniel Pratt, of Alabama, were significant names in that period in connection with the manufacture of cotton goods. As a result of unusual success in securing subscriptions in Charleston, Gregg established, in 1848, the Graniteville factory, which even survived the war and around which there developed an interesting village life. He felt that factory building would not only improve the life of his own section, but would, by making the economic life of the North and South similar to a greater degree, tend to abate sectionalism. Pratt operated planing, flour and grist mills, an extensive cotton gin factory, and probably the leading cotton factory in Alabama between 1840 and 1850.[46] De Bow, the great Southern economist,

44. Slason Thompson, *A Short History of American Railways* (New York and London, 1925), 97, 119, 148.
45. Emory R. Johnson, T. W. Van Metre, G. G. Huebuer and D. S. Hauchett, *History of Domestic and Foreign Commerce of the United States,* vol. I (Washington, 1915), 240–247; Lippincott, *op. cit.,* 141–144.
46. Broadus Mitchell, *The Industrial Revolution in the South*

was an advocate of the use of slave labor in manufacturing. Writing in 1852, he expressed the opinion that
slavery would not expand into any existing territories,
or any that might be acquired, and that all the slaves
the South had could not long be profitably employed in
agriculture.[47] Congressman J. H. Lumpkin, of Georgia,
at the same time was urging the Southern people to
put aside their prejudices against manufacturing, since
its development, he contended, would increase consuming power, and hence aid agriculture. He claimed that
there were "upwards of one hundred cotton mills" in
the states of South Carolina, Alabama, Tennessee and
Georgia, and that they were "consuming annually more"
than a hundred thousand bales of cotton."[48]

Though other arguments, such as the checking of
emigration to the West, and a means of becoming independent of the North, were urged in behalf of manufactures, various factors tended to check their growth.
The agricultural philosophy of the section was not con-
sonant with such development. Fluid capital and skilled
labor were not abundant.[49] If slaves were widely used
in factories, such a practice might result in their elevation and freedom. In the face of these difficulties, the
output in value of Southern cotton mills increased from
one and one-half million dollars in 1840 to over four

(Baltimore, 1930), 67–70; Albert B. Moore, *History of Alabama
and Her People*, 3 vols. (Chicago and New York, 1927), vol. I,
406–409.
47. *De Bow's Review of the Southern and Western States*
(New Orleans), vol. V, 182–185.
48. *Ibid.*, vol. XII, 41–43.
49. It should be noted, however, that some Southern capital
which might have been invested in industrial enterprises was
used in the acquisition of Northern lands. See Paul W. Gates,
"Southern Investments in Northern Lands before the Civil
War," *Journal of Southern History*, vol. V, May, 1939, 155–185.

and a half million in 1860. The total value of goods manufactured in the section in 1840 was $34,000,000, and in 1860 nearly $100,000,000.[50] Iron manufacturing was prevalent to some extent in many parts of the South. It was that industry in Virginia, inseparably connected with the name of Joseph R. Anderson, which played a significant part in enabling the South, in the face of great difficulties, to fight a war for four years.[51] In connection with general industry, mention should be made of coal mining, especially in the states of Maryland, Missouri, Kentucky, Tennessee and Virginia. Slight progress in that industry had been made in Alabama.[52] Tobacco manufacture made noticeable strides from 1840 to 1860. The value of the capital invested in that enterprise in the United States, if cigars are excepted, almost tripled during the twenty-year period, while the value of the product increased from $5,819,-568 in 1840 to $21,820,535 in 1860. More than half of the product was turned out in Virginia, where Richmond factories alone, in 1860, produced goods worth $4,838,995.[53]

The large planter, with broad acres, numerous slaves, sufficient leisure to read and travel, and sufficient means

50. Philip G. Davidson, "Industrialism in the Ante-Bellum South," *South Atlantic Quarterly* (Durham, 1928), vol. XXVII, 405–425.

51. Kathleen Bruce, *Virginia Iron Manufacture in the Slave Era* (New York and London, 1931). See especially 179–230 and 273–324.

52. Emory Q. Hawk, *Economic History of the South* (New York, 1934), 304–307. According to Hawk, the coal mined during the five-year period, 1856–1860, was 8,500,000 tons.

53. Robert, *Tobacco Kingdom*, 164–165, 190. Dr. Robert points out that, grain milling enterprises excepted, tobacco factories "exceeded all other industries in capital investment, value of raw material, and value of product." (p. 170). The above statement has reference only to Virginia.

to entertain lavishly and to send his sons to college, was the social ideal of the Old South. That an undue proportion of the wealth of the section was in the hands of the small group of very large planters is undoubtedly true; yet, as facts presented earlier in this chapter suggest, the majority of the people were of the middle class, and they probably lived about as comfortably as others of that class in different sections. That small group exercised great political influence and power; yet a recent writer has suggested, with some degree of proof, that except possibly in the case of South Carolina the slaveholding aristocracy never controlled the politics of the cotton states.[54] Another writer has pointed out that many who were officially connected with the Confederate government during the Civil War came from very humble origins.[55] At least political democracy, as exemplified by removal of restrictions on the suffrage, the equalization of representation in large part in legislative bodies, and the exercise of a greater degree of popular control by voters, had been practically achieved in the South by 1860.[56]

The homes of planters or prosperous farmers ranged

54. Daniel M. Robison, "From Tillman to Long: Some Striking Leaders of the Rural South," *Journal of Southern History,* vol. III, August, 1937, 289–310, especially 289–291.

55. Burton J. Hendrick, *Statesmen of the Lost Cause* (New York, 1939), 9.

56. Fletcher M. Green, *Constitutional Development in the South Atantic States,* 1776–1860 (Chapel Hill, 1930). Professor Green treats the five states of Maryland, Virginia, North Carolina, South Carolina and Georgia. He shows that by conventions to revise the constitutions in Maryland and Virginia, and by amendments to constitutions in the other states in the 1850's, most of the remaining undemocratic features were removed except in South Carolina, 254–296. For conclusions as to nearly complete victory for political democracy, in the face of stiff opposition, see 297–304.

all the way from the colonnaded mansion to the double log house,[57] though the former symbolizes the ideal. Concerning the lighter side of life, it may be suggested that horse-racing and fox-hunting, at least in parts of the South, afforded amusement or entertainment to many. In the *American Farmer* one reads of a "Horse College" in a Virginia county, of eight blooded horses being sold near Petersburg, Virginia, for nearly $8,000 and of a pack of hounds that caught three grey foxes in one day and thirty-seven during a hunting season.[58] Critics of the Southerner often called him hot-tempered and too impatient of opposition and criticism. If he were, that tendency or trait was offset by his hospitality.[59] In the Southern environment, where population was sparse, and where there was no great diversity of interests, it was natural that the family should evolve as a strong social unit. The home was the chief center of all interest and all life, and parental and filial relations were mutually affectionate.[60] Philip A. Bruce's characterization of the social environment into which Robert E. Lee was born in 1807, while not altogether true of Lee, was applicable to many Southerners: "Season after season, year after year, they tilled the ground; raised thoroughbred horses; intermarried with the members of neighboring families—; attended the services

57. Francis P. Gaines, *The Southern Plantation* (New York, 1924), 168.

58. *American Farmer*, vol. X, 268, 398, vol. VIII, 206.

59. In Allan Nevins, *American Social History as Recorded by British Travellers* (New York, 1923), 133, see remarks to that effect by Charles Augustus Murray, a British traveller, and similar remarks by the Duke de La Rochefaucault Liancourt, a French traveller, in H. T. Tuckerman, *America and her Commentators* (New York, 1864), 95.

60. Arthur W. Calhoun, *Social History of the American Family*, vol. II (Cleveland, 1917), 330–331.

of their church; danced at the country balls; were present at the local races; shot partridges, wild turkeys and wild ducks in forest, field or stream; hunted the fox with packs of trained hounds; adored a pretty woman; played cards; and were not averse to a mint julep at any hour of the day." [61]

There are some interesting aspects of cultural life in the old South. It had more illiterate whites than any section of the country, but it had many men of unusual individual culture. Men like the gifted Joel R. Poinsett and Francis Walker Gilmer, the latter characterized by Thomas Jefferson as "the best educated" man in Virginia, were unusual in any age or society.[62] Wide reading was the habit of those who had time to read. Edmund Ruffin tells us in his diary that he read eight hours a day, and Hugh Blair Grigsby was another planter who read for the mere sake of reading.[63] Thomas S. Dabney's gifts to his wife-to-be during their periods of engagement consisted frequently of works of standard English authors.[64] There was more interest in the natural sciences than has been commonly supposed. That interest was reflected in the inclusion of such courses in the college curricula, in the formation of scientific associations, and in the reviews of scientific works in southern periodicals.[65] The classics were thus

61. Philip A. Bruce, *Life of Robert E. Lee* (Philadelphia, 1907), 13.

62. Richard B. Davis, *Francis Walker Gilmer: Life and Learning in Jefferson's Virginia* (Richmond, 1939), 90.

63. William and Mary College Quarterly (Williamsburg, Virginia), vol. XVII, 64.

64. Susan D. Smedes, *A Southern Planter* (New York, 1900), 32.

65. Thomas Cary Johnson, *Scientific Interests in the Old South* (New York and London, 1936) represents a full treatment of this subject.

not of all-absorbing interest. In literature the South was more of a consumer than a producer. When literature is mentioned one instantly thinks of William Gilmore Simms, Henry Timrod, Paul Hamilton Hayne and others, yet cannot visualize any such galaxy of names as might be quickly mentioned to exemplify Northern literary production. One writer has called the southern section "a fertile field for newspapers," but "a graveyard for magazines." [66] Many of the latter were launched, particularly in Charleston, but did not survive. Two periodicals that did come to have lasting fame were the *Southern Literary Messenger* and J. D. B. De Bow's *Review*.

In respect to education, the planter section was hampered in several ways. Many had the ideal of private education, and the feeling that the state should provide educational facilities only for those who could not provide them themselves. Slavery, aristocratic conceptions of society, sparseness of population and difficulties of travel were all barriers to public education. Yet before 1860 all the Southern states except South Carolina made constitutional provisions for education and provided permanent public-school funds, which represented at least a form of indirect taxation for school purposes. North Carolina made definite constitutional provisions for taxes to support schools, and South Carolina was the only Southern state which supported its public educational system solely by annual legislative appropriations.[67] The planter section had a larger number of

66. R. S. Cotterill, *The Old South* (Glendale, California, 1936), 299.
67. Edgar W. Knight, *Public Education in the South* (Boston and New York, 1922), 118–119, 156–157, 169, 188–189; Cotterill, *op. cit.*, 282–291. Cotterill concludes that the free schools of the South were inferior to those of the Northeast, but perhaps

colleges in proportion to white population than the remainder of the country, and, as Professor Dodd points out, a much larger number of college students, proportionately, than even the New England states.[68]

not to those of the Northwest. Edgar W. Knight, in *The Influence of Reconstruction on Education in the South* (New York, 1913), presents significant data to show that school conditions in the South compared favorably with those elsewhere in the United States except in most of the New England states. See pp. 94–100. An interesting account of education in the South, written in popular style, may be found in Charles W. Dabney, *Universal Education in the South*, vol. I (Chapel Hill, 1936).

68. Dodd, *The Cotton Kingdom*, 111–112.

II

The Development of the Slavery Controversy
to 1852

THERE were some indications during the last quarter of the eighteenth century that the institution of slavery might, within a reasonable time, become extinct in the American states. Prior to the American Revolution, some of the colonies, notably Virginia, had tried to restrict the foreign slave trade, but colonial laws of a restrictive character were disallowed by the British government. During the war with England and after, that trade declined; and since profit from the trade had constituted the principal Northern concern with slavery, its falling off meant the lessening of Northern interest in the whole institution.

At a time when the American colonies were fighting a war to free themselves from the control of England, and their leaders were giving sanction in the Declaration of Independence to certain "inalienable rights" to which men were said to be entitled, it was natural that voices should be raised against the institution of slavery. Among those voices Jefferson's was most prominent, though it should be pointed out that the great Virginia reformer was fully conscious of the social problem involved in emancipation, and predicted that great evils would follow that step, unless it was accompanied by colonization of the freed Negroes. Jefferson proposed in

1784 that slavery, after 1800, be prohibited in all the Western territories, and, though that proposal was not adopted by Congress, the prohibition was made effective for the Northwest in 1787.[1] During the Confederation period the states north of the Mason and Dixon line made provision for gradual emancipation, but that process was not completed in some of them until well into the nineteenth century. In the Northern states it was not difficult to yield to the anti-slavery trend of the Revolutionary period. The slaves were not numerous; climatic conditions were such that they seemed more of a burden to provide for than an essential element in economic life; and the paucity of numbers meant that emancipation presented no great problem of social adjustment.[2]

When the Constitution was made there were approximately 700,000 slaves in the United States, the large majority of them, it goes without saying, in the Southern states. Cotton production at that time was unimportant, but tobacco, rice and indigo were the great staple crops in the production of which slave labor seemed essential. Despite the considerable number of slaves, some of the members of the Constitutional Convention of 1787 saw in the signs of the times an early end to the institution.

1. It is significant to note that Jefferson in 1819–20 favored neither the proposed slavery restriction on Missouri nor the Missouri Compromise. Diffusion of slavery, he thought then, would make the problem easier to handle than congestion. For Jefferson's views see Matthew T. Mellon, *Early American Views on Negro Slavery* (Boston, 1934), 101–122.

2. Three works that deal in part with the eighteenth century trends in respect to slavery are Phillips, *American Negro Slavery*, B. B. Munford, *Virginia's Attitude Toward Slavery and Secession* (New York, 1909), and W. E. B. DuBois, *The Suppression of the African Slave-Trade to the United States of America, 1638–1870* (Boston, 1896).

It was not deemed wise, however, to give Congress control over slavery in the states; in fact had there been an attempt to do so no Union would have been formed. The Constitution recognized and protected slavery, directly or indirectly, in a number of ways. Georgia and South Carolina, in particular, objected to giving Congress unrestricted control over commerce, because such control might be exercised so as to prohibit entirely the foreign slave trade. The power over commerce in that respect was restricted by a provision to the effect that Congress might not prohibit for twenty years such persons as the states cared to import, but might tax them ten dollars per head in the meantime. In apportioning representation and in the laying of direct taxes, five slaves were counted as three. In case of insurrection or domestic violence, state authorities might call upon the Federal Government for aid, a clause which made it obligatory to aid should slave insurrections occur. Not only did slavery seem to be protected in the slave states, but it seemed to be guaranteed in case slaves went into free states. Without a dissenting vote, the states in the Constitutional Convention, all of which with the possible exception of Massachusetts had some slaves at the time the Constitution was made, placed the following clause in that instrument: "No person held to service or labor in one State, under the laws thereof, escaping into another, shall, in consequence of any law or regulation therein, be discharged from such service or labor; but shall be delivered up on claim of the party to whom such service or labor may be due."

The foreign slave trade was prohibited by Congress in 1808, but the prohibition was never entirely effective, and that phase of the slavery question never ceased entirely to be a matter of controversy. Under the act effective in 1808, importation of slaves was made punishable, after considerable debate, by a prison sentence, but in 1820 such action was branded as piracy and made punishable by death. A treaty negotiated with England in 1842, when Tyler was President, for co-operation between that country and the United States in suppressing the African slave trade was not very successful in practice; and, as pointed out elsewhere,[3] the question of the foreign slave trade became more controversial in the fifties than it had been at any time since its legal prohibition.

The application of Missouri for admission to statehood in 1819 brought on the most spirited sectional controversy over slavery that had yet arisen. Questions of the balance of power, of political advantage, of constitutional right and of the ethics of slavery all entered into the debate. Missouri, already a slave territory, if admitted without restriction, would have given the slave states a majority of two in the Senate, though they were already considerably surpassed in strength in the House by the free states. Northern opposition to the three-fifths ratio, manifest over a period of time, played its part in making the debate spirited. John Quincy Adams had declared that the ratio, by increasing Southern strength in the electoral college, had decided the election of 1800, and Timothy Pickering had denounced that constitutional provision as sufficiently unjust to afford "adequate ground to demand a separation of the sections."[4]

When Missouri applied for admission, James Tall-

3. See Chapter IX.
4. Henry H. Simms, *Life of John Taylor: The Story of a Brilliant Leader in the early Virginia State Rights School* (Richmond, 1932) 161; Henry Adams, *Documents Relating to New England Federalism, 1800–1815* (Boston, 1877), 343 *et seq.*

madge, of New York, in the House proposed as a condition of admission that Congress prohibit further introduction of slaves into Missouri, and that children born of slaves there be free at the age of twenty-five years. Northerners, such as Tallmadge and Timothy Fuller, of Massachusetts, in the House and Rufus King in the Senate, contended that, under the power to admit new states, Congress might impose conditions upon them, and further, that since slavery was incompatible with a republican form of government as guaranteed to the states by the Constitution, it was the duty of the legislative body to impose the restriction. They claimed that Congress, after the twenty-year restriction had passed, might not only forbid the foreign slave trade, but the importation of persons from state to state. Southerners, such as Philip P. Barbour, of Virginia, in the House and William Pinkney in the Senate, contended that a community entering the family of states had a right to come in on a basis of equality with the other states, and they claimed that, if the Northern argument as to what constituted a republican form of government were accepted, Congress would have power to emancipate the slaves in all the states. The slave trade clause of the Constitution, they claimed, applied only to the foreign slave trade. King, in denouncing the three-fifths ratio, contended that it was as logical to allow other property representation as to allow it to slave property.[5]

The Tallmadge Amendment was accepted by the House but not by the Senate, with the result that a

5. For the various arguments presented, see Edward King, *The Life and Correspondence of Rufus King, Comprising his Letters, Private and Official, his Public Documents and his Speeches* (6 Vols., New York, 1894), Vol. VI, 690–710; Simms, *Life of Taylor*, 162–163, 168–169; John W. Burgess, *The Middle Period* (New York, 1897), 61–95.

compromise was engineered under the terms of which Missouri was to be admitted without restriction, but in the remainder of the Louisiana Purchase territory north of 36° and 30′ slavery was to be forbidden. In the House the Southern vote on the compromise was thirty-eight to thirty-seven in favor, and in the Senate fourteen to eight in favor. The passage of the compromise measure meant that Missouri was authorized to form a government; but when that state or territory presented its constitution for formal acceptance by Congress, the lower House of that body refused admission to the state on the ground that its constitution contained a clause making it the duty of the legislature to prevent the entrance of free Negroes. A hot debate ensued during which some said that Missouri was already a state by virtue of the authorization to form a government, but others insisted that formal acceptance of the constitution was necessary for admission. Henry Clay suggested a second compromise which, as finally adopted, contained a pledge from the Missouri Legislature that the state would not enact any law which would interfere with the rights to which any citizen of a state was entitled under the Constitution of the United States.

The rise of the abolition movement was a very significant factor in the development of the slavery controversy. That movement prior to the 1830's was not sectional, but in mild form was making progress in the upper tier of slave states. The general and militant defense of slavery which became pronounced in the South by 1840 was not in evidence before 1830, though after the Missouri debates, during which many Southerners were apologetic for what they regarded as a grave problem, there was more of a tendency for them to resent criticism of their institutions and to defend them. One writer has stated that "anti-slavery feeling in Virginia reached its high tide in 1830," [6] though there was not much public discussion of slavery in that state until the great debate on that subject in the Legislature in 1831–32. Another writer, though giving evidence of an increasing pro-slavery sentiment in the 1820's, has stated that in North Carolina slavery before 1831 "seems to have been discussed in a sane way," [7] and still another student of the early anti-slavery movement has presented strong evidence of considerable mild abolition sentiment in Maryland, Kentucky, Virginia, North Carolina and Tennessee. [8]

There were varied factors contributing to the rise of the abolition movement in the North. There was a more diversified intellectual life there than in the South. The tendency toward critical inquiry was more pronounced in the free than in the slave states because the forces that bred conservatism in the South were not present in the North. Southerners often referred to these experimental tendencies as unhealthy "isms," but many Northerners regarded them as the essential prerequisite of progress. Reform movements were numerous, and of course gave added zeal and zest to the abolitionists who

6. Theodore M. Whitfield, *Slavery Agitation in Virginia,* 1829–1832 (Baltimore, 1930) 47, 58.

7. John S. Bassett, *Slavery in the State of North Carolina* (Baltimore, 1899), 7, 98 *et seq.*

8. Alice Adams, *The Neglected Period of Anti-Slavery in America, 1808–1831* (Boston and London, 1908). According to Adams (116–118), more than one hundred anti-slavery societies, approximately three-fourths of all in the United States, were in the slave states in 1827. Jenkins, *op. cit.,* 65–81, holds than the "positive good theory" of slavery was formulated in the twenties, and was accepted by many slaveholders. He, however, questioned "the weight of opinion in the South that had reached the advanced position" by 1829.

regarded themselves as the reformers *de luxe* of the age. Peace societies, woman's rights societies, temperance societies, religious societies for encouraging missionary work, the building of churches or the distributing of Bibles and societies for the abolition of imprisonment for debt comprise a partial list of organized groups at work. Many of the abolitionists, such as Lewis and Arthur Tappan and Gerrit Smith, gave their time and money to encourage some of these movements. In the intellectual realm the gifted Henry David Thoreau, philosopher-poet and essayist, Ralph Waldo Emerson and William E. Channing, the great exponent of Unitarianism, were all abolitionists.

Through such men as Charles Finney and Theodore Weld a religious impulse was imparted to the anti-slavery movement, particularly in the West; and through the action of the British Parliament in providing for gradual emancipation of slaves in the British possessions between 1833 and 1840 precedents weighed heavily in the scales in favor of the abolitionists. It is true that the British Government compensated the slaveholders to the extent of twenty million pounds; but that part of the precedent the abolitionists either criticized or ignored.[9]

Abolition literature was rapidly circulated in the 1830's. Some of the most important monthly abolition publications were the *Anti-Slavery Record, Human Rights, The Emancipator* and *The Slave's Friend.* The

9. An excellent account of the motivation for the abolition movement can be found in Gilbert H. Barnes, *The Anti-Slavery Impulse, 1830–1844* (New York and London, 1933). Intellectual and cultural characteristics of Northern society, which of course had their inception before 1850, are well treated in Arthur C. Cole, *The Irrepressible Conflict, 1850–1865* (New York, 1934), especially 205–242.

Quarterly Anti-Slavery Magazine and lesser periodicals added to the total. The year preceding May, 1836, the American Anti-Slavery Society was responsible for the circulation of 1,095,000 periodicals.[10] This figure does not include periodicals that emanated from numerous other sources.

The abolitionists usually demanded immediate, uncompensated emancipation, though not the immediate bestowal of all civil and political rights upon the Negro. Many prior to 1830 had favored colonization, but after that time they usually denounced such an idea. A Colonization Society had been formed in 1816 with Bushrod Washington as President, subsequently followed by Henry Clay in the same capacity. The Society drew its strength mainly from the middle states and from the northern tier of slave states, and its opposition mostly from the lower South and from New England. Its operations were hampered by several factors. Not only did the abolitionists oppose it because they alleged, among other things, that it was a device to lessen the dangers to slavery by disposing of the free Negro, but slaveholders, of the lower South particularly, discredited its work as much as possible. Even had there not been these factors, it is probable that the expense of colonizing all the Negroes in the United States would have been prohibitive.[11] Madison and others favored

10. See *Third Annual Report of the American Anti-Slavery Society; with the Speeches Delivered at the Meeting*, May 10, 1836 (New York), 35.

11. For a brief account of the Colonization Society, see Albert Bushnell Hart, *Slavery and Abolition, 1831–1841* (New York and London, 1906), 162–164, 237–238, 314–315. Hart points out that the Society spent $1,806,000, and transported to Africa 10,586 Negroes. He estimates that it would have cost $700,000,000 to remove the 4,000,000 Negroes to Africa, 314–

the plan of using the proceeds from the sale of public lands to colonize the Negroes on some of the vacant Western lands in the United States, but objections to that plan are obvious.

The content of abolition literature varied considerably. The attack upon slavery and the South was a medley of mildness, severity, reasonableness and unreasonableness. When the abolitionist contended that there was no problem, economic or social, involved in emancipation, he was unreasonable. When he contended that there was a natural right of liberty for the slave, he was maintaining a reasonable position, and, when he assailed the practical evils connected with the domestic slave trade, there is much to be said for his viewpoint. The abolitionist, however, represented Southern society as much more stratified than it was, and his erroneous representation, in some cases, of slavery as an extremely cruel system in practice and the master as a ruffian without character inevitably caused deep resentment. Theodore Weld, with all of his reputed gentleness and mildness, in his widely read book, *Slavery as It Is,* claimed that the slaveholders "frequently" branded slaves with "red-hot irons," put iron collars with prongs "around their necks," "cut off" their ears and "knocked out" their eyes.[12] The *Anti-Slavery Record,* which prior to May, 1836, had an annual circulation of 385,000,[13] the highest of any abolition publication, declared that the policy of the abolitionists, since 1830, had been to "denounce slaveholding as a sin in all circumstances,

315. The standard work on colonization is Early Lee Fox, *The American Colonization Society, 1817–1840* (Baltimore, 1919).

12. Theodore Dwight Weld, *Slavery as It Is: The Testimony of a Thousand Witnesses* (New York, 1839), 7–10.

13. *Report, op. cit.,* 35.

and to place the determined slaveholder on the list of felons, as worthy to be excluded from the society of honest men as the pickpocket, the counterfeiter, or highway robber. If slaveholders *are* guilty of a worse felony than highwaymen, it is very absurd to approach them smilingly, and reason the matter as if they were high-minded, honorable and honest men." [14] Garrison denounced the South as "one great Sodom," and stated that of the Negro population in the United States "forty-nine out of fifty have more or less white blood in their veins." [15]

The author cannot recount here the woes and insults which the abolitionists experienced in the North. Their presses were sometimes destroyed, they were assailed by mobs, and sometimes murdered, as happened in the case of Elijah Lovejoy, in Illinois. William E. Channing, an abolitionist himself, though sympathizing with those of like mind in their persecutions and in their aims, thought they they were too "vituperative," and that they were harming their own cause by assailing the "character" of slaveholders and by portraying them as "monsters of cruelty and crime." [16]

14. *Anti-Slavery Record,* Vol. II, 100–102.
15. The character of abolition literature is analyzed in some detail in an article by Henry H. Simms, "A Critical Analysis of Abolition Literature, 1830–1840," *Journal of Southern History,* Vol. VI (August, 1940), 368–382. For further analysis see Arthur Young Lloyd, *The Slavery Controversy, 1831–1860* (Chapel Hill, 1939), 49–101. Hart in *Slavery and Abolition* states that the Census of 1860 showed that about one seventh of the Negroes were mulattoes. He feels that the Census enumeration was incomplete, but calls attention to the fact that some of the mulattoes were children of mulattoes, 80.
16. *The Works of William E. Channing* (6 Vols., Boston, 1846), George Channing, Editor, Vol. II, 128–129, 132–133, 168–170.

The South was profoundly affected by the abolition activities. The growth of the cotton kingdom was no doubt a factor in the development of the Southern idea of slavery as a "positive good," but those with no material considerations at stake were apprehensive of the possible harmful results of the circulation of abolition literature in their midst. In 1829, David Walker, a free Negro in Boston, published a pamphlet known as the *Appeal,* in which he urged the slaves to rise and cut their masters' throats. The pamphlet was circulated in the South, and led directly to the passage of more repressive slave codes in Georgia and North Carolina.[17] Whether that publication did or did not have any connection with Nat Turner's Insurrection in 1831, it is not difficult to see why such a connection seemed logical. By the middle thirties anti-slavery societies had disappeared in the South (with the exception of one society in Kentucky), and freedom of discussion was curtailed to a greater extent than it had been before 1830.

Despite the urging of President Andrew Jackson that Congress forbid the sending of incendiary materials through the mails, and of Calhoun that Congress pass

17. Clement Eaton, "A Dangerous Pamphlet in the Old South," *Journal of Southern History,* Vol. II (1936), 323–334. It is sometimes said that Southerners did not read what the abolitionists claimed. Yet in 1851 the *Mobile Advertiser* bitterly condemned the Southern "fire-eating papers" for publishing "the vilest abolition speeches, reports and papers which contain the most bitter abuse of the masters." That paper stated that such a practice was both unlawful and dangerous to Southern society, and it quoted the *Tuscaloosa Monitor* and *Selma Reporter* as in agreement with its position. See *Advertiser,* Jan. 29, 1851. Some Southerners evidently felt that what was in a Southern newspaper was subject to more effective control than were abolition tracts indiscriminately circulated by those hostile to slavery.

a law which would protect the states in the alleged right to forbid the entrance of abolition literature, that body refused to interfere with the power of the Federal Government to transport the mails. In some of the Southern States in 1835 and 1836, notably Virginia and South Carolina, the governors were suggesting to the legislatures that they request Northern legislatures to suppress abolition societies.[18] Some such requests were made, but no affirmative action was taken.

Anti-slavery petitions caused spirited debate in Congress from 1835 until the House restriction on such petitions was removed in 1844. The petitions asked particularly for the abolition of slavery in the District of Columbia, but they included requests that the domestic slave trade be forbidden, that Arkansas not be admitted as a slave state nor Texas annexed to the United States, and that the fugitive slave law be repealed. In 1836 the House passed a rule which required the laying on the table, without consideration, all petitions touching the question of slavery. On the one hand it was alleged that Congress had exclusive control over the District of Columbia, and hence the power to prohibit slavery there; on the other, that Maryland and Virginia had ceded the land for the District, and that slavery should not be forbidden without their consent. What did the right of petition mean? Some seemed to think that such right was not satisfied until the House took some action on the prayer of the petition; others contended that, under

18. Hart, *Slavery and Abolition*, 236–237; Henry H. Simms, *Life of Robert M. T. Hunter* (Richmond, 1935), 34–35. Postmaster-General Amos Kendall had given a ruling in 1835 to the effect that postmasters might withhold abolition materials from delivery, but a law of Congress passed in 1836 held invalid such a ruling.

the power to make rules for its procedure, the House could treat petitions as it chose, but could not prevent them from being sent to that body.

After the passage of the "gag resolution" in 1836, the abolitionists, under the direction of a committee of three composed of Theodore Weld, Henry Stanton and John G. Whittier, launched, with considerable success, a popular campaign to secure petitions. In the 1840's, Weld played a leading part in aiding those who were attempting to remove the restrictions upon anti-slavery petitions. Notable among that group in Congress were John Quincy Adams, whose position, according to Barnes, was not always consistent on the right of petition as such, Joshua R. Giddings and Seth M. Gates. Henry A. Wise and Henry Pinckney were among the main opposing leaders from the South. The "gag rule" was finally rescinded in 1844.[19]

The controversy over abolition material in the mails and over petitions widened the abolition appeal, because the policy of the South led many in the North to say and feel that the former section was trying to curb freedom of speech and the right of petition. The South, however, felt that the abolitionists were attempting to intermeddle with a problem which was not theirs, and that they were using the halls of Congress to try to accomplish indirectly through agitation a goal they could not achieve directly.

The period from 1840 to 1850 was a decade during which national expansion reached its zenith. Unlike the period from 1850 to 1860, when the expansionist tend-

19. An excellent discussion of all phases of the controversy over petitions—the legal aspects, the strategy involved, and the popular petition campaign—can be found in Barnes, *The Anti-Slavery Impulse*, 109–145.

encies existed mostly in the South, it was an era in which the "manifest destiny" idea, North and South, seemed well on its way to realization. Our principal interest here with that territorial growth consists in its implications in connection with the slavery controversy. The Mexican province of Texas became independent in 1836 and after a period of nine years, during which the Van Buren Administration was apathetic toward annexation and the Tyler Administration aggressive in its behalf, became a part of the United States. As early as 1836 Benjamin Lundy made the charge, which he often repeated, that the war for Texan independence was waged for the purpose of establishing slavery there, and the annexation ultimately of Texas to the Union as a slave state. In 1836 Lundy established a paper in Philadelphia known as the *National Enquirer,* for the purpose of demonstrating the charge which he had made.[20] John Quincy Adams fully subscribed to the view expressed by Lundy; and, though Adams had once tried to acquire Texas himself, he held, in 1843, in a paper signed by him and twelve of his associates in the House of Representatives, that the Union was no longer binding upon the free states, if annexation were consummated.[21]

The desire for new slave territory undoubtedly had

20. *National Enquirer* (3 Vols., Philadelphia, 1836–1838), Vol. I, August 3, 17, 24, 31, 1836. In a pamphlet by Benjamin Lundy, *The War in Texas* (Philadelphia, 1836), he stated that it was clear "That the immediate cause and the leading object of this contest originated in a settled design, among the slave-holders of this country . . . to wrest the large and valuable territory of Texas from the Mexican Republic, in order to re-establish the system of slavery; to open a vast and profitable slave-market therein; and ultimately, to annex it to the United States." Page 3.

21. George P. Garrison, *Westward Extension, 1841–1850* (New York and London, 1906), 141.

something to do with the movement to annex Texas.
The fear that England might acquire a controlling economic interest there and bring about the abolition of
slavery accentuated the slavery factor in the situation.
But Lundy and Adams overstated their case. The expansionist impulse was strong; cheap and fertile lands
lured many Southwestward who were not slaveholders;
and the discipline or the feeling of party was such that
annexation seemed more of a party issue than a sectional issue. John Henderson, of Mississippi, was the
only Southern Whig senator who voted for Calhoun's
treaty for annexation, while only three Whig senators
from the South and two Whig members of the House
from that section favored the joint resolution to make
Texas a part of the Union.[22] In the light of subsequent
controversies over the Missouri Compromise line, it is
significant to note that that line was extended to the
state of Texas in the act of admission.

From the time of the admission of Texas as a state
into the Union, the most absorbing slavery question of
a controversial nature was that of the status of the "peculiar institution" in the territories of the United States.
The controversy with Great Britain over Oregon had
ended in the acquisition of most of that territory, and
the war with Mexico, concluded in 1848, had resulted
in the acquisition of California, New Mexico and Utah,
names which collectively signify a much greater extent
of territory than that included in the present-day states

22. The various factors in the Texas situation are well treated
in *ibid.*, 110–114, 117–118, 120–121, 152–153; Eugene C.
Barker, "Notes on the Colonization of Texas" and "The Influence
of Slavery on the Colonization of Texas," *Mississippi Valley
Historical Review*, Vol. X, No. 2, 1923, 141–152, and Vol. XI,
No. 1, 1925, 3–36, respectively: George P. Garrison, *Texas: A
Contest of Civilization* (Boston and New York, 1903).

of those names. In 1846, soon after the beginning of the
Mexican War, David Wilmot introduced in the House
of Representatives a proviso to the effect that slavery
should be forbidden in any territory that might be acquired as a result of the war. It is probable that Wilmot
had political reasons for introducing the measure. He
had supported the Polk Administration in all of its
measures, including the Walker Tariff, though he was
the only member of the House from Pennsylvania to
support the lower tariff. Having incurred the enmity
of a protectionist constituency by his action, he sought
to keep his political fences intact by associating himself
conspicuously with the anti-slavery forces.[23]

There were five suggested methods for the settlement
of the slavery question in the territories. One, complete
prohibition, has already been mentioned. The antithesis
of that principle was to permit slavery, with protection,
in the territories until such time as states were formed,
which would have the right to decide the matter for
themselves. It seemed logical, some suggested, to let the
people of a territory decide the matter during the territorial existence. Other possible methods were to leave
the status of slavery to the Supreme Court or to extend
the Missouri Compromise line through the territories.
The Southern members of Congress were strongly in
favor of the last solution, but the Northern members,
particularly in the House where they were able to pass
the Wilmot Proviso, opposed its extension. Armistead
Burt, of South Carolina, proposed, in 1847, that Oregon

---

23. Richard R. Stenberg, "The Motivation of the Wilmot
Proviso," *Mississippi Valley Historical Review*, Vol. XVIII,
March, 1932, 535–541. The origin of, and struggle over, the
Wilmot Proviso are treated at length in Charles B. Going, *David
Wilmot Free Soiler* (New York and London, 1924).

be organized as a free territory because it was north of the Missouri Compromise line, and, though his proposal was supported overwhelmingly by Southerners, the Northern view that Oregon should be free because such a principle was in accordance with the Northwest Ordinance finally prevailed.[24]

In the debate over slavery in the territories, Northerners contended that the power given Congress under the Constitution to make needful rules and regulations for the territories and other property belonging to the United States carried with it the power to exclude slavery. They stressed the three-fifths ratio and the incompatibility of free and slave labor in the same community as objections to slavery in the territories. Southerners held generally that, under the Constitution, each and every citizen had an equal right to take his property to the territories, and that Congress, in making needful rules could prepare the territories for admission to statehood, but might not deprive a person of his property there. It was claimed also that Southerners played a leading part in winning the war with Mexico, and hence should not be deprived of any economic or political advantages that might come as a result of the victory.[25]

What with free state legislatures passing resolutions endorsing the Wilmot Proviso and slave state legislatures protesting bitterly against it, and Congress convulsed by angry debates, it seemed that political parties would become sectionalized in the presidential campaign and election of 1848. However, political strategy

24. Jesse T. Carpenter, *The South as a Conscious Minority* (New York, 1930), 107.
25. A particularly good brief analysis of the Southern legal argument in regard to slavery in the territories may be found in Carpenter, *op. cit.*, 148–155.

made it otherwise. The Whigs chose Zachary Taylor, of Louisiana, who, though the possessor of several hundred slaves, was believed to have moderate views in regard to matters of policy concerning slavery. They did not adopt any platform when their convention met, though immediately after most of the delegates to the convention held a ratification meeting at Philadelphia and drew up meaningless resolutions. The Democrats nominated Lewis Cass, of Michigan, who was known to favor squatter sovereignty as a means of settling the slavery question in the territories. In their platform, however, the Democrats offered no specific suggestion as to the settlement of the territorial dispute. The Free-Soilers chose as their candidate Martin Van Buren. Two results of the election deserve comment. Parties not only did not become sectionalized, but each major party demonstrated that it was definitely a national organization. Cass carried eight free and seven slave states, and Taylor, seven free and eight slave states. Van Buren polled 300,000 popular votes, a figure in striking contrast to the 62,000 which James Birney, the Liberty party candidate, received in 1844. The difference was no doubt due to several facts. The Free-Soil platform contained planks on economic subjects, and that of the Liberty party did not. Those who placed the Wilmot Proviso above every other consideration found refuge with the Free-Soilers, and Van Buren no doubt received some personal support from his Democratic friends.

During the brief time that Taylor was President, the territorial status of slavery was not the only controversial matter pertaining to that institution. For years the questions of slavery and the slave trade in the District of Columbia had been debated, but no final action had been taken concerning them. Texas and New Mexico were engaged in a boundary dispute, the former of course a slave state and the latter an unorganized territory where the status of slavery was as yet undecided. The controversy over fugitive slaves was in large part the product of two factors. One was the underground railroad, a system by means of which the escape of slaves from their masters was facilitated. The other was the decision of the Supreme Court of the United States in the case of Prigg vs. Pennsylvania. Under a Pennsylvania state law Prigg had been arrested for forcibly taking a slave from the state. The Supreme Court declared the Pennsylvania act unconstitutional on the ground that under the Constitution and Federal law pursuant thereto a slave might be recovered. It held, however, that states need not render assistance in returning slaves, though under the law of 1793 there was provision for such assistance.

Clay and Douglas [26] were responsible for the form which the compromise measures assumed. In their final form they provided that California be admitted as a free state; that New Mexico and Utah be organized as territories without restriction as to slavery, but to be admitted as states with or without slavery as their constitutions might provide at the time of admission and that during the territorial condition the Supreme Court might adjust disputes that arose over slavery; that the debt of Texas be assumed in return for her surrender of the territory in dispute with New Mexico; that the slave trade be abolished in the District of Columbia; that the

26. Frank H. Hodder, "The Authorship of the Compromise of 1850," *Mississippi Valley Historical Review*, Vol. XXII, March, 1936, 525–536, holds that Douglas not only had much to do with framing the compromise measures, but in pushing them to final passage.

return of fugitive slaves should be effected by Federal authority, and that citizens, if necessary, should aid in their rendition.

Most of these measures were originally in one bill, but as finally passed were separate measures. Zachary Taylor was not a friend of the "omnibus bill." He had encouraged the people of California, who had had no form of territorial government, to draw up a state constitution and apply for admission to the Union, and he desired that the inhabitants of New Mexico do the same thing. He did not favor delay so as to secure a balance in regard to sectional advantage in the settlement of a number of controversies. Some of the Southerners were particularly incensed at the effort to bring California in as a free state. If the effort succeeded, they knew that all chance would be gone to use its territorial organization as a factor in driving bargains on other points, and they realized, too, that the sectional balance in the Senate would be gone. The point, however, which they emphasized was that California had been organized as a state in a revolutionary manner. The President, they alleged, invited its people to call a convention, and paid the expenses of its members out of the United States Treasury without authority; and the convention admitted members not elected and extended its authority over comparatively vacant territory. Ten Southern senators entered a protest to the Senate the day after the California bill was passed.[27]

Of the three most prominent men in public life in 1850, one, Calhoun, opposed the Compromise, and two, Clay and Webster, favored it. Early in 1849, Calhoun, as spokesman for a caucus of Southern members of Congress, had prepared an "Address" to the Southern peo-

27. Simms, *Life of Hunter*, 64–65, 67–68.

ple, in which he bitterly criticized abolition propaganda, the attempts to deprive the South of equality in the territories, and the violation of the fugitive slave clause of the Constitution. That clause, it was emphasized, was placed in the Constitution without the dissenting vote of any state. Instead of rendering up slaves, as the Constitution demanded, Northern people were aiding them to escape, which action, it was charged, represented a double infraction of the fundamental law of the land. The Southern Whigs were generally hostile to the "Address," and only a total of forty-eight members of Congress signed it.[28] Calhoun's speech on the Compromise, which was his last and which he was too weak to deliver himself, was similar in tone to the "Address." He stressed the fact that slavery had been excluded from three-fourths of the territory of the Union, and emphasized his belief that the South, as a minority section, must insist upon her "rights" in the Union. Webster felt that economic laws made it impossible for slavery to exist in the new territories, so he felt that the free states could gain their objective without giving the South the "taunt" of a Wilmot Proviso. He upheld the fugitive slave law on the ground that the South was entitled, under the Constitution, to the return of fugitive slaves, and he expressed the opinion that peaceable secession was an impossibility. Webster's arguments were strikingly similar to those of Clay. The Kentuckian, too, had deplored disunion, and had emphasized his conviction that the laws of nature had settled the question of slavery in the territories.

28. *Ibid.*, 61–62; William M. Meigs, *Life of John C. Calhoun* (2 Vols., New York, 1917), Vol. II, 426–432; Arthur C. Cole, *The Whig Party in the South* (Washington, 1913), 138–140; Elizabeth Merritt, *James Henry Hammond, 1807–1864* (Baltimore, 1923), 92.

Chase and Seward both condemned the Compromise. Seward denounced the fugitive slave law as "unjust, unconstitutional and immoral." In reference to the fugitive slave provision of the Constitution, he declared that "The Constitution contains only a compact, which rests for its execution on the states." The New York Senator claimed that the Constitution did not recognize slaves as property, and that there was a constitutional right to prohibit slavery in the territories, but added that "There is a higher law than the Constitution, which regulates our authority over the domain, and devotes it to the same noble purposes. The territory is a part, no inconsiderable part, of the common heritage of mankind, bestowed upon them by the Creator of the universe. We are his stewards, and must so discharge our trust as to secure in the highest attainable degree their happiness." [29]

Though strong and generally successful efforts were made both North and South to get public opinion to accept the Compromise, serious obstacles had to be overcome in both sections. In the North the fugitive slave law was the main barrier to acceptance. Giddings in the House declared that sending slaves back would be "murder," because they would perish in five years on sugar plantations, and in seven on cotton plantations. Chase wished to leave the whole matter of returning slaves to the states, and declared that the Prigg decision "practically expunged the fugitive servant clause from the Constitution." In this general debate during the session of 1850–51, some interesting viewpoints were expressed concerning the fugitive slave law. John McClernand, of Illinois, held the underground

29. George E. Baker, *The Works of William H. Seward* (5 Vols., Boston and New York, 1887), Vol. I, 64–67, 71–75.

railroad responsible for the law, said that the Constitution would not have been adopted without the fugitive slave provision in it, and that Giddings should have criticized the Constitution, not the law. Rhett claimed that the federal law was unconstitutional, and that it devolved upon the states either to return slaves or pay for them. Clay contended that the Federal Government, under the "necessary and proper" clause could carry into effect all powers where there was no specification as to how they were to be made effective. Davis was not willing to use force in Massachusetts to enforce the law, because such would infringe the sovereignty of the state and the known will of the state. Other states, however, might pass judgment on the conduct of Massachusetts and determine whether the bonds of Union still remained.[30]

In 1851, a slave named Shadrach was rescued by a mob of Negroes in Boston, and one named Jerry by a mob in Syracuse. In the face of these alarming developments Fillmore did take steps to enforce the law.[31] What should be emphasized, however, is the predominant sentiment in the North for the Compromise. Democrats such as Douglas and Cass and Whigs such as Clay and Webster, by lending their best efforts to create a public sentiment favorable to the settlement of 1850, offset to a considerable extent the opposition of Seward, Chase, Giddings, and others. "Union meetings" to endorse the

30. All of these remarks are in *Globe*, and *Appendix to Globe*, 31 Cong., 2 Sess.: Giddings' remarks, Dec. 9, 1850, 14–15; Chase's, *Appendix*, Feb. 22, 1851, 309; McClernand's, *Globe*, Dec. 9, 1850, 16; Rhett's, *Appendix*, Feb. 24, 1851, 317–319; Clay's, *Appendix*, Feb. 24, 1851, 320–321; Davis', *Globe*, Feb. 18, 1851.
31. Theodore C. Smith, *Parties and Slavery, 1850–1859* (New York and London, 1906), 23–24.

Compromise were held in many of the cities of the
North, meetings which were said by a prominent Southern journal to be taking "truly national grounds" on the
subject of slavery.[32]
There was a rather vociferous minority of extremists
in the South, who, alleging the admission of California
as one of their main grievances, threatened the acceptance of the Compromise in that section. The failure
of the Nashville Convention in 1850, however, suggested acquiescence in the settlement as the general
sentiment of the South. After meeting in June and ad-
journing, the Convention came together again in November with greatly reduced membership, and con-
tented itself in denouncing the Compromise measures,
asserting the right of secession, and recommending that
the South cut off commercial relations with the North.
Had South Carolina seceded, the strong conservative
sentiment in the South in the early fifties might have
found itself put to a severe test. The question in that
state was whether to secede alone or wait for the co-
operation of the other states. Robert B. Rhett favored
secession. Langdon Cheves and R. W. Barnwell favored
co-operation. In the ensuing test of strength the co-
operationists won.[33] The *Savannah Republican* declared
that, even if South Carolina had an abstract right to
secede, she had no moral right to do so and expose the
other states to civil war without consulting them. The
Southern Advocate called the anti-Compromise meetings "Rhettite failures." [34]

32. *Mobile Advertiser,* Jan. 8, 1851.
33. Laura A. White, *Robert Barnwell Rhett: Father of Secession* (New York and London, 1931), 103 *et seq.*
34. *Savannah Republican,* May 23, 1851; *Southern* (Huntsville, Ala.) *Advocate,* Feb. 5, 1851.

In Mississippi the Compromise forces, headed by
Henry S. Foote, won in a state election over their opponents, championed by John A. Quitman and Jefferson Davis, and in Georgia a state convention endorsed
the Compromise, but warned of secession in case it was
violated. The action of Georgia was a potent obstacle
to secession on the part of South Carolina.[35] In Virginia
there was considerable anti-Compromise sentiment.
Hunter had been particularly hostile to the admission
of California, and Henry A. Wise criticized the Compromise and claimed that Virginia was "sold out" to it
by Thomas Ritchie, powerful and influential editor of
the *Richmond Enquirer*, because he wanted his public
printing contract renewed. However, the Virginia Legislature overwhelmingly endorsed the measures of
1850.[36]

The presidential election of 1852 represented a climax
to the efforts to keep the Compromise of 1850 a finality.
The Democrats, putting aside such possibilities as Cass,
Douglas and Marcy, chose Franklin Pierce of New
Hampshire as their candidate, and adopted a platform
strongly endorsing the slavery measures of 1850. Pierce
had written a letter giving his unequivocal endorsement
to the measures, and that letter had been used to good
advantage in the convention in securing him the nomination. William R. King, of Alabama, was chosen as his
running mate.

The three possible Whig choices were Webster, Fillmore, and Winfield Scott. The latter had most of his
support in the North; Fillmore was the first choice of

35. J. F. H. Claiborne, *Life and Correspondence of John A.
Quitman* (2 vols., New York, 1860), Vol. II, 115, 146–148;
Richard H. Shryock, *Georgia and the Union in 1850* (Durham,
1926), 300–355.

36. Simms, *Life of Hunter*, 68–70.

the Southern Whigs and Webster the second.[37] Scott received the nomination, but a platform was adopted which at least represented the possibility of holding the Southern strength of the party, because it endorsed the Compromise. William A. Graham, of North Carolina, was chosen for Vice-President. The Free Democrats, as the Free-Soilers now called themselves, chose John P. Hale for President and George W. Julian for Vice-President.

The election resulted in a decisive victory for Pierce, though his popular majority over Scott was not as impressive as his majority in the electoral college. Pierce had 254 electoral votes and Scott 42, which he received from the states of Massachusetts, Vermont, Kentucky and Tennessee. The popular vote was Pierce, 1,601,474, Scott, 1,386,580 and Hale, 156,667.[38] Undoubtedly some of the Webster Whigs refused to support Scott, for Webster himself, as one of the last acts of his life, advised his friends to support Pierce. Because of Scott's close relations with Seward, the Southern Whigs feared that he had free-soil tendencies, and hence many refused to support him.[39] These factors help to explain the defeat of the Whig candidate.

37. Cole, *Whig Party in the South*, 223–224, 232, 257.
38. Edward Stanwood, *A History of the Presidency from 1788 to 1897* (Boston and New York, 1928), 257.
39. Cole, *The Whig Party in the South*, 259–263.

III

The Repeal of the Missouri Compromise

THE settlements embraced in the Compromise of 1850
and the results of the presidential election of 1852,
which seemed to place the stamp of finality upon the
Compromise, gave the country for a brief period a
greater degree of calm than it had experienced for some
years. However, there were some factors which still
kept sectional feeling alive. *Uncle Tom's Cabin,* resistance in parts of the North to the Fugitive Slave Law of
1850, proposals for the annexation of Cuba and for the
granting of free homesteads in the public land domain,
all provoked controversy.[1] But the most controversial of
all sectional issues, that of the status of slavery in the
territories, seemed to have been settled, until it was revived by the introduction of the Kansas-Nebraska Act
in 1854.

The name of Stephen A. Douglas is inseparably connected with that Act, though other political leaders fig-
ured in the developments that led to the bill in its final
form. One of those leaders was David R. Atchison of
Missouri. During the session of Congress of 1852–53,
he had voted to organize Nebraska territory with slavery forbidden, but only because he felt that the Missouri
restriction could never be repealed. However, he re-

1. All of these factors are discussed elsewhere in some detail.

58

versed his position when he engaged in a contest for the senatorship with Thomas H. Benton in 1853. Benton held that, under existing laws, whites could and should take up land in Nebraska, and pledged himself to vote to organize the territory when the next session of Congress convened. In order to counteract the expansion appeal thus made by Benton to the prospective Nebraska settlers in Missouri, Atchison appealed to the slaveholders by expressing himself in favor of repeal of the Missouri restriction, and by pledging himself not to vote for the territorial bill unless the restriction was removed. Douglas and Atchison were close friends, and no doubt the latter urged Douglas to action, especially since the Missouri Legislature, which chose the senator, would not be elected until the summer of 1854.[2] When Douglas first framed his measure, it did not expressly call for the repeal of the Missouri Compromise, but did, after it was known to him that Archibald Dixon, a Whig Senator from Kentucky, would offer an amendment for repeal.

Since "charges of free soil sympathy and prejudice" were being made against President Pierce, there was doubt as to whether he would sign the measure proposed by the Illinois Senator. Pierce did believe that the law of 1820 was unconstitutional, but, instead of outright repeal, he preferred a measure which would guarantee "rights of persons and property" in accordance with the Constitution, and would leave it to the Supreme Court to decide what those rights were. However, the Southerners who heard his proposal would accept nothing short of repeal. When Douglas, on a Sunday in January, 1854, interviewed Pierce, he was

2. P. Orman Ray, *The Repeal of the Missouri Compromise* (Cleveland, 1909), 102–106, 109–141, 200–234.

accompanied by Jefferson Davis, Secretary of War, David Atchison, James Mason, and Robert M. T. Hunter, Senators, and John C. Breckinridge and Philip Phillips, members of the House of Representatives. This group succeeded in getting the President to agree to sign the measure,[3] which in its final form expressly repealed the Missouri Compromise, left it to the people of the territories to determine the nature of their domestic institutions, "subject only to the Constitution of the United States," but provided that, in all cases involving the title to slave property or the question of personal freedom, there might be an appeal to the territorial courts and ultimately to the Supreme Court of the United States. The bill made provision for two territories instead of one.

In the controversy in Congress over the Kansas-Nebraska Act, much time was devoted to its relation to, or alleged relation to, the territorial settlements in the Compromise of 1850, and to the early policy of the country. "The Appeal of the Independent Democrats," issued January 19, 1854, and signed by Senators Chase, Sumner, and others, after denouncing the measure as "a violation of a sacred pledge," and "a criminal betrayal of precious rights," contended that the Compromise of 1850, instead of virtually repealing the Missouri Compromise, expressly affirmed it, in the clause which declared that nothing in the provision for the settlement of the Texas boundary should be construed to impair the annexation resolution, under which slavery was forbidden north of 36° 30′. The "Appeal" further declared that "The original settled policy of the

3. Roy F. Nichols, *Franklin Pierce: Young Hickory of the Granite Hills* (Philadelphia, 1931), 319–324. Also Henry H. Simms, *Life of Robert M. T. Hunter*, 81.

United States, clearly indicated by the Jefferson proviso of 1784, and by the Ordinance of 1787, was non-extension of slavery." It concluded with the claim that the "dearest interests" of the people were "made mere hazards of a presidential game." [4] The Kansas-Nebraska Act had declared that the Missouri Compromise was "inconsistent with" the principles of the measures of 1850 and hence "inoperative and void." It was not difficult for Douglas to establish that the "principles" of the two compromises were inconsistent, though it is very doubtful whether men like Webster and Clay, in 1850, were trying to establish any specific principle to be applied to future territorial organization. Douglas very plausibly contended, however, that of three proposals at issue in 1850 two had been discarded and one accepted. The Wilmot Proviso had been rejected, and all efforts to extend the Missouri Compromise line to the Pacific had failed after the Proviso had been introduced. Denying the assertion in the "Appeal" that the Missouri Compromise was expressly recognized in 1850, he made the claim, only partially correct as to the extent of territory, that some of the territory north of the old compromise line had actually been incorporated into the territories of New Mexico and Utah. In reference to the policy of the early fathers of the country, the "Appeal" claimed too much. The anti-slavery provision in the Ordinance of 1784 was, of course, not adopted, and when North Carolina, during the years 1789–90, ceded her territory of Tennessee to the United States, it was agreed by the latter that slavery should not be

4. The "Appeal" is in *Congressional Globe*, 33 cong., 1 sess., Jan. 30, 1854, 281–282. It bore the signatures of Salmon P. Chase, Charles Sumner, United States Senators, and of John R. Giddings, Edward Wade, Gerrit Smith, and Alexander De-Witt, members of the House of Representatives.

abolished. As Douglas pointed out, Congress, as in the case of Tennessee, applied the provisions of the Northwest Ordinance in organizing Mississippi in 1798, and the territory of New Orleans in 1805, but specifically excepted the article in that Ordinance which forbade slavery.[5]

Chase showed that Douglas was too sweeping in his claims in regard to the amount of territory once free that had been incorporated into New Mexico and Utah. The Ohio Senator, admitting that the account given by Douglas of the early policy of the country in respect to slavery was correct, claimed that the majority of individuals in Congress in 1784 favored the anti-slavery clause in the Ordinance of that year, even if the states did not pass it. Had the Constitution been properly interpreted, he said, Congress, under that instrument, would have forbidden slavery in all the territories.[6] William H. Seward denounced the South for securing what he called its "equivalents" under the Compromise of 1820 and then preventing the North from receiving its share of the settlement. He claimed that the forefathers prevented the introduction of slavery where it was "practicable," but it was not practicable to do so south of the Ohio River.[7] Southerners brought forward all of the arguments that had been advanced during the preceding decade in regard to equality of rights in the territories, but they, like Douglas, made much of

5. For Douglas' views on the various points discussed, see the *Congressional Globe*, 33 Cong., 1 sess., Jan. 30, 1854, 275–279. For details of North Carolina's agreement with the United States when the farmer ceded Tennessee, see Henry S. Randall, *The Life of Thomas Jefferson* (New York, 1858, 3 volumes), Vol. III, Appendix, 668–669.

6. *Appendix to Congressional Globe*, 33 Cong., 1 sess. Feb. 3, 1854, 133–140.

7. *Ibid.*, Feb. 17, 1854, 150–151.

the claim that the North had really abandoned the Missouri Compromise. She had even repudiated the original Compromise before Missouri was admitted to the Union, they said, for that section succeeded in defeating the admission of the state until there was a second Compromise relative to the anti-Negro clause in her constitution. The North had completed the abandonment of the line as a principle of settlement by the middle of the century.[8]

Historians have long speculated as to the motives that prompted Douglas to bring forward a measure which was so loaded with dynamite as the proposal in 1854. Some have found the explanation in his devotion to the principle of local self-government, others in his desire to get Southern support for the presidency, and others in his wish that Chicago might be the eastern terminus of a transcontinental railroad. It has already been pointed out that the situation in Missouri was one of the factors giving momentum to the movement for repeal of the Act of 1820. For some years before 1854, North-South sectional rivalry had been developing over possible routes for a transcontinental railroad. Memphis, St. Louis, Chicago, Superior (Wisconsin), New Orleans, and other places, each had had its champions as an eastern terminus for the road.[9] The organization of the territory of New Mexico and the purchase of a strip of territory from Mexico by James Gadsden seemed to make practicable a proposed Southern transcontinental

8. Speech of Alexander Stephens in House, *ibid.*, Feb. 17, 1854, 193–197. He pointed out that there were fifty-two northern votes in the House against the admission of Arkansas in 1836. See also Simms, *Life of Hunter*, 82-84.

9. Robert R. Russel, "The Pacific Railway Issue in Politics Prior to the Civil War," in *Mississippi Valley Historical Review*, Vol. XII, No. 2 (1926), 187–201. See also pp. 192–197.

road. Moreover, Jefferson Davis, Secretary of War in Pierce's Cabinet and very influential in the Councils of the Administration, was keenly awake to the interests of his section. Douglas, as Professor Hodder points out, had long been interested in a transcontinental railroad, and realized that it was necessary to organize a territorial government in the Nebraska country, if the Southern advantages were to be overcome. This organization could be made possible only by Southern votes, which would not be forthcoming unless the Missouri restriction were removed. Hodder explains that the separation into two territories was the result of conflicting railroad interests in Missouri and Iowa.[10] As a practical politician, Douglas could not proclaim that his measure was for the purpose of thwarting Davis' Southern transportation schemes, but the *Chicago Times*, the powerful Douglas organ in Chicago under the editorship of James W. Sheahen, expressed in glowing terms what it felt the Kansas-Nebraska Act meant to the Northwest. Referring to a land grant by Congress to Iowa to aid in construction of four railroads and a branch road, this paper said that they were four of the Chicago railroads extended "to the Missouri river, over one of the richest states in the Union." By that Act, it continued, "He [Douglas] opened Nebraska to the people of the Northwest, and he opened a way to the Pacific through Nebraska from the Missouri river. Let these roads be built to the Missouri, and who doubts that the first road to the Pacific commences at a point connecting with these roads, which in fact are but extensions of Chicago railroads. Was this no boon, no advan-

10. Frank H. Hodder, "The Railroad Background of the Kansas-Nebraska Act," in *Mississippi Valley Historical Review*, Vol. XII, No. 1, June, 1925, 3–22.

tage to Chicago? Did this great act deserve at the hands of a Chicago meeting insult, calumny, outrage and violence?—It was said that in opening these Territories, that a railroad might find its way hence to the Pacific, he agreed that the people who might settle there, might have African slavery if they thought fit to have it. He did do so. He could not consent to shut Chicago out of a fair competition for the route to the Pacific, on the miserable plea that it was unsafe to trust the people of Nebraska and Kansas, with a right possessed by the people of Kentucky and Iowa, of Missouri and Illinois. —He struck down the Missouri restriction, declared the people competent to govern themselves, and by so doing laid an empire at the feet of Chicago. For this Chicago mobbed him. For this the bells tolled the people to riot and disorder; for this the pulpits thundered with anathemas." [11]

Whatever may have been the motive of Douglas in sponsoring the Kansas-Nebraska Act, the charge so often made by his enemies that he was indifferent to the moral aspects of slavery and wished to extend the institution does not stand the test of analysis. He did believe in white supremacy, and in the superiority of the white to the black; but, as his most sympathetic biographer points out, he regarded slavery as ethically wrong and did refuse slaves as a wedding gift from his father-in-law.[12] The Illinois senator was convinced that his

11. *Daily Chicago Times*, May 18, 1856.
12. George Fort Milton, *The Eve of Conflict: Stephen A. Douglas and the Needless War* (Boston and New York, 1934), 149–150, 34–35. The first marriage of Douglas was to Martha Denny Martin, daughter of a prosperous North Carolina planter. She did own slaves, and in managing her estate in Mississippi, Douglas thus had some indirect connection with the "peculiar institution."

measure would not result in the extension of slavery. He felt that there might be a few scattered slaves in the Nebraska country, "but when labor becomes plenty, and therefore cheap, in that climate, with its production, it is worse than folly to think of its being a slaveholding country—I have no idea that it could." [13]

An examination through the press of the popular currents of reaction to the Kansas-Nebraska Act reveals an intense bitterness of feeling on the part of the opposition press in the North, and an indifference or lack of enthusiasm for it on the part of many of the Southern papers. The *Boston Atlas* termed the supporters of the bill "aggressors" and "agitators," and predicted that they would "open a question which they will not be able to close." The *Ohio State Journal* characterized the measure as "monstrous," and the *New York Tribune* regarded it as "a conspiracy against human nature" which was "transacted by one hundred and fifteen thousand slave-owners, whose votes and influence Douglas and his rivals seek as the road to presidential honors." The *New York Independent*, a religious journal, which had among its special contributors George B. Cheever, Henry Ward Beecher, and Mrs. Harriet B. Stowe, denounced the legislation as a crime which would "blacken with a damning guilt the soul of every man who lends himself to the perpetration of it." [14]

Should the vote in Congress be taken as an indication, it might be said that the South was overwhelmingly in favor of the Kansas-Nebraska Act. Only two

13. *Congressional Globe*, 33 Cong., 1 Sess., Jan. 30, 1854, 279.
14. *Boston Atlas*, Jan. 27, 1854; *Ohio State Journal*, March 14, 1854; *New York Tribune*, Feb. 11, 1854; *New York Independent*, Feb. 2, 1854.

Southern senators, Houston and Bell, and nine Southern representatives, seven of them Whigs, opposed the bill.[15] Once the proposal was before them, it was natural for political representatives to favor it, and to work up enthusiasm for it as the debate progressed. But the section they represented, though feeling that the Missouri restriction was a grievance, came only slowly to accept repeal with any degree of enthusiasm. The *Mobile Daily Advertiser,* though willing to support repeal, and though feeling that the restriction was "unfair and unconstitutional," doubted the value of re-opening the slavery agitation, which would aid the "abolitionists." The repeal act was "barren of practical benefit" to the South, the section cared "little" for it, and not "a single Southern journal" was demanding repeal when Douglas proposed it. It was said to be a Northern measure. *The Arkansas Whig,* in opposing the bill, declared that the South never asked for it, and the *Memphis Eagle and Enquirer,* though pointing out that it embraced the principle of equality for its section, felt that it would be of little practical benefit, because slaves could not be used to advantage in the northwestern territory. The *Savannah Republican* thought that the constitutional principle of the bill was correct, but regretted the renewal of the strife over slavery, and predicted the political death of Douglas. The *Raleigh Register* doubted "the utility of disturbing" the Compromise, the *Columbia* (S. C.) *Times* saw in the disturbance of it the removal of an odious restriction that wounded Southern pride but doubted that the removal would be of "any practical, positive good" to the South, but the *New Orleans Crescent* opposed the Act, be-

15. James F. Rhodes, *History of the United States from the Compromise of 1850* (New York, 7 volumes), Vol. I, 489.

cause the South was growing "weaker" and would be at a disadvantage if slavery agitation were revived. Papers such as the (Arkansas) *True Democrat* and the *Richmond Enquirer* strongly supported repeal of the Missouri restriction, but the latter felt it necessary, in the face of Northern claims of Southern indifference to repeal, to explain why the section apparently showed so little interest in the matter.[16]

As may be noted above one of the points emphasized in a portion of the press was that the territory in question would be of no practical value to slaveholders. Many times was that idea also expressed by Southern members of Congress. Robert M. T. Hunter, a senator from Virginia, momentarily "permitted such an illusion" as slavery extension to enter his mind, but "came to the conclusion that it was utterly hopeless to endeavor to effect any such thing."[17] Senator Andrew P. Butler of South Carolina thought that Webster was right when he said "that the laws of God" would determine the question of the use of slave labor. He felt that the measure would not strengthen slavery, but he favored it because "the south wants her heart lightened—not her

16. Mobile *Daily Advertiser*, Feb. 18, March 9, 30, May 17, June 22, 1854; *Arkansas Whig* quoted in the *True Democrat*, April 25, 1854, and *Memphis Eagle and Enquirer* in same, June 6, 1854; *Savannah Republican*, Feb. 23, 25; *Raleigh Register* quoted in *Richmond Enquirer*, Feb. 3, 1854; *Columbia Times* and *New Orleans Crescent* quoted in *Ohio State Journal*, March 14, 1854; *True Democrat*, April 11, 25, 1854; *Richmond Enquirer*, March 2, 1854. The latter journal explained the absence of popular demonstrations in terms of "the dignity and gravity of the Southern character." It stated also that "all agree that slavery cannot exist in the territories of Kansas and Nebraska."

17. *Appendix to Congressional Globe*, 33 Cong., 1 Sess., Feb. 24, 1854, 224.

power increased." She wanted "equality" and "constitutional justice." [18] Alexander H. Stephens could see no reason why the North should oppose the settlement of the slavery questions by the territories, for that section had such a preponderance of population over the South that it could create free states, if it wished.[19]

The meaning of the Kansas-Nebraska Act was anything but clear. Did it mean that a territorial legislature could prohibit slavery prior to the time that the territory framed a constitution to enter the Union as a state? Was the power given to the territory derived only from Congress, and, if so, could the territory exercise a greater power than Congress could exercise? The *New York Tribune* claimed that the idea that the power over slavery was conferred upon the territorial legislature was a "great fraud." Not only might the governor and the judges, who were appointed by the President, prevent exclusion of slavery by the legislature, but Southerners contended that under the Constitution their property was entitled to protection in the territories.[20] Another Northern journal suggested that what power a territory had it derived from Congress, and that if the territory had the right, so did Congress. It pointed out also that the leading men of the South rejected the idea of territorial exclusion of slavery.[21] Chase emphasized the vagueness of the bill on this point, and

18. *Ibid.*, 235, 240.
19. *Ibid.*, Speech in House, Feb. 17, 1854, 193–197. For additional evidence in confirmation of this point see Elmer LeRoy Craik, *Southern Interest in Territorial Kansas, 1854–1858* (Reprinted from collections of the Kansas Historical Society, Vol. XV, 1916), 335–337.
20. *New York Tribune*, March 1, 1854.
21. *Ohio State Journal*, March 14, 1854.

claimed that it asserted no right of a territorial legislature except what was "subject to the Constitution." [22]
He offered amendments to clarify the point, but they
were not accepted. Meanwhile, some of the Southern
presses were denouncing the "squatter sovereignty"
idea.[23]

In the Senate, Albert G. Brown of Mississippi challenged the claim of Lewis Cass of Michigan that the
territorial legislature could exclude slavery, and contended that when the Michigan senator proved that
Congress could not exclude slavery, he proved that its
creature, the legislature, could not. Brown, who contended that slave property was entitled to protection
in territories until a state constitution was made, was
unwilling to vote for the Kansas-Nebraska Act, if Cass'
construction of it was correct, but did favor the measure
because it left doubtful points to the decision of the
Supreme Court.[24] Hunter expressed views very similar
to those of Brown,[25] and Senator Butler, who indicated
that he would be willing for the Supreme Court to pass
on the matter, spoke in the following vein: "I have,
therefore, no idea that in the vote I shall give upon this
bill, I will be committing myself to any such doctrine
as that of the uncontrolled sovereignty of the people of
the Territories—That [the Constitution] is the monarch
of all it surveys, and it makes Congress the Governor
and trustee, with the power of delegating the agency

22. *Appendix to Congressional Globe*, 33 Cong., 1 Sess., Feb.
3, 1854, 133.
23. *Richmond Enquirer*, March 9, 1854, and *Charleston Mercury* quoted in *Enquirer*, March 13, 1854.
24. *Appendix to Congressional Globe*, 33 Cong., 1 Sess., Feb.
24, 1854, 230–32.
25. Simms, *Life of Hunter*, 86–87.

to administer the trust with a limitation that it must be limited by consideration of equality." [26]

The Supreme Court clause in the Kansas-Nebraska Act was the outgrowth of conferences in the Democratic senatorial caucus, where differences of opinion between Northern and Southern Democrats developed over the details of the bill.[27] In its origins and in its nature, this clause helped pave the way for the later split in the Democratic party.

26. *Appendix to Congressional Globe,* 33 Cong., 1 Sess., 239.
27. Milton, *op. cit.,* 131.

IV

Kansas Difficulties

HAD Kansas been settled in a normal, natural way, it is easily conceivable that it would soon have become a free state, and that Douglas would have secured the transcontinental railroad route which he favored. But immigration to Kansas did not proceed in normal fashion. When the Kansas-Nebraska Act was being considered in Congress, the Massachusetts Legislature, largely as a result of the efforts of Eli Thayer, enacted a measure creating the Massachusetts Emigrant Aid Society with an authorized capital of $5,000,000, only a small part of which was ever subscribed. The purposes of the Society were to make Kansas a free state, and to realize profit in carrying out that venture. Other aid societies came into existence in the same year (1854) and in 1855. The activities and purposes of the societies were given considerable prominence in the Eastern newspapers.[1] Thayer announced at a meeting held in New York to form a Kansas League that the Massachusetts Company would have one thousand emigrants on the way to Kansas by September 1, 1854, and

1. *Boston Atlas*, August 3, 5, 1854; *New York Times*, August 4, 1854. The *Chicago Democratic Press* of March 2, 1855, spoke of the "rumors" in Eastern newspapers of heavy anti-slavery emigration in Kansas and yet to come.

expected to send twenty thousand within a year. He explained that expenses for transportation would be provided, and that homes would be erected for settlers until they could build their own. He predicted that they would "beard oppression in its very den," and would assail slavery in sections of the South after Kansas was made free. *The New York Tribune* assured its readers, in urging emigration, that the Missouri slaveholders were determined to secure both Kansas and Nebraska "as fields for nigger-breeding and nigger-flogging," and that, indeed, there was "no hope of deliverance" from them in "the entire Union," unless freedom won in Kansas.[2]

The Northern emigrant aid movement influenced greatly the developments in Missouri and the currents of sentiment in the South. Atchison and Benjamin F. Stringfellow, pro-slavery extremists, urged the people of Missouri to resist the unnatural and allegedly aggressive efforts of Northern "fanatics" to secure Kansas. In the opinion of Atchison, a free Kansas meant no further extension of slavery and it portended an attack upon the institution in Arkansas, Texas and Missouri. Since Thayer had said as much, that contention seemed plausible. At any rate, Kansas free meant that Missouri except on its Southern border would be encircled by free states, a situation that was felt to be dangerous to the existence of slavery in the latter state.[3] A pro-slavery

2. For Thayer's remarks see *New York Times*, August 4, 1854, and for the *Tribune's* sentiments see issue of June 22, 1854.

3. For a good discussion of Missouri's attitude and of the pro-slavery position in general see James C. Malin, "The Pro-Slavery Background of the Kansas Struggle," in *Mississippi Valley Historical Review*, Vol. X, No. 3, 1923, 285–305. For Atchison's position, see especially 286–294.

group in Kansas issued an address November 20, 1854, urging the defeat of Robert Flenniken, Free-Soil candidate for delegate to Congress, on the ground that "Those abolitionists were literally shipped from the New England states for the avowed purpose of abolitionizing Kansas, with the ultimate view of the more effectually assailing the institutions of our neighboring states of Missouri, Arkansas and Texas." [4]

In June, 1854, President Pierce appointed Andrew H. Reeder, of Pennsylvania, as Governor of Kansas Territory. The appointee, however, did not go to Kansas until early fall, and did not provide for the taking of a census there until the following February. Reeder was suspected of anti-slavery sympathies, all the more because he acquired in the Territory landholdings, which he hoped to sell in small tracts to free state settlers. It was claimed that he delayed the taking of the census, in order that the New England settlers might arrive in sufficient numbers to make Kansas free. [5] Despite the fact that no census had been taken, a territorial delegate was chosen November 29, 1854. In that election, won by John W. Whitfield, the pro-slavery candidate, illegal votes were cast on both sides, [6] though there is little doubt that more of them were cast by Missourians than by the anti-slavery group. When the election of a territorial legislature was held in March, 1855, more than four times as many votes were recorded as there were registered voters. The large majority of illegal votes may be attributed to the Missourians, but some

4. *Kansas Weekly Herald* (Leavenworth), Nov. 24, 1854.
5. See speech of Representative Mordecai Oliver, of Missouri, *Appendix to Congressional Globe*, 34 Cong., 1 sess., March 7, 1856, 167–168; Roy F. Nichols, *Franklin Pierce: Young Hickory of the Granite Hills* (Philadelphia, 1931), 407–411.
6. Malin, *op. cit.*, 295–296.

to the free state group.[7] It is very probable that the Southern group would have triumphed without the invasion from Missouri, for the census showed that there were at that time more people in Kansas from the slave states than from the free.[8] But this preponderance of the Southern element in the settled population of Kansas was short-lived; and had that element, unaided by the Missourians, elected the legislature it is doubtful whether, in the face of a steady migration from the western free states, it could have even temporarily made Kansas a slave state.

The reaction to the developments in Kansas was usually partisan in nature. The *Chicago Press* thought the action of the pro-slavery group "a flagrant outrage," but the *Chicago Times* felt that the North was the aggressor, that it had caused the trouble by sending men to Kansas at "fifty dollars a head."[9] The usually conservative *Mobile Daily Advertiser* declared that the prime cause of the troubles in Kansas were the Emigrant Aid Societies, that they had thrown "down the gage to the Southern settlers."[10] Senator H. S. Geyer of Missouri felt at the time of the passage of the Kansas-Nebraska Act that Kansas would be a free state, but now he thought that the activities of the Societies had checked the tendency in that direction.[11] On the other hand,

7. Reports of the Committees of the House of Representatives, Cong., 1 Sess., 1855–56. Report No. 200, 2–34, 73–74, 82–84; see also Leverett Spring, *Kansas: The Prelude to the War for the Union* (Boston, 1885), 47–51.

8. Spring, *op. cit.*, 43; Craik, *op. cit.*, 346; Theodore C. Smith, *Parties and Slavery*, 1850–1859 (New York and London, 1906), 126.

9. *Chicago Press*, April 3, 1855 and *Times* quoted in *Press*, April 13, 1855.

10. May 19, 1855.

11. *Appendix to Globe*, 34 Cong., 1 Sess., April 8, 1855, 465.

Senator Hale, claiming that the Societies not only had a right to exist but had been "invited" to do so by the passage of the Kansas-Nebraska Act, construed the action of the Missourians as that of invasion and conquest.[12] Some of the papers that had sprung up in Kansas did not use language quite as dignified as that cited above. Emigrants sent by the Aid Societies were characterized as "miserable serfs," "miserable scum," "lawless banditti" and "paupers and cutthroats," [13] while those who came from the South were called "bar-room rowdies," "blacklegs," and "border ruffians" who were "parading the country chopping single persons, who chance to fall into their hands, to pieces, and frightening women and children." [14]

If it be granted, as Senator Hale contended, that the Kansas-Nebraska measure represented an "invitation" to the Emigrant Aid Companies to come into existence, it is nevertheless unfortunate that the invitation was accepted. The numbers they were sending or were going to send to Kansas were much exaggerated. In fact, a considerable number who went to the Territory were disappointed and left without registering a claim after they found that the economic situation was not what it had been represented as being.[15] The organized Missouri exodus on the election date in 1855, which natu-

12. *Ibid.*, Feb. 28, 1856, 104–107.
13. *The Squatter Sovereign* (Atchison), May 1, 1855, July 1, 1856.
14. *Herald of Freedom* (Lawrence), April 7, 1855, Feb. 16, 1856. In the East the *Boston Atlas*, condemning the Missouri invasion as a "systematic conspiracy to force slavery on Kansas," declared that, "in all that constitutes manly character, the New England emigrant is as far above the Missouri tools of slavery as the heavens are above the earth." (April 4, 1855).
15. See letter of Kansas emigrant in *New York Times*, Jan. 18, 1855; *Lawrence Herald of Freedom*, April 18, 1855.

rally aroused the North, would probably not have occurred had the Aid movement, greatly magnified in
the popular imagination, not stimulated it. It was said
that the Northern emigrant groups were going to aboli-
tionize certain slave areas, but as most of them were
anti-Negro (as will be shown later), it is hardly probable that they meant to make such efforts. Yet in the
South they seem to have been generally regarded as
abolitionists. One who had made a careful study of the
Emigrant Aid Societies has concluded that they stirred
public feeling to a high emotional pitch in the South
and East, but that they "had practically nothing to do
with making Kansas a free state." Migration from the
Western states was the factor that achieved that goal.[16]

Political developments in Kansas after the territorial
election of March, 1855, augured anything but well for
the ultimate success of popular sovereignty. On the
basis of alleged irregularities in six of the eighteen election districts, Reeder rejected eight of thirty-one members of the legislature, and when supplementary elections were held to fill their seats, the pro-slavery group
refused to participate in them. The anti-slavery men
thus elected were, however, unseated by the legislature,
and several free-soilers who had been selected in the
original election resigned their seats.[17] Reeder's original
residence and the seat of the government in Kansas
were in Shawnee Mission, but he directed the legislature to meet at Pawnee, one hundred and forty miles
from the Missouri border, though that was an unde-
veloped town, in which cholera was said to be prevalent.

16. Ralph V. Harlow, "The Rise and Fall of the Kansas Aid
Movement" in *American Historical Review*, Vol. XL, 1935,
1–25. For conclusions stated, see p. 25.
17. Spring, *op. cit.*, 49, 52–53.

The Executive's order was attributed to the fact that
he had extensive landholdings on the military reserva-
tion near Pawnee.[18] Despite the Governor's veto of its
action, the legislative body decided to meet at Shawnee
Mission. Reeder then found himself in a hopeless wran-
gle with that body, and was soon thereafter dismissed
by President Pierce on the ground that he could not approve the former's land contracts with the Indians. The
opposition alleged, however, that the dismissal was due
to the failure of the Governor to be the willing tool of
the slavery interests.[19]

The free-soilers, refusing to accept the pro-slavery
government thus organized, proceeded to establish a
separate one for themselves. Their principal leaders
were Charles Robinson and James Lane, the latter of
whom was instrumental in securing Sharp's rifles and in
making other military preparations which were regarded as essential in resisting the aggressive tactics of
the pro-Southern group. After preliminary conventions
at Lawrence and Big Springs in August and September,
1855, the anti-slavery group met in Topeka in October
and drew up a free state constitution which was to be
submitted to the people. They also made provision for
the election of a governor, a legislature and a member
of Congress. The free state group ratified the Topeka
Constitution in December, and elected a legislature and
governor in the following January. The governorship
went to Robinson. Reeder, in the meantime, had been

18. See speech of Rep. Oliver, of Missouri, *Appendix to Congressional Globe*, 34 Cong., 1 Sess., March 7, 1856, 170; Spring,
op. cit., 55–56.
19. For a favorable view of Pierce's action see Nichols,
op. cit., 408–418 and for a less favorable view see sketch of
Reeder in *Transactions of the Kansas State Historical Society*,
Vol. III (Topeka, 1886), 197–202.

elected as territorial delegate to Congress to contest the seat of Whitfield, the pro-slavery choice.[20]

During the years 1855 and 1856, there was a feeling in the South that that section was not doing what it could or should in the colonizing of Kansas.[21] That feeling, which was stimulated in part by appeals from Missouri to the effect that if they lost the October (1856) election all was lost, helped to lead to the expedition of Major Jefferson Buford, of Alabama, to Kansas in 1856. His four hundred followers, who were armed with Bibles instead of with rifles, were promised forty acres of land, free passage to Kansas and means of support for one year after arrival. When they arrived in May, Kansas was on the verge of a small civil war, a situation which was not very conducive to the success of the enterprise. Some of the group became United States soldiers, others left the Territory because of attacks upon them by the free state supporters, and some cast their lot with the free staters.[22]

It is undoubtedly true that the physical violence which took place in Kansas was greatly exaggerated, and that exaggeration added to the commotion throughout the country. It has been estimated that approximately two hundred men lost their lives by violence in Kansas between 1854 and the time that that Territory was admitted as a state in 1861, but that one-half of

20. Spring, op. cit., 60–70; Smith, Parties and Slavery, 131–134.

21. For such sentiments see Augusta Constitutionalist, Jan. 4, 22, Feb. 10, 1856; Arkansas (Little Rock) True Democrat, Sept. 2, 23, 1856.

22. See Walter L. Fleming, "The Buford Expedition to Kansas," in American Historical Review, Vol. VI, No. 1, October, 1900, 38–48. Buford's followers came not only from Alabama, but from several other Southern states.

those were killed as the result of quarrels over land titles and other provocative frontier questions.[23] This unfortunate aspect of the Kansas struggle may be indicated by several incidents. Late in 1855 Sheriff Sam Jones arrested a free state man for uttering threats against a pro-slavery man who had committed a murder. A mob freed the prisoner and took him to Lawrence, which was guarded by free state men. A Missouri mob marched upon that town, but did not attack it, due to the fact that Jones succeeded in arranging a "truce" with Lane and Robinson, leaders of the Lawrenceites.[24]

But Lawrence was not to be spared. When Sheriff Jones went to serve a warrant against some free-state leaders, presently to be indicted for "treason," he was shot by one of their supporters. A United States marshal then summoned a posse, which consisted mostly of Missourians, and made some arrests in Lawrence, though some of the leaders had fled. Though the marshal did not encounter resistance, the mob, many of its members inflamed by liquor, destroyed a hotel which had been declared to be a "nuisance," broke up the free state presses and committed other depredations. Only two lives were lost. Three days later (May 24, 1856) John Brown, feeling that he was atoning for the "sack of Lawrence" and for the killing of free-staters, led a band that hacked to death five men on Pottawatomie Creek. No such premeditated, cold-blooded murders had taken place in Kansas.

The scene now shifts to Washington. Just on the eve of the weird developments in Kansas in May, 1856, Charles Sumner delivered a long speech in the Senate which he captioned "The Crime Against Kansas." Those

23. Milton, *Eve of Conflict*, 198.
24. Smith, *Parties and Slavery*, 133–134.

portions of the speech which attracted most attention consisted of personal remarks directed against Douglas and Senator Butler, of South Carolina, particularly against the latter, who was not present at the time. "The Senator from South Carolina," he declared, "has read many books of chivalry, and believes himself a chivalrous knight, with sentiments of honor and courage. Of course he has chosen a mistress to whom he has made his vows, and who, though ugly to others, is always lovely to him—though polluted in the sight of the world, is chaste in his sight: I mean the harlot slavery." Referring to a throat affliction that Butler had, Sumner spoke of how the South Carolinian "with incoherent phrase, discharges the loose expectoration of his speech," and declared that the afflicted senator "touches nothing which he does not disfigure—with error, sometimes of principle, sometimes of fact. He shows an incapacity of accuracy, whether in stating the Constitution or in stating the law, whether in details of statistics or diversions of scholarship. He cannot ope his mouth, but there flies a blunder." [25] Some of the Massachusetts Senator's speech was devoted to a bitter denunciation of South Carolina, and much of it to a vigorous attack upon the actions of the pro-slavery group in Kansas, but whatever his theme, his manner and language were calculated to arouse strong antagonism.

Two days after the speech, Preston Brooks, a member of the House of Representatives from South Carolina and a relative of Senator Butler, went to Sumner's desk when the Senate was not in session, rebuked the latter for his attack upon South Carolina and the per-

25. For above quotations, see Charles Sumner, *His Complete Works* (Boston, 1900, Statesman Edition), Vol. V, "The Crime Against Kansas" speech, May 19, 20, 1856, 144.

sonal reflections upon his relative, and then broke his cane to pieces on Sumners' head. As a result, the recipient of the assault was absent from the Senate for more than three years. The House failed to expel Brooks for the attack, but he resigned and stood successfully for reelection in his district. Referring to the constantly repeated allegations that Brooks' action was evidence of "Southern violence" and "ruffianism," Butler pointed out that the first physical encounter (the disgraceful details of which he described) in Congress was between Matthew Lyon, of Vermont, and Roger Griswold, of Connecticut during the 1790's and that neither was expelled, though the House was in session during the encounters. The South Carolinian, had he been present, would "not have submitted" to Sumner's remarks, and did not understand how some of the remarks could have been made in the presence of ladies.[26]

The reaction to the caning was of a varied nature. The Republican *New York Times* called it "a ruffianly attack . . . on one of the most courteous and gentlemanly members of the Senate." There was "not an extenuating circumstance" in the case, and the attack was another proof of the malign nature of the pro-slavery party, "which will respect neither age, nor position, nor genius, nor place."[27] The Democratic *Detroit Free Press* felt that Sumner's speech was "gross, vulgar and unprovoked," but that Brooks' attack was made "in a not very manly way."[28] Though there were many manifestations in the South of sympathy with Brooks, there

26. For Butler's speech, see *Appendix to Congressional Globe,* 34 Cong., 1 Sess., June 12, 1856, 625–634. For further details of Lyon-Griswold affair, see Claude G. Bowers, *Jefferson and Hamilton* (Boston and New York, 1925), 360–361.

27. May 23, 1856.

28. June 14, 1856.

was also some condemnation. The *Augusta Daily Constitutionalist* thought the speech was "a gross outrage" and that Sumner "deserved the beating," [29] and the *North Carolina Standard* was of the same opinion.[30] However, the *Savannah Republican,* while condemning the Senator's speech as "ruthless and malignant," felt that no "sort of provocation" should have led a man to strike "an unarmed Senator" in the Senate chamber,[31] and the *New Orleans Picayune,* though characterizing the speech as one of "insult," condemned the attack as one "to be severely reprehended." [32]

Conditions in Kansas on the eve of the presidential election of 1856 were anything but satisfactory. Two governments existed there, and the adherents of each blamed the other for that political situation, and for the physical violence that had occurred in the territory.[33] After adopting the Topeka Constitution, the anti-slavery group, through its legislature, chose Lane and Reeder as United States Senators, and asked Congress that Kansas be admitted as a state under the Topeka instrument. The measure for admission passed the House in July, but failed in the Senate. Rhodes expresses the opinion that it "would have been a monstrous precedent" to admit Kansas in such fashion, for "the

29. May 27, 1856.
30. May 27, 1856.
31. May 27, 1856.
32. May 27, 1856. This journal felt that the attack would harm the South more than a half dozen such speeches.
33. *The New York Tribune,* May 23, 1856, declared that slavery was responsible for "butchery and arson in the settlers' homes." The *Boston Post,* April 3, 1856, emphasized the fact that the Big Springs convention had resolved to resist the existing authorities and laws "unto blood," and suggested that Sharp's rifles were there in abundance to aid the "bold treason" of maintaining a government that had no legal right to exist.

Topeka Constitution had been adopted by a self-styled convention which had not the authority of law, was irregular, and only represented a faction."[34] However, the government which was recognized as legal by the Federal Administration had been under fire since the Missouri incursion, and had been even more strongly criticized when the legislature passed a very severe slave code. Under that code death was the penalty for inciting a slave insurrection, death or ten years at hard labor for aiding a slave to escape, and two years at hard labor for speaking or writing against the right to hold slaves.[35]

The Democrats, inspired no doubt partly by political reasons, made genuine efforts in the spring and summer of 1856 to settle the Kansas question. Douglas had introduced as early as March a measure for that purpose, but one devised by Toombs and reported from the committee on territories by Douglas in June was acted upon by the Senate. Under its terms, five commissioners to be appointed by the President were to take a census of the bona fide residents in Kansas, on the basis of that census a convention was to be elected, and that convention was to frame a constitution to be submitted to Congress. While the bill was under discussion, numerous amendments were offered to meet Republican objections. Free state men who had been driven from the territory were to be allowed to return and register and, as a significant commentary on the much talked of principle of Congressional non-interference, territorial laws especially obnoxious to anti-slavery adherents were repealed. The Republicans were invited to offer any

34. Rhodes, Vol. II, 151.
35. Smith, *Parties and Slavery*, 129.

other amendments they regarded as desirable.[36] Though the Republicans objected to the presidential appointment of the commissioners, Amos A. Lawrence, on the basis of information from Pierce concerning the probable personnel of the commission, wrote to a member of the House that it was satisfactory.[37] The Toombs bill passed the Senate in July, 33 to 12, but received scant consideration in the House.

Why did the Republicans reject such a measure? It was evident by that time that, as had been said so often, slavery would amount to little in Kansas, and even the author of the bill had said four months earlier that he expected it to be a free state.[38] Hale said that there was "much in it [the bill] to approve," but he could not trust those in power in Kansas, he did not like past developments there, and he preferred to settle the Kansas matter after a new president entered office.[39] Seward regarded it "as a bill of concession," confessed that it gave freedom "an equal chance" with slavery, a chance that he was not willing it should have.[40] He wanted congressional exclusion of slavery, and not popular sovereignty, yet was willing to admit Kansas under the Topeka Constitution. The *New York Tribune* admitted that there were some "fair-seeming provisions" in the Toombs measure, but it assigned recent developments in Kansas as an excuse for not accepting it. That journal also chided Douglas for saying that Congress had no power over acts of a territory, and yet

36. Rhodes, Vol. II, 147–150.
37. Nichols, *Pierce*, 476–477.
38. *Appendix to Congressional Globe*, 34 Cong., 1 Sess., Feb. 28, 1856, 116.
39. *Ibid.*, July 2, 1856, 768.
40. *Ibid.*, July 2, 1856, 789–790.

had supported the proposition that Congress repeal some of those acts.[41] The Republican defeat of Toombs' proposal gave the opposition press a chance to take the offensive in Kansas matters, and that it did. They enumerated the fair provisions of the bill, pointed out that the Republicans had insisted upon admitting Kansas under the "irregular" Topeka Constitution, and claimed that the Republicans were willing even that bloodshed might continue in Kansas in order that their party might use the situation there to advance its fortunes in the ensuing presidential election.[42]

The Kansas-Nebraska Act produced marked results upon political parties. It represented the death blow to the already weakened Whig party. Some of the Whigs, North and South, found refuge in the Know-Nothing group, but many in the former section entered the ranks of the new Republican party, and in the latter, those of the Democratic party. Though the Democratic party was strengthened in the South, it was weakened in the North by the defection of Anti-Nebraska Democrats, who, combined with the old Free-Soilers and a portion of the Whigs, composed the Republican party, the main principle of which was exclusion by Congress of slavery in the territories.

While the political battle lines were being formed for the presidential election of 1856, a heated contest occurred in the session of Congress, 1855–56, for the Speakership of the House of Representatives. During the nine weeks' struggle, many candidates were paraded

41. July 4, 7, 1856.
42. *Detroit Free Press,* July 4, 6, 8, 12, Sept. 19, 1856; *Cincinnati Enquirer,* September 26, 1856; *Leavenworth Weekly Herald,* July 26, 1856; *Boston Post,* July 2, 4, 12, 1856; *New Orleans Daily Picayune,* July 8, 10, 1856. *The Picayune* supported Fillmore during the campaign.

before the House—William Aiken of South Carolina and William A. Richardson of Illinois, Democrats; Lewis D. Campbell of Ohio and Nathaniel Banks of Massachusetts, Republicans, and Henry M. Fuller of Pennsylvania, a Know-Nothing. The balloting showed much bitterness of feeling between Democrats and Know-Nothings,[43] a situation which aided the Republicans, who were themselves rent with discord as a result of personal rivalries. After much discussion, a plurality rule was adopted, in accordance with which a candidate receiving a plurality on the fourth successive ballot was to be declared elected. On Feb. 2, 1856, on the 133rd ballot, Banks was chosen Speaker. Toombs wrote privately of his concern at the election of Banks, for it had given the Republicans great hope, and once they got power, it would "finally result in division of the South, which will be the most fatal result that could happen to us."[44] A Southern paper alleged that Banks was "the very blackest Republican of all" and that he boasted that he represented "the strongest anti-slavery district in the Union," while a Northern journal called the Massachusetts man's election a "revolution," a step in a struggle between "two nations," involving "a question of power which, once settled, will not soon be subject to a new disturbance."[45] Despite the sectional feel-

43. Know-Nothing journals in the South, such as the *New Orleans Daily Picayune* (Feb. 5, 1856), and the *Savannah Republican* (Jan. 17, 1856), emphasized with approval the discord between those groups. The candidates mentioned above do not exhaust the list which received support.

44. Toombs to Thomas Thomas, Feb. 9, 1856, 361, in Vol. II of *The Correspondence of Robert Toombs, Alexander H. Stephens and Howell Cobb.* Edited by U. B. Phillips, in The Annual Report of the American Historical Association for the year 1911. (Washington, 1913).

45. *Arkansas True Democrat,* Jan. 8, 1856: *Cincinnati Com-*

ing aroused by the contest, a prominent Southerner said some years later that Banks was "one of the ablest" speakers he had seen in that position, and "without doubt the most impartial." [46]

The Republicans had made great political gains since the party had been organized in 1854, and they therefore faced the presidential election year, 1856, with high hopes. Chase and Seward were possible presidential candidates, John McLean, a Supreme Court justice, was supported by many of the older men and conservatives in the party, but John C. Fremont, a youthful explorer who seemed to possess the dash that many of the younger men wanted, was chosen as the standard-bearer. William L. Dayton, of New Jersey, was his running mate. Through Banks, the Fremont supporters skilfully schemed to gain the support of a considerable group of anti-slavery Know-Nothings, and thus strengthened Republican chances.[47] The party platform declared it the duty of Congress to prohibit slavery in the territories, claimed that the Pierce Administration had been trying to force slavery on Kansas and denounced the Ostend Manifesto, a declaration by United States ministers of aggressive designs against Cuba.

The Democrats, as in 1852, accepted the Virginia and Kentucky Resolutions as their constitutional creed, and the Kansas-Nebraska Act, whatever that meant, as their

mercial quoted in *Cincinnati Enquirer*, Feb. 5, 1856. For an interesting account of the details of this contest, and an interpretation of its outcome as a sectional victory, see Fred. H. Harrington, "The First Northern Victory" in *Journal of Southern History*, Vol. V, No. 2, May, 1939, 186–205.

46. Stephens *Correspondence*, Alexander Stephens to J. Henly Smith, Feb. 4, 1860, 460.

47. Allan Nevins, *Frémont Pathfinder of the West* (New York and London, 1939), 424, *et. seq.*

main political principle. Though Toombs wrote as late as February, 1856, that the party could not do "much better" than to nominate Pierce, Howell Cobb, as early as December, 1854, expressed privately the view that "the renomination of General Pierce is certain and inevitable defeat," and he felt that the same fate would befall anyone who had been personally connected with the bitter fight over the Nebraska bill. He thought that Buchanan was the logical candidate, and probably the only one who could win.[48] Cobb's view prevailed, and James Buchanan, from the pivotal state of Pennsylvania, was chosen for the Presidency and John C. Breckinridge of Kentucky, for Vice-President.

The Know-Nothings were hostile to immigration and to Catholicism, but were in a quandary over the slavery question. That group had elements of strength in the South as well as in the North, for there were elements in the former section which did not care to associate themselves with the Democratic party, and, what is more significant, saw through the medium of the Know-Nothing party a chance to check the great floods of immigration which were hostile to slavery and were constantly increasing the political strength of the free states. Though it lost some of its Northern support by so doing, the party took a position on the question of domestic institutions in the territories which was supposed to mean popular sovereignty. Millard Fillmore was named for President, and Andrew J. Donelson, of Tennessee, for Vice-President.

A lively campaign followed, or was actually in swing before the nominations were made. Extreme statements

48. Toombs *Correspondence*, Vol. II, Toombs to Thomas Thomas, Feb. 9, 1850, 361; Howell Cobb to James Buchanan, Dec. 5, 1854.

were the order of the day, whether made in reference
to Kansas or other factors that might arouse the emo-
tions. The *Boston Atlas* said of Frémont before he was
nominated that the Californian "knows it to be a contest between civilization and barbarism, . . . —between humanity and cruelty." [49] The *Richmond Enquirer* pictured the opposition to the Democrats as composed of those who threaten "the safety of the South,
the perpetuity of the Union, the sanctity of religion,
purity of morals and security of property," and, in denouncing the editor of the *New York Herald* for desert-
ing the Republicans for allegedly ulterior motives, declared that the paper was "born in a brothel and reared
among the inmates of the penitentiary." [50] It was asserted that Frémont could never carry on the government in the South, for "no true or decent Southern
man would accept office under him; and our people
would never submit to have their post-offices, custom-
houses and the like, filled with Frémont's Yankee abolitionists." [51] Bitter resentment was expressed at the statements of Republicans that they would, if triumphant,
fill the Southern offices with anti-slavery men. [52] Jere-
miah Black wrote to Howell Cobb that the thought that
the Republican candidate might be elected "is enough
to startle one," but concluded that, if he were elected,
he would not follow as rash a policy as his supporters
were suggesting because for "three-fourths" of them
the campaign was "a wild, heartless and unprincipled
hunt after office." [53]

49. April 9, 1856.
50. June 23, 11, 1856.
51. *North Carolina Standard*, Sept. 12, 1856.
52. *Richmond Enquirer*, July 8, 1856.
53. *Cobb Correspondence,* Black to Cobb, Sept. 22, 1856,
382–383.

During the campaign Fillmore made a speech at Albany in which he said that it would be "madness and folly" to think that the South would submit to a sectional president such as Frémont,[54] an utterance which the *New York Tribune* denounced as "treasonable."[55] The conservative Northerner, Rufus Choate, wrote a letter, given considerable publicity, in which he said that a national party to keep slavery out of "Utah, New Mexico, Washington or Minnesota" was "about as needful and about as feasible as a national party to keep Maine for freedom." A government under Republican control, he felt, would appear to the South "an alien government" and "a hostile government," and such a party [Republican] "flushed by triumph" and "cheered onward by the voices of the pulpit, tribune and press" would produce disastrous consequences.[56] Fillmore's supporters in the South represented him as a conservative nationalist, who took a middle ground between the radical extremes represented by both of the other parties.[57] Replying to Southern threats of disunion, the Republicans claimed that such utterances were so much gasconade, that the South would not run the risk of losing protection to slavery by dissolving the Union.[58]

It has been pointed out in the preceding chapter that there was much difference of opinion as to the meaning of the Kansas-Nebraska Act. Those differences of interpretation played a considerable part in the campaign of 1856. The Republicans pointed out that the Democrats construed the Act differently in different parts of

54. For account of speech, see *Chicago Times,* July 10, 1856.
55. July 4, 1856.
56. *True Democrat,* Sept. 2, 1856.
57. For such views, see *New Orleans Picayune,* Oct. 10, 23, 1856; *Mobile Daily Advertiser,* Feb. 28, June 11, 1856.
58. *New York Times,* July 1, 3, Oct. 23, 1856.

the country, and their claims were well founded.[59] The result in the popular vote in the election was 1,838,169 for Buchanan, 1,341,265 for Frémont and 874,534 for Fillmore.[60] The Republicans derived consolation from the fact that the free states showed such a preponderance of votes over those of the slave states,[61] and from the further fact that, in their estimation, the vote for Frémont represented "the flower of American manhood, and the highest moral, religious and intellectual life of the nation," while that for Buchanan, stood, in large part, for "lazy unthrift" and for "hostility to free schools" and to "religion."[62]

During the turbulent period in Kansas following Reeder's dismissal, Wilson Shannon and John W. Geary had each served as Governor of the Territory, but with the advent of the new Administration Buchanan gave that position to Robert J. Walker, who had been born in Pennsylvania, but had had his interesting public career as a citizen of Mississippi. Frederic P. Stanton, of Tennessee, who became the new territorial secretary, went to Kansas ahead of Walker to assist in preparations for the election of members of a convention, which was to frame a constitution preparatory to admission of the Territory as a state. For the purpose of electing this convention, the territorial legislature provided that a cen-

59. For Republican claims see *Boston Atlas*, May 19, 1856, and *New York Times*, July 14, 22, 1856; for Northern Democratic view that territorial legislature could prohibit slavery, see *Albany Atlas and Argus* quoted in *Times*, July 22, 1856. The *Richmond Enquirer* (June 6, 9, 1856), claims that the Cincinnati platform repudiated squatter sovereignty, but points out that the *Richmond Whig* took the opposite position.
60. Edward Stanwood, *A History of the Presidency, 1788 to 1897*, Vol. VII (Boston and New York, 1928), 276.
61. *Boston Atlas*, Dec. 12, 22, 1856.
62. *Chicago Daily Press*, Nov. 10, 1856.

sus should be taken during March, 1857, that a month thereafter should be given for clearing up all errors, or alleged errors, in the taking of the census, and that the apportionment of members of the convention should be based on that enumeration.[63] Registration of voters was, of course, to follow. The census was defective, and registration took place in only sixteen of the thirty-four counties.

An addition to the charge that the legislative districting of the Territory for electing convention delegates was unfair to the free state element—a charge for which there was some basis—the Republicans also laid the defective census and registration at the door of the proslavery group.[64] It is significant to note that the *New York Tribune* at one time advised the free state men in Kansas to note all errors of "omission and commission" in census taking and registration, to see to it that "no voter" is "illegally enrolled or left off the voting lists," and at another it said "to vote at the election, *or to seek to be enrolled as a voter at it*" would be an acknowledgment of "Border-Ruffian" control in Kansas. It advised the free-staters to keep their own government, and carry on "a perpetual protest" against the other "oppressive" one.[65] In fact, the Republicans themselves were responsible, in part, for the very situation they deplored in the Territory. In some counties they drove out the census-takers, or used threats and force to keep them from functioning. In others they refused to take the census. Since under the laws of Kansas counties were attached to other counties for civil and political pur-

63. For details of Act, see *Leavenworth Journal*, Feb. 5, 1857.
64. *New York Tribune*, August 17, 1857.
65. For these inconsistencies, see issues of March 31 and April 11, 1857. Words underlined above by author.

poses, it is an error to regard as separate units the eighteen or nineteen counties in which no registration took place. When it is said that census-takers were prevented from functioning in three counties, ten units are included. In three separate units there was no population, and in some of the others it was sparse.[66]

Some of the free-staters were Democrats and some Republicans, and not by any means all of them refrained from registering or tried to hamper that process. When the convention delegates were elected in June, something more than 2,100 votes were cast of a total of 9,251 registered,[67] which indicates that the anti-slavery group could easily have won the election, had it participated. Though it regarded the policy of the pro-slavery government in Kansas as unfair, the Republican *New York Times* had urged the free-staters to vote, since it believed that they could thus control the convention, and a free state paper in Kansas said after the Lecompton convention had met that the consequences that flowed from the June election would not have ensued, had not "pensioned letter writers" in the Territory "filled columns of Republican papers with falsehoods," and thus prevented the anti-slavery group from

66. For an analysis of Kansas laws and of census difficulties, see speech of Senator Trusten Polk, of Missouri, *Congressional Globe*, 35 Cong., 1 Sess., March 11, 1858, 1062. For difficulties, see also *Lecompton National Democrat*, August 20, Sept. 3, 1857. Spring says that for the "condition of things [in Kansas] the pro-slavery party was not wholly responsible. Free-State men perplexed the enumeration by embarrassments of omission and commission, and were not ill pleased at the starved and skeleton returns." Spring, *Kansas*, 212.

67. *Reports of Committees of the House of Representatives*, 36 Cong., 1 Sess., 1859–1860. *Covode Report*. See letter of Walker to Buchanan, June 28, 1857, 115–119.

electing the convention delegates.[68] The *Boston Post* well expressed the Democratic attitude toward developments in Kansas when it declared the Republicans "want and mean to have Kansas to use in the presidential struggle of 1860."[69]

In his inaugural address in May, 1857, Walker indicated that he believed Kansas was destined to be a free state, and that the constitution to be drawn up by the forthcoming convention should be referred to the people, or Congress should refuse to admit the Territory as a state. Other Southerners themselves had said that they expected Kansas to be free, but not when they were acting in the same official capacity as Walker, hence some in the South criticized him for expressing such views where he did, though others upheld him in so doing. The main point of controversy, however, was over the question as to whether the constitution should be submitted to the people for ratification. As far as the relations between Buchanan and Walker are concerned, it is evident that the former promised the Governor that he was willing "to stand or fall" on the question of submitting the constitution to the voters. On the basis of information given him by Walker in regard to political groups in the Territory, Buchanan felt that, if the Kansas situation could be cleared up in accordance with the principle he suggested, it would result in a triumph for the Democratic party there on the basis of the union

68. *New York Times*, April 10, 1857; *Kansas Herald of Freedom* without date quoted in *Boston Post*, Feb. 22, 1858.

69. August 20, 1857. The *Cincinnati Enquirer*, Sept. 18, 1857, charged that the Republicans did not vote for convention delegates, so that they might, for political reasons, keep Kansas matters unsettled.

of pro-slavery and anti-slavery Democrats.[70] Some in the South held that it was the wise and proper procedure to refer the constitution,[71] but many there contended that it was not necessary, that many states had been admitted without referring their instruments, that through the convention to frame a constitution the people really spoke in their sovereign capacity, and that Walker had no authority to say that reference was an essential condition of the admission of the state. The campaign for submission was viewed as an effort on the part of the Republicans to keep up agitation for political purposes after they had refused to vote in the election of delegates to the convention.[72]

In the Lecompton Convention there was a close struggle over the question of submitting the constitution to popular vote, but the proposal by John Calhoun to do so lost by one vote,[73] and then a compromise was effected under the terms of which it was decided to submit the Constitution to be accepted with or without the slavery clause attached. If one voted for the constitution with slavery, his action signified the willingness to admit further slavery; if he voted for the con-

70. See Walker's letter to Buchanan, June 28, 1857, *Covode Report*, 115–119, and Buchanan's to Walker, July 12, 1857, *Ibid.*, 112–113.

71. The *Richmond Inquirer* held that view (see issues of June 26, July 11, Oct. 27, 1857), and so did Henry A. Wise of Virginia (See Simms, *Hunter*, 138–139). The *Daily Picayune* thought it "fair" to refer it, but not legally necessary to do so (June 23, July 8, 1857).

72. For these various views see *Mobile Daily Register,* June 11, Sept. 16, 1857; *Arkansas True Democrat,* July 7, 1857; Simms, *Hunter,* 88–91; *Toombs and Cobb Correspondence,* Toombs to W. W. Burwell, July 11, 1857, 403–404 and Lucius Q. C. Lamar to Howell Cobb, July 17, 1857, 405–406; *North Carolina Standard,* June 27 and July 4, 1857.

73. *Covode Report,* 157–172.

stitution without slavery, it meant no further admission, but in either case it was a vote to protect the little slave property in Kansas. This was not a direct method of submitting the slavery question, but Buchanan held that it submitted what was the fundamental point of the dispute, and that the few slaves there should not be summarily confiscated. If the people desired to change their constitution after they became a state, they could do so at any time,[74] and in this view he was no doubt correct.[75]

Much of the controversy over the Lecompton Constitution, which was accepted with the slavery clause after the free state men refused to vote, consisted in stating again the arguments that had been made before the convention met. A pro-slavery minority, so the Republican argument ran, had deprived the anti-slavery majority of its political rights in Kansas, and was trying to force that majority to accept its will.[76] The anti-slavery group had its chance in the spring of 1857 and muffed it, so the pro-Lecompton argument ran, and now they were refusing to admit a slave state which had been more "regular" in reaching the goal of statehood than had California.[77] Many Northern Democrats were hostile to the Lecompton proceedings, even if that hostility was not reflected to a great extent in the Senate vote on admission of Kansas under the Lecomp-

74. See message to Congress Dec. 8, 1857 in *Works of James Buchanan*, edited by John B. Moore (12 Volumes, Philadelphia and London), Vol. X, 146–151.

75. See discussion by Philip Auchampaugh, *James Buchanan and his Cabinet* (Duluth, Minnesota, 1926), 27.

76. See remarks of Seward, *Globe*, 35 Cong., 1 Sess., March 3, 1858, 942; *New York Times*, March 9, 1858.

77. *Augusta Constitutionalist*, Feb. 3, 4, 1858; *Savannah Republican*, Jan. 9, 30, Feb. 16, 1858.

ton Constitution. Douglas felt that the instrument as presented was a violation of the Kansas-Nebraska Act, a vitiation of the principle of popular sovereignty, and he came to a dramatic break with Buchanan over the President's willingness to admit Kansas as a state. Walker also broke with the President, and the skies were not bright for the Democratic party.[78]

The Lecompton Constitution was acceptable to the Senate, but it failed of acceptance in the House, where a motion to resubmit the entire instrument prevailed. But did Congress have the authority to force a territory, when that embryonic state was making a constitution, to submit it to popular vote as a prerequisite of statehood? Many said no, whereupon William H. English, an anti-Lecompton Democrat, engineered a compromise between the Senate and House positions, under which the House view prevailed, but with the added stipulation that, if Kansas rejected the Constitution, she would have to wait for admission until she had the population equal to the ratio necessary for a representative in Congress. If the instrument were accepted, the Territory would receive a liberal grant of public land. The latter provision was described at the time as a "bribe," [79] and has been so regarded by many historians since. However, it was a customary practice for Congress to donate land to states when they were admitted. Minnesota, when admitted in 1857, was given a tract as large as the one offered Kansas under the English measure. The Grow bill, which provided in 1856 for the coming in of Kansas as a free state, had an identical provision, and when that hectic Territory became a

78. Milton, *Eve of Conflict*, 270–273, gives a good account of this phase of the controversy.
79. *New York Times*, April 22, 26, 1858.

free state in 1861 she received the donation called a "bribe" in 1858.[80] When resubmitted the Constitution was rejected by a large majority. It is significant to note that the free state group participated in the regular election of a territorial legislature several months after they refused to take part in the election of delegates to the constitutional convention, and that they won handsomely in that election.[81] In a premature state election held on January 4, 1858, they won again. It appears that they were nearly always victorious when a victory did not mean the removal of Kansas from the realm of controversy.

80. See article by Frank H. Hodder, entitled "Some aspects of the English Bill for the Admission of Kansas," in *American Historical Association Report,* 1906, 201–210.

81. Spring, *Kansas,* 216–220.

V

The Supreme Court and the
Slavery Controversy

THE Dred Scott decision, in 1857, came as the climax
to a controversy of a legal nature, which, in respect to
two points in particular, had been going on for some
time. One was the question as to whether slaves were
regarded as property under the Constitution, and the
other, whether the Supreme Court should be the arbiter
in regard to the status of slavery in the territories. The
Republicans usually contended that slavery, as a personal relationship between master and slaves, might be
established by states, but existed as such only by reason of positive local law, and that Congress could not
maintain or establish slavery anywhere. To do so,
argued Chase, would be a violation of the Fifth Amendment to the Constitution. Wade would "never" acknowl-
edge the "title" to a slave as property, and Senator
James Shields, of Illinois, declared that Northern feeling revolted at the Southern contention that the Constitution protected the right of property in slaves.[1]

There were several provisions in the Constitution
which, in the minds of Southerners, showed that the

1. For Chase's view see *Appendix to Globe,* 33 Cong., 1 Sess.,
Feb. 3, 1854, 137–138; for Wade's see *ibid.,* Feb. 6, 1854, 339;
and for Shield's see *Globe,* 31 Cong., 1 Sess., April 5, 1850.

instrument did place the property stamp upon the slave. It provided that slaves imported might be taxed during the twenty-year period when Congress could not forbid the foreign slave trade, and it made mandatory the return of slaves escaping from one state to another. Five slaves were to be counted as three persons in apportioning representatives and in the laying of direct taxes. It was obligatory upon the Federal Government to aid the states in suppressing insurrections, and the reference was conceivably to slave insurrections. As was true of slave codes in the states, the Constitution seemed to imply that slaves were both persons and property. Senator Dixon, of Kentucky, held that, under the Constitution, a master's ownership of his slave was as complete as that of his land or horse, and Senator J. M. Berrien, of Georgia, pointed out that slaves had been taxed, according to valuation, along with land and dwelling-houses when the Federal Government levied a direct tax during the early years of the nineteenth century.[2]

⌐The question as to whether the Supreme Court should be the final arbiter on the status of slavery in the territories had been discussed at length for ten years before the Dred Scott decision was given. After Senator John M. Clayton, of Delaware, made the proposal in 1847 that the Court should settle that annoying question, a considerable difference of opinion de-

2. See *Appendix to Globe*, 33 Cong., 1 Sess., Feb. 4, 1854, 142–143, for argument of Dixon, and *ibid.*, 30 Cong., 1 Sess., June 28, 1848, 877–878, for that of Berrien. The latter was correct in his assertion in regard to taxing slaves as property. A direct tax was imposed in 1798, 1813, 1815 and 1816, and was applied in part to slaves each time. See Simms, *Life of John Taylor* (Richmond, 1932), 131. They were taxed by head in 1798, and according to valuation the other three times.

veloped in regard to the proposal. Free-Soilers and
some of the Whigs opposed it, other more conservative
Whigs favored it, and Southern Democrats, though
some were inclined at first to distrust the court, came
gradually to accept Clayton's view.[3] Under the Compromise Acts of 1850, provision was made for referring
to the court controversies over the title to slave property in the territories, and when the Kansas-Nebraska
Act was framed the same kind of provision was made,
because the Democrats differed as to the power of a
territorial legislature over slavery.

The Dred Scott case had been a matter of litigation
for years before it was decided by the Supreme Court
of the United States. Scott had lived temporarily with
his owner, Dr. John Emerson, in the free state of Illinois
and also in territory made free by the Missouri Compromise Act of 1820. After Dr. Emerson's death, Scott,
in 1846, sued Mrs. Emerson for his freedom, and
though the Negro received a favorable decision in one
Missouri court, the supreme court of that state held
that he was a slave, despite the temporary residence in
a free state and in free territory. The two-to-one decision of the latter court appears to have been a politically partisan one, for the tribunal had frequently before that time allowed slaves their freedom when they
returned to Missouri after residing in free territory.
Before 1852, when the Missouri supreme court decision
was given, Mrs. Emerson had married Dr. C. C. Chaffee, of Massachusetts, who was an abolitionist member
of Congress from that state from 1855 to 1859. When
the case, after 1852, went to the United States circuit
court, it is thus conceivable that Chaffee, an abolition-

3. Charles Warren, *The Supreme Court in United States History* (2 Volumes, Boston, 1935), Vol. II, 207–217.

ist, may have been the defendant; but to avoid such a peculiar situation Scott and his family were transferred to J. F. Sanford, of New York, a brother of Mrs. Chaffee, and an executor of Dr. Emerson's estate. Dred Scott, claiming to be a citizen of Missouri, was thus suing Sanford, a citizen of New York.[4]

Sanford held that the United States circuit court did not have jurisdiction in the case, because Scott was a Negro and hence not a citizen. However, the court heard the argument, and found in favor of Sanford, after which an appeal was taken to the Supreme Court of the United States. That tribunal, when it finally considered the case early in 1857, was undecided as to what points to consider. Four judges had held that the plea in abatement, that is, Sanford's contention that the lower court did not have jurisdiction, could be considered, and four that it could not. Nelson was at first undecided, but finally took a negative position, and on February 14, 1857, was authorized to write the decision of the Court, affirming the contention that Scott was a slave because the Missouri supreme court had so ruled. Neither jurisdiction of the lower Federal court nor the question of slavery in the territories was to be considered, when Nelson wrote his decision.[5]

The evidence strongly suggests that the reason the Dred Scott decision, as finally given, did cover so many points is to be found in the determination of two judges, Benjamin R. Curtis and John McLean, to give dissenting opinions covering all phases of the case. Evidence of this character exists in letters written by Justices

4. See Frank H. Hodder, "Some Phases of the Dred Scott Case," in *Mississippi Valley Historical Review*, Vol. XVI, June, 1929, 3–22. See pp. 6–7 for above discussion.
5. Hodder, *op. cit.*, 9–12.

Catron and Grier to James Buchanan before the latter was inaugurated March 4, 1857. Catron had written to Buchanan urging him to write Grier "how necessary" it was to take advantage of the "opportunity" now presented to settle the agitation over slavery in the territories, and the President-elect did write Grier a letter. What had brought the majority of the Court to a conclusion to give a decision on all the controversial points in the case had happened, however, before Buchanan wrote the letter, for Catron himself said in his communication mentioned above that the reason the constitutionality of the Missouri Compromise would be decided was because "a majority of my Brethren will be forced up to this point by two dissentients." Grier wrote of the history of the case in greater detail. He stated that the first question which presented itself was the right of a Negro to sue in the courts of the United States. A majority of the court were of the opinion that the question did not arise on the pleadings and that we were compelled to give an opinion on the merits. After much discussion it was finally agreed that the merits of the case might be satisfactorily decided without giving an opinion on the question of the Missouri Compromise; and the case was committed to Judge Nelson to write the opinion of the court affirming the judgment of the court below, but leaving both those difficult questions untouched.

"But it appeared that our brothers who dissented from the majority, especially Justice McLean, were determined to come out with a long and labored dissent, including their opinions and arguments on both the troublesome points, though not necessary to a decision in the case. In our opinion, both the points are in the case and may be legitimately considered. Those who held a different opinion from Messrs. McLean and Curtis on the powers of Congress and the validity of the Compromise Act feel compelled to express their opinion on the subject, Nelson and myself refusing to commit ourselves." [6]

\\Professor Hodder, who feels that the two anti-slavery judges were mainly responsible for the decision, does not assign them very laudable motives for insisting on it. He claims that Curtis, wishing for financial reasons to resign from the Court and build up a law practice, had to overcome some earlier feeling developed against him because of his pro-slavery decisions, and felt that the Dred Scott case afforded him an opportunity to ingratiate himself into the favor of the people of Massachusetts. McLean, he points out, had engaged frequently in political discussion while a member of the Court, and had for many years been a candidate for the presidency. He still felt that his age would not forbid his candidacy for that office in 1860.[7] In considering the factors that influenced individual judges, mention should be made of the fact that Justice Campbell, one of the pro-slavery judges, reversed, in his decision in

6. *The Works of James Buchanan,* Edited by John Bassett Moore (12 Volumes, Philadelphia and London, 1910), Vol. X, Catron to Buchanan, Feb. 19, 1857, 106, Grier to Buchanan, Feb. 23, 1857, 106–108. Also Hodder, *op. cit.,* 11–12.

7. Hodder, *op. cit.,* 12–15. Professor Francis P. Weisenburger, in *The Life of John McLean: A Politician on the United States Supreme Court* (Columbus, 1937), deals at length with McLean's political ambitions and career. He does feel, however, that McLean was sincere in his convictions on the question of slavery in the territories, though influenced by political considerations in giving his decision. For latter point, see 195–210. On political activities, see also Warren, *op. cit.,* Vol. II, 269–272.

the Dred Scott case, his former position to the effect
that Congress did have the power to prohibit slavery
in the territories.[8]

Even if the main responsibility for the Dred Scott
decision does not rest upon the South, though many
have maintained for years that it did, it is no doubt
true that political and environmental circumstances
played their part in determining the constitutional arguments advanced by all of the judges, with the exception
probably of Nelson, who gave the decision he had once
been directed to write. Five of the judges came from
the slave states, though there were not "five slaveholding judges," as the *New York Tribune* was wont to say.[9]
Curtis had been a Whig, McLean was an Ohio Republican, and Grier a Pennsylvania Democrat. Stripped of
its many and controversial technicalities, it was a decision in which six judges held that the Negro was not a
citizen of the United States and that Congress had no
constitutional power to prohibit slavery in the territories, two took the reverse position on those points, and
one, Nelson, as stated above, simply held that Scott
was a slave because the state of Missouri had so decreed.

Separate decisions were given by each judge, and
each did not always arrive at similar conclusions by
similar processes of reasoning. However, the arguments
of Chief Justice Taney for the majority and of Justice
Curtis for the minority are generally regarded as the

8. E. I. McCormac, "Justice Campbell and the Dred Scott
Decision," *Mississippi Valley Historical Review*, Vol. XIX, June,
1932, 565–571.

9. *New York Tribune*, March 13, 16, 1857. Milton says that
none of the members of the Court owned slaves, though he
quotes Beveridge to the effect that Catron and Daniel may have
had one or two house servants. *Eve of Conflict*, 249.

strongest for their respective positions. Taney did not deny that a state might confer citizenship upon Negroes, but he held that such action did not make him a citizen of the United States. He gave a long historical disquisition to show that all the states, at the time the Constitution was made, imposed inequalities upon the Negro, and concluded that the makers of the Constitution regarded them as a subordinate and inferior class who "had no rights or privileges but such as those who held the power and the Government might choose to grant them." A person who was a citizen in a state, the Chief Justice contended, had only such rights in the several states as were "secured to him by the laws of nations and the comity of States."

After elaborating the above thesis, Taney went on to say that it was a matter of record in the Federal circuit court that Dred Scott was born a slave, and if he were not free he was not a citizen. It was the function of the Supreme Court to examine the record of the lower Federal court to see if any error existed there, for if the former court remained silent upon any point in that record, such silence would lead to "misconstruction" and "mischief" in the future. Taney held that Dred Scott was still a slave, because the Missouri Compromise Act was unconstitutional, and hence had not made free the territory into which the Negro had been taken. The territories were acquired by the Government for the whole people, and Congress could not prevent a citizen from sharing them with his property. Clauses in the Constitution permitting the states to carry on the foreign slave trade for twenty years, and pledging that fugitive slaves should be returned to their owners, were cited by the Chief Justice as proof of recognition of slaves as property. He claimed that the only power that

Congress had over slavery was "the power coupled with the duty of guarding and protecting the owner in his rights," and concluded that, if Congress could not exercise powers of prohibiting slavery in the territories, "it will be admitted, we presume, that it could not authorize a Territorial Government to exercise them."[10]

Curtis held that those were citizens of the United States who were or could be citizens of the states under the Articles of Confederation. He showed that Negroes were citizens in some states when the Articles existed, and contended that, if they were citizens of a state, they were citizens of the United States. He admitted, however, that a citizen of a state would not necessarily have in another state all the rights he had in the one that gave him citizenship. The power of Congress to make all needful rules and regulations for the territories gave that body, said Curtis, ample authority to prohibit slavery in them. He stressed the word "all," and emphasized the point that an exception to "needful rules" would be made in the case of slavery, if Congress did not prohibit it. From his argument the conclusion naturally followed that the lower Federal court did have jurisdiction in the case of Scott, and that the judgment should be reversed and a new trial ordered.[11]

10. See Taney's decision in *Reports of Cases Argued and Adjudged in the Supreme Court of the United States*, Howard, Vol. XIX, U. S. Report 60 (Washington, 1857), 399–454. Taney of course denied the jurisdiction of the Federal circuit court, since he denied that Scott was a citizen owing to the fact that he was not only a Negro but also a slave. After Scott's return to Missouri, that state, the Court held, had the right to determine whether the Negro's sojourn in the free state of Illinois entitled him to freedom.

11. See *ibid.*, 564–633, for complete decision of Curtis. See also Benjamin R. Curtis, *A Memoir of Benjamin Robbins Curtis, with Some of his Professional and Miscellaneous Writings* (2 Vols., Boston, 1789), Vol. II, especially 213–245, 272 *et seq.*

It has been frequently claimed that the part of the Dred Scott decision declaring the Missouri Compromise Act unconstitutional was *obiter dictum*. Why should the court after declaring that the lower Federal court had no jurisdiction because a Negro was not a citizen then enter into the slavery phase of the case? A Southerner, gifted with unusual legal acumen, answered that question soon after the decision had been given. He said that because the judges gave one reason why the lower court did not have jurisdiction was no reason why another could not be given. To prove that Dred Scott was a slave strengthened the contention that he was not a citizen.[12]

An examination of a considerable number of newspapers North and South indicates that there was more immediate discussion of the Dred Scott decision in the North than in the South. The Republican press was, as a rule, bitter in its denunciation of the majority of the Court. One Republican journal declared that the decision was "a wicked and false judgment," which was "deficient in every element which should entitle it to respect," and that "any slave-driving editor or Virginia bar-room politician" could have reasoned as well as Taney.[13] The *Boston Atlas* declared that the decision represented "the deadliest blow which has been aimed at the liberties of America since the day of Benedict

12. See Speech of Judah P. Benjamin in Senate, *Globe*, 35 Cong., 1 Sess., March 11, 1858, 1069–1071. For similar argument against *obiter dictum* charge, see Edward S. Corwin, "The Dred Scott Decision in the Light of Contemporary Legal Doctrine," *American Historical Review*, XVII, Oct., 1911, 52–69. Corwin, however, criticizes in some respects Taney's legal reasoning on the power of Congress over slavery in the territories.

13. *New York Tribune*, March 10, 11, 12, 1857. That paper said that if slaves were recognized as property by the Constitution, as the Court said, they might be carried into any free state.

Arnold," and the *Boston Chronicle* applied the term "scoundrels" to a "majority" of the members of the court.[14] However, the powerful *New York Times*, though deploring the decision and feeling that it would produce a stronger reaction against slavery, held that it was "the law of the land," that the authority of the Court must not be denied, and that the violent utterances against that tribunal were "unsound and unsafe." [15]

The views of two Northern Democratic journals typify the immediate response of that segment of the press to the decision. The *Cincinnati Enquirer* claimed that it vindicated completely "the doctrine of the Nebraska Bill and that it was the "ablest [decision] which has perhaps ever proceeded from this venerable tribunal." It criticized McLean for having volunteered an opinion on the subject of slavery in the territories years before that subject came before him judicially.[16] The *Boston Post*, in denouncing the "anarchical" utterances of those who assailed the Court, pointed out that the judges had no agency in bringing the case before them, and performed only their constitutional duty in deciding it. "Lying" and "falsehood" were the terms that journal hurled at those who claimed that the decision legalized slavery in the free states. The *Post* contended that, in recognizing the sovereignty of Missouri over slavery in her borders, the Court recognized state control over slavery, except in the case of the mandatory return of fugitive slaves.[17]

14. *Boston Atlas*, March 9, 1857, and *Boston Chronicle* quoted in *ibid.*, March 13, 1857.
15. *New York Times*, March 7, 11, 1857.
16. *Cincinnati Enquirer*, March 8, 10, 17, 1857.
17. *Boston Post*, March 10, 12, 14, May 30, 1857.

Such Southern journals as did express themselves naturally showed elation at what they regarded as a legal victory. The *Charleston Mercury* felt that those in the South known as "secessionists" had simply been a step ahead of the Court "in declaring what was the law of the land." The *Richmond Enquirer* characterized the decision as a great victory for the Union and the Constitution, and declared that the "abolitionists" would now have to wage warfare against the government itself, if they continued to maintain their principles. The case, that paper claimed, "was instituted and prosecuted" entirely by those who "complain of the result." [18]

In June, 1857, it was announced in the newspapers that Chaffee, as owner of Scott, had taken the proper steps through Taylor Blow in Missouri to give the Negro and his family their freedom.[19] Seward, in a speech in the Senate in 1858, in claiming that the Dred Scott case was on the docket through "design," spoke of "the defending slaveholder" for whom Scott had played "the political game unwittingly," and from whom he received "as a reward" his freedom. "The defending slaveholder" was of course really an abolitionist, so Seward's remarks drew from Judah P. Benjamin, Senator from Louisiana, the retort that it was known that the man who freed Scott "was a Black-Republican compeer in the other House, of the Senator from New York, Mr. Chaffee of Massachusetts." [20]

When Lincoln and Douglas, as candidates for the

18. *Charleston Mercury,* March 17, 1857; *Richmond Enquirer,* March 10, 13, 21, 1857.

19. *Illinois State Journal,* June 3, 1857; *Arkansas True Democrat* quoting *St. Louis Evening News,* June 9, 1857.

20. See Seward's remarks in *Globe,* 35 Cong., 1 Sess., March 3, 1858, 941, and Benjamin's in *ibid.,* March 11, 1858, 1071.

United States Senate in Illinois, were engaged in a series of debates, the Supreme Court policy was the subject of a spirited controversy between them. Both of
those contestants, in the fifties prior to the Dred Scott
decision, had accepted the Supreme Court as the arbiter
on the question of the status of slavery in the territories.
Douglas had placed the Supreme Court clause in the
Kansas-Nebraska Act, and Lincoln in 1856, seven
months before the Dred Scott decision, had expressed
his attitude in the following language: "Do you say that
such restriction of slavery [in the territories] would be
unconstitutional, and that some of the states would not
submit to its enforcement? I grant you that an unconstitutional act is not a law; but I do not ask and will not
take your construction of the Constitution. The Supreme
Court of the United States is the tribunal to decide such
a question, and we will submit to its decisions; and if
you do also, there will be an end of the matter. Will
you? If not, who are the disunionists—you or we?" [21]

How far the decision given was from the "end of the
matter" may be seen by Lincoln's utterances after. He
was willing to accept the decision in the particular case
in which it was given, but not as a rule of political action. He felt that the judgment of the Court was "erroneous," and, in working for a reversal of that judgment, he would, in spite of the decision, vote to prohibit
slavery in the territories, were he in Congress. Lincoln
delayed some time before making the charge that the
Dred Scott decision represented a conspiracy, but in his
"House-Divided" speech in 1858 he said that the language of the Kansas-Nebraska Act, Buchanan's reference in his inaugural address to the forthcoming judg-

21. Lincoln, *Works*, Vol. I, 220. Speech at Galena, Illinois,
August 1, 1856.

ment of the Court and other circumstances indicated that "Stephen, Franklin, Roger, and James" had "all understood one another from the beginning," and had worked in concert to have the Court give its decision.[22] Douglas, in the face of Lincoln's repeated assertions of the latter's belief in the conspiracy charge, pointed out that Buchanan was in England at the time that the Kansas-Nebraska Act was passed, that the Dred Scott case was not then on the Supreme Court docket, and that the abolitionists who brought the case before the Supreme Court had, since the decision, freed Scott. Douglas pronounced the charge against himself "an infamous lie."[23]

In the debates, Douglas emphasized the duty of obedience to the Supreme Court ruling by Republicans as well as by Democrats, but Lincoln saw in the recent decision a possibility that Democrats did not all construe it alike, even if he did have to admit that it ran counter to the Republican policy of prohibiting slavery in the territories. Hence at Freeport he asked Douglas a question which was designed to show the difference between the popular sovereignty idea of the senator and the apparent legal character of the decision. The question was, "Can the people of a United States Territory, in any lawful way, against the wish of any citizen of the United States, exclude slavery from its limits

22. *Ibid.*, 228, speech at Springfield, June 28, 1857; 243, "House-Divided" speech June 16, 1858; 255–260, Speech at Chicago, July 10, 1858. References are of course to Douglas, Pierce, Taney and Buchanan.

23. *Lincoln-Douglas Debates* (Sparks Edition), 108, 121–122, 158, 179–180, 290. Buchanan had said in his inaugural that there would be a decision. That statement was on the basis of information he had from Justice Catron, and was emphasized by Lincoln as an indication of collusion.

prior to the formation of a State constitution?" Douglas answered to the effect that the people of a territory might exclude it by refusing to pass local police regulations essential to the maintenance of slavery. By "unfriendly legislation," a term he used, he therefore really meant the absence of positive legislation.[24]

Seward also charged that the Dred Scott decision was the result of conspiracy, and threatened to make a Supreme Court that would see matters of constitutional interpretation as the Republicans did. "Let the Court recede," he said. "Whether it recedes or not, we shall reorganize the Court, and thus reform its political sentiments and practices, and bring them into harmony with the Constitution." [25]

Some months before Douglas enunciated his Freeport Doctrine, Benjamin gave a careful account as to how the Supreme Court clause became a part of the Kansas-Nebraska Act. Southerners claimed that they had a right under the Constitution to hold slave property in the territories during the territorial existence, and Northern Democrats felt that the territorial legislature could decide the slavery question before statehood. The clause "subject only to the Constitution" was incorporated in the measure, with the intention of leaving that clause to the construction of the courts, but later that intention was made specific by the clause providing for

24. *Ibid.* 152, 161. The *Chicago Times*, virtually parroting Douglas, explained the Freeport Doctrine as follows: "The Dred Scott decision negatives the power of Congress and of the territory to prohibit persons taking slaves to the territories. But whatever rights people have under the Constitution, they can exercise or not, as they please. They can pass laws for the protection of slave property, or not; a failure to pass such laws is fatal to slavery. That is the whole case." August 31, 1858.
25. *Globe*, 35 Cong., 1 Sess., March 3, 1858, 941–943.

appeal to the Supreme Court in all matters involving the right to slave property.[26] Douglas early in 1859 had engaged in a debate in the Senate with Albert G. Brown and Jefferson Davis, of Mississippi, over the respective merits of popular sovereignty and protection for slave property in the territories, and, as a result of that debate, decided to prepare an article expounding his popular sovereignty doctrine as a constitutional principle and not simply as a matter of practical policy.[27] These developments helped set the stage for the Davis-Douglas debate in the Senate early in 1860.

In the late summer and the fall of 1858, Davis made speeches in the Northeast, in which, it was alleged later by Douglas and by Senator Pugh of Ohio, he virtually accepted Douglas' Freeport Doctrine. The Mississippian, however, claimed that they quoted only a part of one of his speeches in question, and hence did not fairly represent his position.[28] March 1, 1860, Davis offered

26. *Ibid.*, Feb. 8, 1858, 615–616.

27. Milton, *op. cit.*, 366–369, 386–388. The article was published in *Harper's Magazine* in September, 1859.

28. Jefferson Davis, *Constitutionalist. His Letters, Papers and Speeches.* Collected and Edited by Dunbar Rowland (10 Volumes, Jackson, Mississippi, 1923). For controversy see Vol. III, 344–347, Vol. IV, 121–125, 130. The clause quoted by Douglas and Pugh from a speech which Davis made at Portland, Maine, August 24, 1858, was as follows: "If the inhabitants of any territory should refuse to enact such laws and police regulations as would give security to their property or to his, it would be rendered more or less valueless, in proportion to the difficulty of holding it without such protection. In the case of property in the labor of man, the insecurity would be so great that the owner could not ordinarily retain it. Therefore, though the right would remain, the remedy being withheld, it would follow that the owner would be practically debarred by the circumstances of the case, from taking slave property into a territory where the sense of the inhabitants was opposed to its introduction. So much for the oft repeated fallacy of forcing slavery upon any com-

to the Senate some earlier resolutions now revised, which denounced attempts of abolitionists to intermeddle in Southern affairs, declared that acts in Northern states designed to nullify the fugitive slave law were revolutionary and unconstitutional, affirmed the sovereignty of the states, and the "duty of Congress" to protect "constitutional rights in a territory," provided the executive and judicial branches of the general Government or the territorial legislature could not or would not provide such protection.[29]

In debating the resolutions, Douglas claimed that the Court clause in the Kansas-Nebraska Act was applicable only to cases that might arise under territorial enactments concerning slavery, and that non-intervention by Congress meant that that body could not prohibit, abolish or protect slavery in the territories. Insistence upon congressional protection for slavery or congressional exclusion of it would, he feared, produce the "irrepressible conflict." Davis countered with the claim that

munity." In the same speech, however, Davis claimed that what was property in the states was property in the territories until they became states, and that the policy of the Democratic party was not to prohibit or establish slavery anywhere, "not to interfere on the one side or the other, but protecting each individual in his constitutional rights, to leave every independent community to determine and adjust all domestic questions as in their wisdom may seem best." Vol. III, 299–302. In speeches in New York before the end of that year (1858), Davis contended that it was the function of the Government "to protect, not to destroy property," and that it could not establish or create property. In Mississippi, in the same year, Davis proclaimed the right of protection for property and emphasized that part of Taney's decision in which he said that Congress, he presumed, could not authorize a territory to do what the national legislature could not do. Vol. III, 320, 333, 347.

29. *Ibid.*, Vol. IV, 203–204. Davis' position on the question of slavery in the territories was approved by the Senate. The Democrats voted overwhelmingly in favor.

Douglas confessed that the inhabitants of a territory derived what power they had from the organic act of Congress, and that, therefore, logic dictated that they could not exercise a greater power than could Congress. He pointed out that Taney, in fact, had said that the territory could not be authorized to prohibit slavery, if Congress had not that power itself. The right to have slave property in the territories was derived, Davis contended, from the Constitution itself, and the main function of the general Government was to give protection to property, where states were unable to do so. Taney in the Dred Scott decision had spoken of the duty of Congress to guard and protect the owner in his rights, so it does seem that Davis was much nearer in accord with the Chief Justice than Douglas, though in the light of the existing sectional and political situation, the policy of the latter may have been more practicable.[30]

While Davis had much support in the South for his idea of congressional protection for slavery in the territories, dissent was frequently expressed. Toombs said privately, if not publicly, that the Davis resolutions were inspired by hostility to Douglas, that, though he agreed with them in the main, he thought it "folly to raise and make prominent such issues now." Stephens claimed that Davis' position on the status of slavery in the territories represented an abandonment of the historic Southern position of non-intervention by Congress.[31] Typical of the argument against Stephens' position was that of the *Richmond Enquirer* which held

30. For Douglas' argument, see *Appendix to Globe* 36 Cong., 1 Sess., May 15, 1860, 307–308, 314, and for Davis', *ibid.*, May 16, 1860, 454, 460.

31. Toombs, *Correspondence*, Toombs to Stephens, Feb. 10, 1860, 460–462; Louis Pendleton, *Alexander H. Stephens* (Philadelphia, 1908), 154–155.

that, if property had a right to exist in territories, it was entitled to protection, and if the other branches of the Federal Government did not co-operate with the Federal courts in making their decisions effective, then such decisions were "a dead letter." [32]

Before the Supreme Court of the United States passed upon the validity of the fugitive slave law of 1850, that act had become controversial from a number of angles. A fugitive slave was an object of particular commiseration or pity, and it was natural that there should be a strong disinclination to return him to his master. In fact, there was a strong inclination to prevent the owner or his agent from effecting the return of the slave. The controversy over this phase of the slavery question was all out of proportion to the number of fugitive slaves. [33] Yet the argument accentuated considerably the feeling between the free and slave states.

In the North there was, to some extent, an appeal to the "higher law" as a principle which justified one in refusing to aid in the rendition of fugitive slaves, or actually in thwarting the rendition. Seward, in giving expression to the "higher law" doctrine, gave it a broader application than simply to the fugitive slave controversy, and Horace Mann, a member of the House of Representatives from Massachusetts, declared that the

32. *Richmond Enquirer,* Nov. 11, 1858, June 30, 1859.
33. *The American Annual Cyclopaedia of the Year,* 1861 (New York), Vol. I, page 579, states that, according to the Census returns, the number of fugitive slaves was 1,011 in 1850, and only 803 in 1860. This estimate is no doubt too small. An outstanding authority on the fugitive slave question estimates that 40,000 slaves were aided in their escape through Ohio, 1830 to 1860, and more than 9000 in the same period through Philadelphia. Those figures did not, of course, include the total escaping. See Wilbur H. Siebert, *The Underground Railroad from Slavery to Freedom* (New York, 1898).

doctrine that "there is no higher law than the law of the state is palpable and practical atheism." [34] In 1852 William Hosmer published a book on *The Higher Law in its Relations to Civil Government,* which he dedicated to Seward. The "higher law," so the argument ran, banished all sin and protected the rights of all, and hence left much to the decision of the individual conscience. In the case of civil law, "the duty of obedience" depended "entirely on the character of the law." Slavery was contrary to the law of God, so not only should the fugitive slave law be broken, but also those parts of the Constitution that sanctioned slavery.[35]

Not only Southerners but also many Northerners denounced the "higher law" doctrine. Hunter admitted that, if the laws of God and of man came into conflict, the former should be obeyed, but he did not feel that a man should take an oath to the Constitution, if he felt that the instrument was contrary to the law of God. Douglas had "no faith in the Union loving sentiments of those" who would not carry out the Constitution in good faith, for it was upon the Constitution that the Union rested. He, too, felt that they should not take an oath to that instrument, if they believed that it violated "the Divine law." [36]

When many Northern states passed laws known as "personal liberty laws," which were either in conflict with the provisions of the fugitive slave law of 1850 or

34. See *Appendix to Globe,* 32 Cong., 1 Sess., August 23, 1852, 1075, for Mann's remarks.

35. William Hosmer, *The Higher Law in its Relations to Civil Government: with Particular Reference to Slavery and the Fugitive Slave Law* (Auburn, 1852), 27–32, 75–79, 158–161, 175–176.

36. See Simms, *Life of Hunter,* 121–123, for views of both Douglas and Hunter.

hampered its prosecution, the legal aspects of the fugitive slave question were warmly debated. The personal liberty laws, which were passed from time to time in as many as eleven states, varied considerably, but among other provisions had the following: slaves were secured the benefits of writ of habeas corpus and of trial by jury, counsel was provided for their defense, no state facilities might be used in effecting the return of the fugitive, and in some cases depositions were not admitted as evidence and "two credible witnesses" were required to prove the master's claim. Connecticut and Wisconsin had both the provisions in regard to depositions and two witnesses, and Michigan and Massachusetts had virtually the same provisions when they required two witnesses. Since the Federal law of 1850, even if it did make the return of slaves easy, declared that satisfactory proof of slave ownership might be given the judges or commissioners by deposition or affidavit, it is difficult to harmonize those portions of the state enactments with the Federal law. Yet there were stiff penalties for violating the state laws. Vermont, for a time at least, declared free any slave that entered the state.[37] In fact, any part of the process of substituting in the states a different method of procedure for returning slaves from that provided in the Federal law can scarcely be harmonized with the idea of the supremacy of Federal law. The *National Intelligencer* concluded that four of the states—Vermont, Massachusetts, Michigan and Wisconsin—had statutes that were "clearly

37. *Annual Cyclopaedia, op. cit.*, 575–579, summarizes the state enactments and the provisions of the Federal law. It should not be overlooked that one alleged purpose of the state enactments was to protect the free Negro, whose liberty, under the operation of the Federal law of 1850, seemed insecure.

unconstitutional," and a careful student of the fifties declared that the "personal liberty acts," though not professing nullification, were "the most practical nullification laws ever set in motion by states against a law of the United States." [38]

Two of the fugitive slave cases that came up for consideration under the law of 1850 attracted unusual attention. One was the case of Anthony Burns in Boston in 1854 and the other that of Booth in Wisconsin. Anthony Burns was an escaped slave who was returned to his owner, but only after a mob in Boston stormed the courthouse where Burns was and killed an assistant to the United States marshal who had the fugitive in charge.[39] The *Boston Post,* which claimed that a man had been killed for doing his "constitutional duty," soon after was denouncing the Massachusetts Legislature for substituting its own laws, characterized as "treasonable" and "shameful," for the rendition of fugitive slaves for those of Congress.[40] The *True Democrat* denounced the proceedings in the Burns case and characterized the Massachusetts "personal liberty act" as "nullification." [41]

The case of Sherman Booth in Wisconsin arose out of the fact that he had aided a fugitive slave to escape. He was convicted in the United States district court in 1855 of violating the fugitive slave law, but was freed under

38. *National Intelligencer,* Dec. 11, 1860, quoted in Vol. III, 30, of John G. Nicolay and John Hay, *Abraham Lincoln: A History* (10 Vols., New York, 1890); E. D. Fite, *The Presidential Campaign of 1860* (New York, 1911), 66.

39. For brief account of this case and further litigation growing out of it, see *Judicial Cases Concerning American Slavery and the Negro,* Edited by Helen T. Catterall, with Additions by James Hayden (5 Volumes, Washington, 1936), Vol. IV, 521–523. See also *Boston Post,* May 29, 31, 1854.

40. *Boston Post,* May 29, 1854, May 19, 1855.

41. *Arkansas True Democrat,* August 7, 1855.

a writ of habeas corpus by the Wisconsin supreme court on the ground that the Federal law was unconstitutional. On March 7, 1859, the United States Supreme Court unanimously upheld the fugitive slave law of 1850, and rebuked the Wisconsin court for interfering with the Federal authority.[42]

Between 1855 and 1859, James Doolittle, a candidate for the United States Senate in Wisconsin, had taken strong state rights ground in his defense of the action of the Wisconsin court, and had been applauded by Republicans there for that position. March 19, 1859, after the United States Supreme Court decision, the Wisconsin Legislature passed state rights resolutions which in the following language were about all that proponents of state sovereignty could ask: "Resolved, that the Government formed by the Constitution of the United States was not made the exclusive or final judge of the extent of the powers delegated to itself; but that, as in other cases of compact among parties having no common judge each has an equal right to judge for itself, as well of infractions as of the mode and measure of redress.

"Resolved, that the principle and construction contended for by the party which now rules in the councils of the nation, that the General Government is the exclusive judge of the extent of the powers delegated to it, stop nothing short of despotism, since the discretion of those who administer the Government, and not the Constitution, would be the measure of their powers; that the several states which formed that instrument,

42. Catterall, op. cit., Vol. IV, 91–97. This was the second writ issued by the Wisconsin court, as it had issued one freeing Booth from detention before a grand jury indicted him. See Catterall, 91–94.

being sovereign and independent, have the unquestionable right to judge of its infractions; and that a positive defiance of those sovereignties of all unauthorized acts done under color of that instrument is the rightful remedy." [43]

Wade praised the Wisconsin Court for its stand in defense of Virginia principles, and contended that a state "crowded to the wall by the General Government" was "to judge whether she shall stand on her reserved rights." [44] The *New York Tribune* claimed that a "broader" question of state rights was now raised than the one raised by the Virginia and Kentucky Resolutions. The question now was how to combat a Court over which there was not popular control. That paper felt from Carl Schurz's utterances at Milwaukee that Wisconsin was "no more likely to submit quietly to this decision of the Supreme Court in favor of its own exclusive authority than the States of Pennsylvania, Virginia and Georgia have done on some other occasions. We trust they will not." [45] Down South the *Richmond Enquirer* was rebuking Wisconsin for "nullification." [46]

Toombs, in a long speech in the Senate early in 1860, described the legal machinery, beginning with the New

43. James F. Sellers, "Republicanism and State Rights in Wisconsin," in *Mississippi Valley Historical Review*, Vol. XVII, Sept. 1930, 213–229. See complete quotation of Resolutions and discussion of Booth case in Samuel Tyler, *Memoir of Roger B. Taney* (Baltimore, 1922), 393–398. Sellers points out that the Wisconsin court did not issue another writ after the United States Supreme Court decision because Byron Paine, who was now on the Wisconsin court, had served as counsel for Booth, and would not take judicial action in the case. The other two judges divided on the question of another writ, 226.

44. Warren, *op. cit.*, 264–266.

45. *New York Tribune*, April 1, 1859.

46. *Richmond Enquirer*, April 2, 1859.

England Confederation in 1643, which had been developed for the return of fugitive slaves, and claimed that the Northern "personal liberty laws" ran counter to the Constitution, Federal law and the Supreme Court decision in 1859. The compact, he contended, had thus been broken by the North.[47]

47. *Appendix to Globe,* 36 Cong., 1 Sess., Jan. 24, 1860, 89–91.

VI

The Controversy over the Free Negro

To WHAT extent was the controversy between the free and slave states moral in nature? To what extent was the agitation against slavery the result of genuine interest in the elevation of the Negro? How far apart were the racial philosophies and practices of the free and slave states? The above questions cannot be answered with mathematical precision, but historical data can be presented which will throw light upon the answer to them.

In the North there was much talk of the Declaration of Independence, with its idea of equality, and of the early anti-slavery views of the man who penned the words of the great Declaration. Benjamin F. Wade denounced the slaveholder as guilty of "nefarious acts and selfishness" in maintaining slavery, and declared that the institution was contrary to the Declaration of Independence, which he characterized as "a declaration from Almighty God, that all men are created free and equal, and have the same inherent rights."[1] Abraham Lincoln declared that the phrase "all men are created equal" was used by Jefferson not because it was of any "practical use" in securing independence

1. *Globe*, 31 Cong., 1 Sess., Feb. 6, 1854, 339.

from England, "but for future use." [2] James Doolittle, a Senator from Wisconsin, in a speech in New York in 1860, declared that the Republicans acknowledged Jefferson "as their leader and chieftain." [3]

Northern Democrats, in challenging the assertions that Jefferson had views similar to those of the Republicans in the 1850's, pointed out, and correctly, that he signed bills for the government of territories in which slavery was not forbidden, and that he opposed both the proposed restriction on Missouri and the Missouri Compromise. [4] Some Southerners, such as Harper and Dew, denied the great Virginian's doctrine of equality, but others, emphasizing the fact that he was a slaveholder himself, denied that he meant to apply his doctrine to slaves. [5]

The much discussed slavery views of Jefferson which were given a variety of interpretations, may be briefly summarized. He felt that slavery was an evil, harmful to both white and black, but that, if the institution were abolished without colonizing the slaves, the two races, so dissimilar in many ways, could not live harmoniously together. That feeling probably helps to explain why he at his death freed only five of his slaves. Jefferson believed that, if slaves were scattered over a wider area, they could be more easily emancipated than if congested, and hence his opposition to territorial restriction on slavery in 1820. Furthermore, he thought party poli-

2. Abraham Lincoln, *Complete Works, Comprising His Speeches, Letters, State Papers and Miscellaneous Writings.* Edited by John G. Nicolay and John Hay (2 Volumes, New York, 1920), Vol. I, 231–232. Hereafter cited as Lincoln, *Works.*
    3. Quoted in *Boston Post,* April 30, 1860.
    4. *Boston Post,* April 30, May 2, 1860; *Detroit Free Press,* August 30, 1854.
    5. See latter view in *Arkansas True Democrat,* April 14, 1857.

tics was involved in the attempt to impose restrictions on Missouri when she applied for admission to the Union.[6] It should be borne in mind that the views of the author of the Declaration of Independence developed at a time when the sectional controversy over slavery was not intense. What with the rise of the Northern abolitionists and the development of the bitter political struggle over slavery after Jefferson's death, it is difficult to say what his views would then have been.

It is not to be denied that the trend of world thinking was hostile to slavery during the nineteenth century, that the Southern defense of the institution was in some respects extreme, and the Northern assault upon it in some respects sound. Yet when one weighs the moral aspects of the slavery controversy, he has to consider the sentiments in regard to the free Negro, who was an inevitable consequence of emancipation. Sentiment in the free states in regard to him was not radically different from that of the slave states, despite the lip service paid to equality by many in the North. On the whole, he had greater freedom of movement in the North than in the South and a greater degree of civil and political rights. In 1860 he was neither a citizen nor a voter in the slave states, and was a citizen in only a portion of the free states and a voter in a still smaller portion. The privilege of suffrage was accorded the Negro in the New England states, with the exception of Connecticut, and in New York, but in the latter he was subject to a property qualification not imposed on the whites. Incidentally, only approximately one-tenth of the free Negroes in the North were in the six New England states, and in the entire free state section that type of

6. Mellon, *Early American Views on Negro Slavery*, 105–109.

population did not equal its numbers in the land of slavery.[7]

Legal enactments hostile to the Negro were more numerous in the Northwest than in the Northeast. Between 1803 and 1807 the Ohio Legislature passed a series of "Black Laws," which required a Negro entering the state to give a certificate of freedom and to deposit bonds to the amount of $500 guaranteeing his good behavior, and forbade him to serve in the militia or testify against a white person. The more obnoxious of those laws were repealed about the middle of the century, but the Ohio Constitution formed in 1850 still forbade suffrage to the Negro and refused him service in the militia.[8] The Illinois Constitution of 1848, which was ratified by a large majority, included a clause prohibiting free Negroes from entering the state, and her Legislature in 1853 gave effect to the clause by providing fines for entering, and compulsory labor if the fines were not paid. When that state drafted a new Constitution in 1862, barely a month before Lincoln's preliminary Emancipation Proclamation, there was submitted to popular vote a separate clause again prohibiting free Negroes from entering, and it was adopted by a majority of more than 100,000—a vote of almost two and one-half to one.[9] After pointing out that there was some sympathy for the blacks among the abolitionists and the people of the northern part of the state, a care-

7. For figures, see Chapter I.
8. Frank U. Quillin, *The Color Line in Ohio* (Ann Arbor, 1913), 20–24, 38–40, 88.
9. John C. Hurd, *The Law of Freedom and Bondage in the United States* (2 volumes, New York, 1862), Vol. II, 136; N. Dwight Harris, *The History of Negro Servitude in Illinois and of the Slavery Agitation in that State, 1719–1864* (Chicago, 1904), 235–236, 239.

ful student of the Negro in Illinois has concluded however that "In fact, the antipathy of the whites for the
Negroes and the desire to keep the colored people out
of everything—politically and socially—seem to have
increased with the growth of the agitation for their
freedom." [10]

The Iowa Constitution of 1846 had declared that "All
men are, by nature, free and independent, and have
certain inalienable rights," yet the Legislature of that
state in 1851 passed an act to prevent free Negroes from
coming into the state, and providing penalties if they
did.[11] Oregon had a very severe anti-Negro clause in
the Constitution of 1859 under which she was admitted
to the Union. Negroes not only were prevented from
entering the state, but those there could not hold any
real estate, maintain a suit or make a contract. That
clause, submitted to the voters separately as was the
anti-slavery one in the same constitution, actually received a heavier vote than the latter.[12] By the stagger-
ing vote of 108,513 to 20,951, the people of Indiana in
1851 approved a Negro-exclusion article in their Constitution.[13] The Negro was not forbidden to enter Pennsylvania, but it is difficult to find his lot harder anywhere than as depicted in that state by Turner in his
excellent monograph, *The Negro in Pennsylvania*. He
concludes that "At the time, therefore, when the Civil
War burst upon the country pro-slavery advocates
could with some reason point to the treatment of the
Negro in states like Pennsylvania, and could feel that

10. Harris, *op. cit.*, 233.
11. Hurd, *op. cit.*, 177.
12. *Ibid.*, 217. The vote was 8,640 to 1,081 in favor of the
anti-Negro provision, and 7,727 to 2,645 for the anti-slavery
one.
13. *Ibid.*, 130–131. Also Quillin, *op. cit.*, 9.

De Tocqueville was right when he said twenty-five years before, that race prejudice was stronger in those states which had abolished slavery than in those states where it still remained." [14]

Some of those who proclaimed loudest the doctrine of equality, and strongly condemned the philosophy and the institutions of the South, at times almost reduced its slavery problem to insolubility. Senator Wade, in making a speech in 1860 in which he advocated the plan, then perhaps impossible, of colonizing the Negroes in Central America, uttered the following language: "There is in these United States a race of men who are poor, weak, uninfluential, incapable of taking care of themselves. I mean the free Negroes, who are despised by all; outcasts upon the face of the earth, without any fault of theirs I know of; but they are the victims of a deep-rooted prejudice and I do not stand here to argue whether that prejudice be right or wrong. I know such to be the fact. It is there immovable. It is perfectly impossible that these two races can inhabit the same place, and be prosperous and happy." [15]

Lincoln's utterances on slavery indicate not only the dilemma in the problem, but the dilemma in which he seemed to find himself also. He felt that a slave was the equal of any other person in the "right to eat the bread she earns with her own hands without asking leave of any one else," [16] but he doubted whether that degree of freedom would satisfy an emancipated slave. He de-

14. Edward R. Turner, *The Negro in Pennsylvania, 1639–1861* (Washington, 1911), 146, 149.
15. A. G. Riddle, *The Life of Benjamin F. Wade* (Cleveland, 1886), 229–231.
16. *Works,* Vol. I, 231–232. Speech at Springfield, Illinois, June 26, 1857.

clared at Peoria, Illinois, in 1854 that, if the slaves were freed and "kept among us as underlings," he was not certain that step would better their condition, yet his "own feelings" were hostile to the idea of making "them politically and socially our equals." He thought that colonization was the best solution, but that could not be suddenly accomplished, so he concluded that, "if all earthly power were given" him, he "should not know what to do as to the existing institution." [17] Four years after the Peoria speech Lincoln, speaking at Chicago, gave utterance to a more lofty conception of race relations. He said that, if one man said that the Declaration of Independence did not apply to the Negro, another could easily say that it did not apply to some other man, and he urged his audience to "Let us discard all this quibbling about this man and the other man, this race and that race and the other race being inferior, and therefore they must be placed in an inferior position. Let us discard all these things, and unite as one people throughout this land, until we shall once more stand up declaring that all men are created equal. . . . I leave you, hoping that the lamp of liberty will burn in your bosom until there shall no longer be a doubt that all men are created free and equal." [18]

During the Lincoln-Douglas debates, which took place in 1858 after Lincoln's Chicago speech, Douglas, who renounced any idea of race equality, repeatedly asked his opponent questions relative to the latter's Negro views. Finally, in Southern Illinois, Lincoln replied in the following language:

17. See Peoria speech, *Works,* Vol. I, Oct. 16, 1854, 184, 186, 187, 195, 197.
18. *Works,* Vol. I, 260. Speech at Chicago, July 10, 1858.

"I will say, then, that I am not, nor ever have been, in favor of bringing about in any way the social and political equality of the white and black races; that I am not, nor ever have been, in favor of making voters or jurors of Negroes, nor of qualifying them to hold office, nor to intermarry with white people; and I will say, in addition to this, that there is a physical difference between the white and black races which I believe will forever forbid the two races living together on terms of social and political equality. And inasmuch as they cannot so live, while they do remain together there must be the position of superior and inferior, and I as much as any other man am in favor of having the superior position assigned to the white race." [19]

After this utterance, Douglas accused his opponent of having one set of racial ideas for northern Illinois and another for the southern part of the state where anti-Negro sentiment was stronger, and the *Chicago Times*, elaborating the same theme, referred to "his [Lincoln's] greater than Sam Patch leap from the platform of Negro equality to that of perpetual Negro subordination." [20]

James Doolittle, Republican Senator from Wisconsin, felt that freeing the slaves would lead to the "Africanization" of the Gulf states, admitted that there was strong prejudice against the Negroes in the free states, and characterized the problem as to what to do with them as "the burning question of the hour." He introduced a resolution in the Senate in 1859, proposing

19. *The Lincoln-Douglas Debates of 1858*. Edited by Edwin E. Sparks (Springfield, Illinois, 1908). The quotation is from Lincoln's speech at Charleston, Illinois, 267–268. See Lincoln's definite rejection of the idea of Negro citizenship, 303. For Douglas' remarks, see 225–226, 301–302, 329–344.

20. *Chicago Times*, Sept. 24, 1858.

colonization of Negroes in Central America, but it received scant consideration.[21]

The strong and radical anti-slavery utterances of William H. Seward seem to have been dictated more by opposition to the political and social system of the South than by love for those who were in a condition of slavery. He told an Iowa audience in 1860 that the sectional contest was one "between aristocracy and democracy," and that Iowa had no Negroes and would not have any; that the Negro had less to do with the controversy "than anybody in the world."[22] The Republican *New York Times,* often sharply critical of the South, declared that "Even could every slave be set free tomorrow, there would still remain the tremendous responsibility and burden of providing for a black population numbering scarcely less than four million souls. That so great a mass of colored people is to remain, in freedom and equality among us, cannot for a moment be supposed."[23]

21. See speech of Doolittle at Buffalo, July 4, 1859, as reported in *New York Times,* July 9, 1859.

22. Speech of William H. Seward at Dubuque, Iowa, Sept. 21, 1860, in *Works of William H. Seward* (5 volumes, Boston and New York, 1887), Edited by George E. Baker, Vol. IV, 370–372. "He [the Negro] has just as much to do with it as a horse or a watch in a justice's court, when two neighbors are litigating about its ownership. The controversy is not with the Negro at all, but with two classes of white men, one who have a monopoly of Negroes, and the other who have no Negroes. One is an aristocratic class, that wants to extend itself over the new territories, and so retain the power it already exercises; and the other is yourselves, my friends, men who have no Negroes and won't have any, and who mean that the aristocratic system shall not be extended. There is no Negro question about it at all. It is an eternal question between classes—between the few privileged and the many underprivileged—the eternal question between aristocracy and democracy." P. 372.

23. July 9, 1859.

Brief reference must be made to the attitude of Northern Democrats toward the Negro question. After Arkansas had passed a law providing for the expulsion of free Negroes from the state, and when some of the other border states were threatening to do the same thing, Democratic journals in Michigan and Pennsylvania demanded laws in those states excluding that class of people.[24] Congressman Brodhead, of Pennsylvania, thought that his state would be overrun by a "worthless population," should emancipation occur, felt that there could never be any kind of equality between the races, and claimed that the slaves of the South were far better cared for than the free Negroes of the North. Senator George Pugh, of Ohio, hoped ultimately for liberty for the slave, but felt that freedom had not helped him so far, and that "the condition of free Negroes, in the non-slaveholding states, is worse even and more pitiable, than that of the slave." Senator John B. Weller, of California, said that he had never lived in a slave state, and did not advocate slavery, but that he was weary of so much talk of the Declaration of Independence from those who denied its principles to the Negroes in their midst.[25]

An argument not infrequently advanced by free-

24. *Detroit Free Press,* March 11, 1860; *Philadelphia Press,* Jan. 17, 1860. The former paper declared that, "if slavery here is unprofitable, free Negroes are a thousand times more so. . . . witness the Negro colonies wherever they are found in the North. Witness the British West India Islands where emancipation has resulted in the ruin of both races."

25. For Brodhead's remarks, see *Globe-Appendix,* 30 Cong., 1 Sess., June 3, 1848, 650, and for those of Pugh and Weller, respectively, see *Appendix to Globe,* 34 Cong., 1 Sess., May 26, 1856, 617–618 and *ibid.,* 33 Cong., 1 Sess., Feb. 13, 1854, 198–200.

soilers against permitting slavery in the territories was
that the presence of the Negro there would not be for
the best interest of the whites. When James Burrill, a
Senator from Rhode Island, was advocating the anti-
slavery restriction on Missouri in 1820, he declared that
he was "not only averse to a slave population, but also
to any population composed of blacks, and of the infi-
nite and motley confusion of colors between the black
and the white." [26] David Wilmot, in advocating his
famous Proviso in 1847, made it clear that he was plead-
ing "the cause of the rights of white freemen," of those
of his "own race and own color," and that he had "no
squeamish sensitiveness upon the subject of slavery,
nor morbid sympathy for the slave." [27] Senator John A.
Dix, of New York, thought it was the "sacred duty" of
Congress to reserve the territories of the West for the
white race by excluding slavery and thus preventing
the entrance of a different race, which "counts nothing
in the estimate, physical or intellectual, of the strength
of the body politic," and against whose elevation "public opinion at the North presents an insuperable barrier." [28] Since slaves in the territories meant ultimately
free Negroes and the West was hostile to the latter,
there was thus presented a strong reason, according to
Representative Julius Rockwell, of Massachusetts, why
slavery should be prohibited in the territories.[29] Prohibition of slavery in the territories, said Lincoln, meant

26. *Annals,* 16 Cong., 1 Sess., Jan. 20, 1820, 217.
27. Charles B. Going, *David Wilmot Free Soiler* (New York,
1924), 174.
28. *Appendix to Globe,* 30 Cong., 1 Sess., June 26, 1848, 862,
865–866; *Globe,* 30 Cong., 2 Sess., Feb. 28, 1849, 293.
29. *Appendix to Globe,* 30 Cong., 1 Sess., June 27, 1848,
792–793.

separation of the races there, and such separation would
prevent amalgamation, an idea "abhorrent" to nearly all
whites.[30]

When the free-soilers met in a Convention at Big
Springs, Kansas, in 1855, they declared that "the best
interests of Kansas require a population of white men,"
and when the Topeka Convention met later in that
year, it referred to the people, separately from the
Constitution it drew up, a clause prohibiting free
Negroes from entering the prospective state. That
clause was approved by a vote of more than three to
one.[31] Douglas chided much the Republicans in the
Senate over their willingness to admit a state, when the
group asking for admission had voted to exclude
Negroes, but Seward frankly replied that he was interested in the white man in Kansas, not the Negro,
while Wade and Senator Henry Wilson emphasized the
fact that the clause, though not to their liking, was not
actually part of the Constitution.[32]

The Negro question centered sharply into the debate
over the admission of Oregon as a state, but at that time
the controversy was so intertwined with political factors as to be very confusing. The prospective state, as
pointed out earlier in the chapter, had an anti-Negro
clause in its Constitution, but also an anti-slavery one.
It was at the time Democratic in its party leanings.
Senators William P. Fessenden and Henry Wilson op-

30. Lincoln, *Works*, Vol. I, 231–232. Senator Doolittle wished,
by excluding slavery from territories, to prevent "Africanization"
of the West. See George M. Stephenson, *The Political History
of the Public Lands from 1840 to 1862* (Boston, 1917), 195,
199.

31. Spring, *Kansas*, 63–67, 71.

32. *Appendix to Globe*, 34 Cong., 1 Sess., Dec. 3, 1855, April
4, 14, 1856, 286, 363–364, 382–394.

posed the admission largely on the grounds of the anti-
Negro provision, but Lyman Trumbull, of Illinois, defended Oregon's right to exclude Negroes, yet opposed
admission partly because of the state's alleged lack of
sufficient population. Douglas contended that, since
both the free and slave state groups had forbidden the
Negro to enter Kansas and each group in Congress had
approved the action, the principle of exclusion had
been accepted. Some Southern Senators opposed Oregon's admission, ostensibly for other reasons, but probably because she was a free state. In the end a majority
of the Southern and of the Republican Senators voted
to admit the state.[33]

The Negro clause was still being debated when the
measure for admission of Oregon came up in the House
in 1859. Representative James Wilson, of Indiana, criticized the clause, but admitted during a running debate
with John Sandidge, of Louisiana, that he believed
"that the Republican party" was "as much opposed to
Negro equality as the Democratic party." Linus
Comins, of Massachusetts, regretted the presence of the
anti-Negro provision, but said that "candor, however,
compels me to say, that it is but in accordance with the
spirit which prevails throughout the West towards free
blacks."[34] However, political party considerations had
overshadowed all else by this time. The Democrats at
the previous session of Congress had refused to accept
the Crittenden-Montgomery bill, which proposed to
submit the Lecompton Constitution to the people of
Kansas, but empowered them to form a constitution

33. *Congressional Globe*, 35 Cong., 1 Sess., May 5, 19, 1858,
1964–1967, 2205. The vote was thirty-five to seventeen in favor
of admission.
34. *Globe*, 35 Cong., 2 Sess., Feb. 11, 1859, 974, 986.

and a state government, in case they rejected the Lecompton instrument. The Republicans contended that they were deprived of Kansas, a Republican state, by the defeat of the Crittenden measure. Benjamin Stanton, a Republican from Ohio, who thought it wise to exclude Negroes from Oregon, summed up the controversy over the admission of that state in these words: "I will not stultify myself by professing to ignore what I know to be the operating causes which control the votes of members on this floor, in voting for and against the admission of Oregon. . . . I am not prepared here, nor will I sit by and aid in adopting one rule for the admission of a Republican State, and another rule for the admission of a Democratic State. That, aside from the Constitution of Oregon, is the true secret of the position of parties in this House on this question." [35] The Democrats in the House, most of the Southerners included, voted to admit a Democratic state, though a free one, and most of the Republicans voted against the Democratic state, even if it were a free one. [36]

35. *Ibid.*, Feb. 12, 1859, 1005. Reference to the rule for admitting Kansas is to the provision in the English bill relative to the population the state must have before admission. Representative Grow tried to repeal the English bill at this time. *Ibid.*, Feb. 10, 1859, 946.

36. *Ibid.*, Feb. 12, 1859, 1001. The vote in favor of admission was 114 to 103. Fifteen Republicans voted in favor, and 18 Southern Democrats and 12 Southern Know-Nothings against. See *Mobile Advertiser*, March 1, 1859. After the Senate had voted to admit Oregon, that territory, in 1858, prematurely elected state officials, and its legislature chose two United States Senators. In these elections there was a three-cornered race among regular Democrats, independent or national Democrats and Republicans. The regular Democrats won in all the contests. See Charles H. Carey, *History of Oregon* (Chicago and Portland, 1922), 536. Such an outcome no doubt influenced the members of the two major parties in casting their votes in the House in 1859 on admission of the state.

The *Mobile Advertiser* lamented the fact that the majority of Southern Democrats had been willing to add another free state to help diminish the power of the South in the Union, while the *Mobile Register* hailed the admission of another Democratic state. The *Boston Post* criticized the Republicans for their alleged inconsistency in objecting to the exclusion of Negroes from Oregon and condoning the exclusion in Kansas, and claimed that "the real sin of Oregon" was "its democracy." [37]

Despite the unsatisfactory conditions under which the Negro generally lived in the North and the hostile sentiment he often encountered in the section,[38] there is some evidence of active sympathy for him. In small degree educational advance was made, good examples of which were the opening of the doors of Oberlin College to Negroes in the 1830's, the establishment of Wilberforce University for them in 1856, and the erasing, through the efforts of Charles Sumner and Wendell Phillips, of the color line in the Massachusetts public schools in 1855.[39] Northern leaders frequently denounced laws in some of the Southern states, notably South Carolina, which provided for imprisonment of Negro seamen while they were in Southern ports.[40] The

37. *Mobile Advertiser*, March 1, 1859; *Mobile Register*, Feb. 19, 1859; *Boston Post*, Jan. 17, 1859.

38. For evidence of this view, in addition to that already presented, see two Negro historians, George W. Williams, *History of the Negro Race in America from 1619 to 1880* (New York and London, 1885), especially 111–112, 131–132, 149–157, and Carter G. Woodson, *The Negro in Our History* (Washington, Sixth Edition, 1932), especially 249, 254, *et seq.*

39. Woodson, *op. cit.*, 255–260.

40. See remarks of Representatives T. J. Turner, of Illinois, and Joseph Mullin, of New York in *Appendix to Globe*, 30 Cong., 2 Sess., Feb. 23, 1849, 222, Feb. 26, 1849, 311–312, and of

abolitionists assailed race prejudice, numerous and vivid examples of which they claimed to see in the free states. Birney thought that Negroes were "subject to more insult" in the free than in the slave states, and Angelina Grimke deplored the fact that "prejudice against color is the most powerful enemy we have to fight with at the North."[41] Theodore Parker wrote Salmon Chase in 1858 that what prevented the slaves from leaving border states was neither the central government nor the activities of "slave-hunters" at home, "but the public opinion of Pennsylvania, Ohio, Maryland and Illinois."[42] Colonizationists, whether considered the friend or enemy of the Negro, were still active during the fifties. David Christy, of Ohio, secured private funds for colonization, and many memorials to the Ohio Legislature requesting appropriations for that purpose. According to Christy, the Legislature refused appropriations to the Colonization Society because of fear that the funds would be used for deporting the colored population from other states. During the decade, however, Pennsylvania and New Jersey made appropriations for colonizing Negroes in Liberia.[43]

Senator John Davis, of Massachusetts, *Appendix to Globe*, 31 Cong., 1 Sess., August 23, 1850, 1626–1628.

41. Henry H. Simms, "A Critical Analysis of Abolition Literature," *Journal of Southern History*, Vol. VI, August, 1940, 368–382. See p. 378.

42. Parker to Chase, March 9, 1858, *Diary and Correspondence of Salmon P. Chase*, 478, in Annual Report of the American Historical Association, 1902, Vol. II (Washington).

43. *African Repository* (67 Volumes, Washington, 1826–1892), Vol. XXVI, 111–112, 166–169, 362–363, Vol. XXVIII, 154, Vol. XXXII, 36. Christy was an agent of the Colonization Society. There was much talk of colonization in the fifties, but, as a solution to the slavery problem, it seemed certainly a hopeless remedy that late in the nineteenth century. Colonization was probably not a practical plan at any time.

The Southerners made no pretensions to either practical or theoretical race equality, but they contended that the slave was usually better provided for than the free Negro in the North, and that the strong criticism of slavery was prompted not by humanitarian considerations, but by political ones. The first of these contentions is well illustrated in the following utterance of Alexander H. Stephens: "Take them [the Negroes] in the North generally, and compare their conditions with those of the South. Take them in Africa; take them anywhere on the face of the habitable globe; and then take them in the Southern States, and the Negro population of the South are better off, better fed, better clothed, better provided for, enjoying more happiness, and a higher civilization than the same race has ever enjoyed anywhere else on the face of the world." [44]

Davis, after making a comparison of the Southern slave with the free black of the North, to the advantage of the former, wanted to know what it was that prompted all the agitation against slavery. "Is it love for the African? No! His civil disability, his social exclusion, the laws passed by some of the non-slave states to prevent him, if free, from settling within their limits, show, beyond the possibility of doubt, that it springs from no affection for the slave. . . . The only conclusion is that you are prompted by the lust of power, and an irrational hostility to your brethren of the South." [45]

Senator Butler, of South Carolina, bitterly exclaimed that the philanthropy of the North was "heated into a flame more to *hate the white race* [italicized in *Globe*]

44. *Appendix to Globe*, 33 Cong., 2 Sess., Dec. 14, 1854, 39.
45. *Appendix to Globe*, 30 Cong., 1 Sess., July 12, 1848, 913. Davis was convinced that "the opposition to slavery is political." *Ibid.*, 912.

than to preserve the black," and that its moral ideals were often inspired "by a criminal ambition and heartless hypocrisy." [46] Other Southerners pointed out that some of the Northern states, in excluding free Negroes, had followed a policy for which Missouri had been denied admission to the Union, and emphasized an alleged inconsistency on the part of Free Soilers, who had once opposed Missouri's admission because of her policy and yet had been willing to admit Kansas, despite the action of the free state group there in excluding Negroes. Those developments, they contended, illustrated the political character of the crusade against slavery.[47]

In case the slaves were freed, "Where are they to go?" queried Mason, of Virginia. "What territory is there within the free states that will receive a class of free blacks?" Senator Underwood, of Kentucky, felt that the sentiment of his state was for the abolition of slavery, if the races could be separated, but concluded that Northern prejudice would confine the Negro to the South, if he were emancipated. He and Mason both referred, by way of one illustration of prejudice, to the attitude toward the emancipated slaves of John Randolph, who were colonized in Ohio, but were scattered through different parts of the state after feeling expressed itself against them in the section in which they had settled.[48]

46. *Ibid.*, 33 Cong., 1 Sess., Feb. 24, 1854, 237.
47. *Ibid.* See remarks of Asa Biggs, Senator from North Carolina, 34 Cong., 1 Sess., July 2, 1856, 759, and of Representative J. H. Lumpkin, of Georgia, August 2, 1856, 1127.
48. *Ibid.*, 30 Cong., 1 Sess., July 6, 1848, 886, June 3, 1848, 701. A traveler in Ohio said that some of the Randolph Negroes expressed a desire to return to Virginia. See letter to *Baltimore Patriot,* as quoted in *African Repository,* Vol. XXVII, 55.

There is a mass of material in the Southern press portraying the alleged condition of the Negro in the North, or denouncing some in that section for their seemingly inconsistent attitude in criticising the South for keeping the Negro in bondage.[49] The tone of the press generally on the Negro controversy is, however, so well mirrored in the *New Orleans Daily Picayune* that the following long quotation is given from that paper. After declaring that the North had worked itself into a frenzy over abolition and giving the Negro the "privileges of freedom," it continues thus: "Now what are those privileges, tested by the condition of those who are already in the North, upon whom it had had the opportunity of expending philanthropy, and its bounty, of demonstrating its theories, and illustrating its zeal and its charity? What have free soil and free labor done for the Africans there? In which one of the states do they increase in numbers or grow into position of respectability as a class? . . . Which one of them has found in them the capacity for self-direction, or the power to rise to a level with the most uneducated and ignorant classes of the white race that surrounds but will not mingle with them? What Northern state desires them as inhabitants, or does more than tolerate them, as a nuisance they would gladly get rid of. Which state would throw open its privileges to any considerable number added by emancipation from the stock of Southern slaves? Is it not in fact true that small as their number is, they are the objects of repugnance to most

49. *Huntsville* (Alabama) *Democrat,* June 23, 1853; *Mobile Register,* Oct. 21, 1858, Jan. 8, 1859; *True Democrat,* quoting with approval article in *Jersey City Benefactor* on condition of Negro in North, Sept. 30, 1853; *Augusta Constitutionalist,* May 7, 1858.

of the states, and that in some of them their intrusion and essential worthlessness has begotten the necessity for legislative acts to exclude them from the state? These theories of benevolence do not include the idea of receiving and supporting, or taking on political probation, with a view to future citizenship among themselves, the helpless and ignorant races, whom they are scheming to set free among us." [50]

It appears, on the basis of the evidence presented in this chapter, that the North and the South, by and large, were not as far apart in their attitude toward the Negro as many have been prone to think; and that seemingly different racial philosophies, which in fact were not so different, could not have been a dominant factor in producing a sectional break and a war. One assays a difficult task indeed when he attempts to decide how much of the opposition to slavery was moral in nature and how much was due to each of several other factors. Political, psychological and economic factors were intertwined with the slavery controversy, and, in the opinion of the writer, did more to produce the tragedy than did any moral factor. Joshua R. Giddings and Theodore Parker might proclaim the potentialities of the Negro, if given opportunity, but Seward said that the Negro had nothing to do with the sectional controversy, that in reality it arose as the result of a contest for political power between aristocratic slaveholders and more democratic elements in the free states. Wade denounced continued "domination of the government" by slaveholders, and expressed his strong feeling against them when he declared that "I am not a Negro-worshipper, as we are sneeringly called, and still less

50. *Daily Picayune*, August 27, 1857.

am I a worshipper of those who claim dominion over Negroes." [51] The South was engaged in a struggle to keep power from passing to a group as hostile to her as the Republican party, and the Republicans, partly because they felt that the South had had an undue proportion of the political plums since the republic was founded, were struggling for power. William T. Sherman was not a politician, but there is food for thought in the way he sized up the sectional situation in 1860. After declaring that "all the Congresses on earth" could not "make the Negro anything else than what he is," and that the only way the two races could live in harmony was in the relationship of "master and slave," he expressed the opinion "that the present excitement in politics" was nothing "more than the signs of the passage of power from Southern politicians to Northern and Western politicians. The Negro is made the hobby, but I know that. Northern men don't care any more about the rights and humanities of the Negroes than the Southerners." [52] Sherman was correct, in the writer's opinion, in attributing much of the excitement to political factors, but time was to prove that he had not correctly gauged the depth of the emotional feeling which those factors and others had produced.

51. *Appendix to Globe,* 34 Cong., 1 Sess., July 2, 1856, 749.
52. *Home Letters of General Sherman,* Edited by M. A. DeWolfe Howe (New York, 1909), Sherman to his wife, July 10, 1860, 178–179.

VII

Exaggeration and Abuse

POLITICAL, psychological, constitutional and economic factors all played some part in producing the break between the sections and the war that followed. However, it seems to the writer that political and psychological factors played the paramount role in producing those unfortunate results. The extreme position taken by some of the public men in both sections of the country, particularly in overemphasizing the significance of the issue of slavery in the territories, no doubt strengthened those men politically in their respective sections, but led to unwarranted fears in the minds of many of their constituents. While many conservative voices were raised in both sections, there were altogether too many in both who indulged in extremes of criticism. That reciprocal abuse undoubtedly played considerable part in developing the emotional fervor which characterized the sectional controversy.

The question of slavery in the territories was a mere abstraction by 1860. Congresses might legislate and courts might adjudicate, but the inexorable laws of nature had decreed that slavery had no place in the Western territories. There had never been more than a few hundred slaves in Kansas, and the sub-zero temperatures of winter had shown the futility of trying to use any slave labor there profitably.[1] The Census shows a total of forty-six slaves in all the territories of the United States in 1860. Kansas had two, Nebraska fifteen, and Utah twenty-nine.[2] In a recent treatise, an able scholar in the field of Southern history has developed the thesis that, since cotton and hence slavery had reached their Western limits by 1850, at least everywhere except in Texas, emancipation of slaves due to economic causes would soon have set in. Slave prices, he points out, had increased much faster, 1850 to 1860, than cotton prices, and hence slaves were being rapidly drawn off from the states of Maryland, Virginia, Kentucky and Missouri. As the new lands in the Southwest were taken up, overproduction and low prices would probably have resulted. The prices of slaves would have dropped and the market for them would have gone, even in the Southwest, after those lands were fully used. That combination of circumstances would have made emancipation a necessity.[3] The author of

1. In writing to Buchanan June 23, 1857, Robert J. Walker said that there had been about 200 slaves in Kansas, but owing to the severe winter that number had been considerably reduced. He gave various temperature readings of from one to twenty below zero during the winter months, and said that he had been told that some of the slaves died as a result of the severe cold. For letter see *Reports of Committees of the House of Representatives*, 36 Cong., 1 Sess. (Report No. 648), 115–119.

2. *Eighth Census, Agriculture*, 247. The total number of slaveholders in the territories was twenty.

3. Charles W. Ramsdell, "The Natural Limits of Slavery Expansion," *Mississippi Valley Historical Review*, Vol. XVI, September, 1929, 151–171. Ramsdell suggests that the social problem involved in emancipation might have been handled by a gradually relaxing system of laws to regulate the life of the emancipated slave. Gray, in his study of Southern agriculture, disagrees with Ramsdell, and holds that the plantation system in 1860, having used only a small portion of the available land, was not about to perish because of lack of room to expand.

the article of course feels that the question of slavery in the territories was of little practical significance.

However, political leaders, North and South, attached much significance to that question. In the South it was frequently said that, if the group in the North trying to prohibit slavery in the territories should be successful, it would then assail the institution in the states. Alfred Iverson, a Senator from Georgia, felt that the Republican party, in order to live, would have to continue the war on slavery as long as the institution lasted. In dramatic fashion he declared that "The demon of abolition, in his most hideous form, has covered them [free states] all over with the footprints of his onward and remorseless march to power. . . . When the present Republican party, or its legitimate successor in some other name, shall get possession of the Government, when it has the President, both Houses of Congress, and the Judiciary, what will stay its hand? It cannot stand still; if it does, it dies. To live and reign, it must go on. Step by step it will be driven onward in its mad career until slavery is abolished or the Union dissolved. One of these two things is as inevitable as death." [4] Lucius Quintus Cincinnatus Lamar, a representative in Congress from Mississippi, queried the Republicans in the following manner: "I ask you if you do not know that when you strike slavery

The growth of railroads, he points out, was making available new lands for production. Lewis C. Gray, *History of Agriculture in the Southern United States to 1860* (2 Volumes, Washington, 1933), 467–477. A New Orleans newspaper, in 1859, declared that the greatest threat to slavery consisted of economic laws. It felt that, if the lower South did not prohibit the introduction of slaves from Maryland, Virginia, Kentucky and Missouri, those four states would become free. The territories, it granted, were won for freedom already. *New Orleans True Delta*, Dec. 4, 1859.

4. *Globe*, 35 Cong., 2 Sess., Jan. 6, 1859, 242–243.

from the Territories you have taken the initial and most decisive step toward the destruction of slavery in the States." [5]

Jefferson Davis declared that the reason Southerners were concerned over slavery in the territories was "simply because of the war that is made against our institutions; simply because of the want of security which results from the action of our opponents in the Northern States. . . . You have made it a political war. We are on the defensive. How far are you to push us?" [6] In a letter written in 1860, the Mississippi Senator expressed more emphatically his view that the Republicans were aiming to strike at slavery in the states. [7] While certain expressions used from time to time by Republicans could be construed to mean a purpose to attack slavery in the states, yet that purpose was not stated in their party platforms, and their leaders, such as Lincoln, Wade and Chase, claimed that interference with the institution in the states was no part of their program.

The strong Southern defense of slavery against the vigorous assaults directed at the institution and the Dred Scott decision legalizing it in the territories were in large part made the bases of Northern claims that the South was trying to spread slavery all over the free states. Horace Mann declared in 1852 that, in looking for room to expand their institution, the slaveholders would try to extend it everywhere, until "even the free states" would be "engulfed with the rest, so that the

5. *Globe*, 36 Cong., 1 Sess., Dec. 7, 1859, 45.
6. Speech in Senate, Feb. 8, 1858, in Vol. III, 173 of *Letters, Papers and Speeches*.
7. Letter to L. P. Connor and others in *Mississippi Free Trader*, Oct. 16, 1860.

dove of freedom will have no spot on the surface of the globe where she can set her foot." [8] After the Dred Scott decision the *New York Tribune* warned New England of the impending "horror" of having the institution of slavery established there.[9]

But the men who probably did most to disseminate the idea of Southern aggression in forcing slavery upon the free states were Lincoln and Seward, the latter already prominent in politics, the former seeking political preferment. The theme of both was that, if slavery did not come to an end, it would be pressed forward until it should become legal in all the free states. It was in accepting the Republican nomination for the United States Senate in Illinois in 1858 that Lincoln gave public utterance and definite form to what came to be known as the "House Divided" speech; but in a private letter three years before he had raised the question as to whether the nation could continue to exist half slave and half free.[10] "A house divided against itself cannot stand," said Lincoln at Springfield. "I believe this government cannot endure permanently half slave and half free. I do not expect the Union to be dissolved—I do not expect the house to fall—but I do expect it will cease to be divided. It will become all one thing or all the other. Either the opponents of slavery will arrest the further spread of it, and place it where the public

8. *Appendix to Globe,* 32 Cong., 1 Sess., August 23, 1852, 1076.

9. "The free hills of Vermont, the lakes of Maine, the valleys of Connecticut, the city where the ancient Oak of Liberty has wisely fallen, may be traversed by the gangs of the Negro-driver, and enriched by the legitimate commerce of the slave-pen." *New York Tribune,* March 11, 1857.

10. Lincoln, *Works,* Vol. I, Lincoln to George Robertson, August 15, 1855, 215–216.

mind will rest in the conviction that it is in the course
of ultimate extinction; or its advocates will push it forward till it shall become alike lawful in all the states,
old as well as new, North as well as South." [11] Anti-
slavery zealots could find considerable comfort in the
above declaration, and conservatives could find some.
When Douglas accused Lincoln of trying to bring about
a war between the sections, the Illinois Republican
claimed that he was making only a prediction and con-
templated no interference with slavery in the states.
However, he continued to warn the North that the
South would never be satisfied until it had legalized
slavery in all the free states.[12]

In his "Irrepressible Conflict" speech at Rochester,
New York, October 25, 1858, Seward claimed that it
was only "accidental" that it was the Negro who was
enslaved, and that the only reason the white laborer
had not been reduced to bondage was because slaveholders had not yet been able to accomplish that object.
It was not the work of agitators, he said, that was producing a collision between slave and free labor, but it
was "An irrepressible conflict between opposing and
enduring forces, and it means that the United States
must and will, sooner or later, become either entirely a

11. *Ibid.*, June 16, 1858, 240. Lincoln claimed that the Dred
Scott decision, carried to its logical conclusions, would legalize
slavery in all the states.
12. One of the best illustrations of this constantly repeated
claim is to be found in the Cooper Institute speech in New York.
Southern people, Lincoln said, would demand the overthrow of
the free state constitutions, for, "Demanding what they do, and
for the reason they do, they can voluntarily stop nowhere short
of this consummation. Holding, as they do, that slavery is morally
right and socially elevating, they cannot cease to demand a full
national recognition of it as a legal right and a social blessing."
Works, Vol. I, Feb. 27, 1860, 611–612.

slaveholding nation, or entirely a free-labor nation. Either the cotton and rice-fields of South Carolina and the sugar plantations of Louisiana will ultimately be tilled by free labor, and Charleston and New Orleans become marts for legitimate merchandise alone, or else the rye-fields and wheat-fields of Massachusetts and New York must again be surrendered by their farmers to slave culture and to the production of slaves, and Boston and New York become once more markets for trade in the bodies and souls of men." [13] Seward had threatened the South with emancipation in a speech in the Senate earlier in the same year (1858). After stating that "the interest of the white races" demanded emancipation, he warned the South that all that remained for it to decide was "whether that consummation shall be allowed to take effect, with needful and wise precautions against sudden changes and disaster, or be hurried on by violence." [14]

Seward's utterances aroused more protest in the South than Lincoln's, because what Lincoln said was not scrutinized very closely until he became the Republican candidate for President. Moreover, Seward's language was more radical than that of his contemporary. Though some in the South thought that not enough emphasis was placed there upon Northern antagonism to Seward's radicalism, [15] others emphasized that the New Yorker's policy was doing much to unite the South in resistance to the North on every point touching slavery. [16]

13. Seward, *Works*, IV, 289–292.
14. *Globe*, 35 Cong., 1 Sess., March 3, 1858, 944.
15. *Savannah Republican*, Sept. 23, 1859.
16. See remarks of Clement Clay, Senator from Alabama, *Appendix to Globe*, March 19, 1858, 145–146; *New Orleans Daily Picayune*, Nov. 7, 1858.

At this point, it should be noted that it was no part of the program of Southerners to extend slavery to the free states. Most of them contended for it as a constitutional right in the territories, but they frankly conceded that in them conditions were such that slavery would never exist. Occasionally a Southerner, such as George Fitzhugh, might express the hope or even the belief that Southern institutions would spread everywhere in the nation, but he was an exception. Indeed, matters of transit or temporary sojourn of servants traveling with masters in free states might and did come up for adjudication by courts, but that was not the same thing as overriding the sovereignty and the sentiment of a state by establishing slavery there.[17]

Several books during the fifties tended, as a result of their extreme nature, to add fuel to the sectional flames. Mrs. Harriet Beecher Stowe's *Uncle Tom's Cabin,* published in 1852, may not, critically examined, have been as severe an indictment of Southern institutions as some

17. As ultra-Southern a journal as the *Richmond Enquirer* declared in 1857 that there were "two insuperable reasons" why slavery could not "yet, if ever, be extended farther North." One consisted of climate and products, the other, sentiment against it. July 23, also Nov. 26, 1857, for same idea. The *Augusta Constitutionalist* conceded that it made little difference how the territorial question was decided, because the right was "practically worthless." Nov. 25, 1858, May 14, 1859. For similar views of Southerners on slavery in the territories, see Chapter III. Jefferson Davis "scarcely knew how to answer so palpable an absurdity" as the claim that the Supreme Court would force slavery on a sovereign state that did not have it, and if Congress tried to do so, the Supreme Court, he felt, ought to declare the act unconstitutional. *Letters, Papers and Speeches,* Vol. III, 302. Yet a special student of the fifties has declared that "current Northern feeling was that unless the South were checked, it would insist on protection to its slaves, not only in the territories, but in the free states." Smith, *Parties and Slavery,* 280.

represented it to be, but, since it portrayed dramatically the worst features of the slavery system, it is entirely probable that that large segment of the Northern public which read it and saw it acted at the theatres received a distorted impression of slavery in practice. Theatres were packed when the play was presented, and the book was read by hundreds of thousands soon after publication.[18]

The book caused a sensation in the South. The *Richmond Dispatch* thought that Mrs. Stowe's reception in England, and the rejoicing in the North at that reception had thrown "discredit" on the institutions and morals of the South.[19] Extracts from the *New Orleans Picayune* afford a fair index as to the novel's reception in the slaveholding section. Commenting upon the fact that the work was to be put upon the stage, the *Picayune* said that it would be "acted by living libellers before crowds of deluded spectators." The South would be represented to the North "as living in a state of profligacy, cruelty and crime-tyrants who fear no God, and cruelly oppress their fellow creatures; and the drama is thus enlisted among the promoters of sectional hatred, a teacher and preacher of national discord, whose end inevitably would be the disruption of the Union." The picture of planter life was no more true than a picture of Northern life which would make "the Polly Bodines,

18. For accounts of the book's reception, see *Chicago Press,* April 10, 1854 and *New York Tribune,* Sept. 19, 1853. The *Tribune* reported that Mrs. Stowe's work was being translated into many languages, that within that short a time approximately one million copies had been printed, that it was played to crowds at a half dozen theatres, and that "songs founded on its more affecting incidents" were "beginning to be sung at nearly every house."

19. *Richmond Dispatch* quoted in *Huntsville* (Alabama) *Democrat,* June 2, 1853.

the Ann Hoags and John W. Websters true representatives of the principles of New York or Massachusetts." [20]

Just as extreme in their way were two books of a sociological nature written in 1854 and 1857, respectively, by a Southerner, George Fitzhugh. They bore the titles, *Sociology for the South, or the Failure of Free Society,* and *Cannibals All! or Slaves without Masters.* In them he represented slavery as the "healthy" and "normal" condition while free society was "a monstrous abortion," in which "three-fourths" of the people were "slaves." The North was full of crime and pauperism, but people in the South were peaceful and happy. He felt that slavery would be entirely abolished or everywhere reinstituted.[21] Fitzhugh wrote in those books so much concerning the Negro problem that one wonders whether that was not uppermost in his mind, yet he applied his principles to society generally, and that application was naturally emphasized by some in the North.[22]

More closely connected with the political controversy during the decade, 1850–1860, than any of the books thus far mentioned was Hinton R. Helper's *Impending Crisis of the South: How to Meet It,* first published in 1857. Helper was originally from North Carolina, but had lived in the North some time before publishing the book. In his treatise, he developed the theme of the economic superiority of the free North to the slaveholding South. The non-slaveholding white could prosper only if slavery were abolished, and to help effect aboli-

20. *New Orleans Picayune,* August 28, 1852.
21. No attempt is made here to cite page numbers, but simply to show the theme of the books.
22. See remarks of Senator Doolittle in Senate, Jan. 3, 1860. *Appendix to Globe,* 36 Cong., 1 Sess., 98.

tion he urged the non-slaveholder to cut off all contacts
with the slaveholder. But he did not stop at so peaceable a suggestion. If immediate, uncompensated emancipation did not take place, he threatened "violence"
and "massacre" to secure it. Slaveholders were compared to the "basest criminals" in prison, and were regarded as worse for society than "robbers, ruffians,
thieves and murderers." [23] Sixty-eight Republican members of the House signed a paper endorsing Helper's
book, and some of them, aided by Horace Greeley and
William C. Bryant, took steps to raise money to print
100,000 copies of a compendium of the *Impending
Crisis* to be circulated as a campaign document in the
presidential election of 1860.[24] The action of the Repub-

23. "We demand our rights, nothing less. It is for you to
decide whether we are to have justice peaceably or by violence,
for whatever consequences may follow, we are determined to
have it one way or the other. Do you aspire to become the victims of non-slaveholding vengeance by day, of barbarous massacre by the Negroes at night? Would you be instrumental in
bringing upon yourselves, your wives, and your children, a fate
too horrible to contemplate?" *Impending Crisis,* 128. "Indeed, it
is our honest conviction that all the proslavery slaveholders, who
are alone responsible for the continuance of the baneful institution among us, deserve to be at once reduced to a parallel with
the basest criminals that lie fettered within the bulk of our
public prisons. . . . Were it possible that the whole number
could be gathered together and transformed into four equal gangs
of licensed robbers, ruffians, thieves and murderers, society, we
feel assured, would suffer less from their atrocities than it does
now." P. 152.
24. The circular endorsing the book, and the proposals as to
the compendium are given in the *New York Herald,* March 9,
1859, as quoted in the *Globe,* 36 Cong., 1 Sess., Dec. 8, 1859, 16.
See also John S. Bassett, *Anti-Slavery Leaders of North Carolina*
(Baltimore, 1898), 16–17. The compendium did not have as
severe passages as the original production.

licans led Representative John B. Clark, of Missouri, to offer a resolution to the effect that no one should be elected Speaker of the House who had endorsed a book that suggested "violence" and proclaimed sentiments that were "insurrectionary." The resolution affected John Sherman, a candidate for Speaker, who, it appears, knew through others that there were "objectionable parts" in the work, but, not having read it himself, thought that such parts had been removed when he gave his signature.[25] Sherman wrote his brother that signing was a "thoughtless, foolish and unfortunate act," and the latter was convinced, after the Speakership contest was over, that he [John Sherman] "will be more careful hereafter in signing papers before he reads them." [26]

The *New York Tribune* endorsed the circulation of the compendium of the *Impending Crisis,* and claimed that the *New York Herald* knew "perfectly well" that Helper "never dreamed of exciting civil war or insurrection at the South." [27] Text books, which generally do not refer to the extreme portions of the *Impending Crisis,* leave one under the impression that the South bitterly resented the publication because it contained an economic thesis to the disparagement of that section. Most of the bitterness, however, was caused by the abusive nature of the book. A thunderous roar went up

25. For Clark's resolution and Sherman's explanation, see *Globe,* 36 Cong., 1 Sess., Dec. 6, 1859, 3, 18, 21. Sherman was not elected speaker. The position went to Pennington, of New Jersey, who had not endorsed Helper's book.

26. *Home Letters of General Sherman,* John Sherman to William T. Sherman, Dec. 24, 1859, 167; W. T. Sherman to his wife, Feb. 10, 1860, 176.

27. *New York Tribune,* Dec. 7, 1859.

from the Southern press, whether radical or conservative, to the effect that the book was slanderous, vile, insulting and insurrectionary.[28]

Books of an extreme nature and exaggerations by politicians as to the importance of issues are not the only uncalled for and unnecessary emotional factors that played a part in rending the nation asunder. Though conservatives in each section tried to apply the brakes, many of the more radically inclined in each seemed to take special delight in criticizing extravagantly Northern and Southern "society," respectively. Some gems of Southern criticism of Northern society may first be given.

L. M. Keitt, a Representative from South Carolina, after pointing with pride to the South's past in the realm of statesmanship, launched into an attack upon the North, because of the alleged prevalence there of crime, pauperism and generally unsatisfactory conditions. "Free society," he said, "points us to its civilization in the splendid aggregate; to its arts and commerce; to its cities and its material monuments; but it does not show us its long array of starving operatives; its crowded jails and fetid hospitals; its breadless boards, and the vast reservoir of human life, poisoned in its well springs, and poured out like water." [29] Senator Butler, of South Carolina, thought that the South was equal to the North in moral and intellectual worth, in the pulpit and in the realm of statesmanship, if not in the mechanical arts. But the North, he claimed, had

28. For criticisms see *Augusta Daily Constitutionalist,* Dec. 17, 1859, *Richmond Enquirer,* Dec. 10, 1860, *New Orleans True Delta,* Dec. 8, 1859, *Charleston Mercury,* Jan. 11, 1860, *New Orleans Picayune,* Dec. 7, 1859.
29. *Appendix to Globe,* 34 Cong., 1 Sess., April 7, 1856, 444.

more pauperism, insanity and "isms" than the South. The only ism for which he had any respect was "Puritanism," but "abolitionism, Maine-liquor-law-ism, strong-minded-womanism, Bloomerism, and all the isms" of the North were "the cankers of theoretical conceit, of impudent intrusion, and cheerless infidelity." [30]

Senator Hammond, of South Carolina, said that one would meet more beggars in one street in New York in a single day than in the South in a lifetime. He characterized the laboring classes in the North as largely slaves in fact, "the very mud-sill of society" who must perform the menial duties which slaves performed in the South. He did not, however, think that "whites should be slaves, either by law or necessity," for they were equal "in natural endowment of intellect." The panic of 1857, he said, due to wild speculation in the North, had cost the South a reduction of $35,000,000 in the price for which the latter sold its cotton to the North. "Thirty-five million dollars, we, the slaveholders of the South, have put into the charity-box for your magnificent financiers, your cotton lords, your merchant princes." Indeed, in normal times, it was the great profits realized from cotton transactions that kept the Northern economic system from collapsing. [31] The North, its "hirelings" and "paupers," constituted a dangerous political element that might appropriate property, but since slaves occupied that relative position at the South and had no political power, and the whites with such power were equal, there would not be the same dangerous agrarian tendency. [32]

The Southern press, and not always the press that was

30. *Ibid.*, Feb. 24, 1854, 236–237.
31. *Ibid.*, 35 Cong., 1 Sess., March 4, 1858, 70–71.
32. *Charleston Mercury*, July 5, 1858.

radical politically, was sometimes more violent in language than the political leaders. The *Richmond Enquirer* declared that free society was "everywhere starving, demoralized, infidel, insurrectionary, moribund!" Such society was declared to be "only prolific of crime, hunger, nakedness, infidelity, revolution and civil war." That journal denounced the religious press of the North for its "violent and bitter philippics" against the South, utterances, it alleged, "more resembling the belchings forth of the infernal pit than the gentle and quiet utterances of the holy gospel." [33] The *North Carolina Standard* charged that the people of the North were so "shrewd and calculating" in regard to making money that they allowed themselves to be easily swayed in spiritual and political matters by priests and politicians, "and with either a spiritual or political hook in their noses, suffer themselves to be led to the devil or to an infraction of the Constitution with equal facility, *provided it costs nothing.* . . . Let them steal a little time from their hot pursuit after *dimes* to judge for themselves in both spiritual and political matters, and the weakened bonds of the Union will be strengthened." [34]

The *New Orleans Picayune* portrayed in dramatic fashion the "desperate" condition of men in New York fighting "starvation" and of paupers in Massachusetts dying in poorly kept almshouses, and claimed an absence of such conditions in the South. Though it granted that many good books were published in New York, it pointed to the many publications of lives of "highwaymen" and "pickpockets" and of stories of an

33. *Richmond Enquirer,* Jan. 19, 1856, Jan. 5, 1857.
34. *North Carolina Standard,* June 20, 1857. Words italicized in the journal.

"undesirable character," expressed the hope that "this spawn of Northern mind could be quarantined out of the South," and asked booksellers to "aid in arresting this tide of demoralization, whose source is in the sewers of the great Babylon, New York, and strive to cultivate the more healthy sentiment existing in the South." [35] Another New Orleans paper deplored the "poor literature" being given to the public in the Northern monthly magazines, and hoped that the increase of such periodicals would accentuate their poor quality to such an extent as to produce toward them an unfavorable reaction on the part of the Southern reading public. "The Northern monthlies," the paper stated, "ignore Southern genius, [and] are governed by a contemptible literary squad, who arrogate to themselves all the decency, all the talents." [36] The criticism of Northern literary productions may have been inspired by the fact that literary efforts in the North seemed generally to be crowned with a greater degree of success than those in the South.

What was the character of the assault of the Northern extremists upon the South? One of their most frequently asserted claims was that the slaveholders constituted an aristocracy which controlled the nation, and humbled and oppressed the Southern non-slaveholder, who was generally represented as in a pitiable condition. Joseph Collamer, a Senator from Vermont, declared that the three hundred and fifty thousand slaveholders represented an "aristocracy," all of whose wants and desires were met by slaves, "but, as respects the rest of the com-

35. *New Orleans Picayune,* Sept. 19, 1858, August 27, Oct. 21, 1859.
36. *True Delta,* May 27, 1859.

munity, five-sixths of them, the free white laboring population, they are depressed, poor, impoverished, degraded in caste, because labor is disgraceful." [37] Only from one-tenth to one-fifth of the people of the South had "any interest in the institution of slavery," claimed Benjamin Wade. Yet the small group that did reigned and domineered "over four fifths of the people of the South," and gagged "the press." That same "slave power" had "molded and controlled the Government ever since its foundation, and it always threatens dissolution of the Union, if an attempt is made to check its absolute dominion." [38]

Lyman Trumbull admitted that one would have to multiply the 350,000 slaveholders by five to get the true proportion of those in the South interested in slaveholding, but held that that small group controlled the general Government, made the non-slaveholders of the South "their dependents," in part, and the freemen of the North their subjects. He claimed that the only interest the non-slaveholders "could have would be to get rid of it [slavery], and to elevate labor in that country to a standard where it would be honorable for free white men to perform it." [39] The 350,000 slaveholders controlling the Federal Government and oppressing the non-slaveholder in the South constituted a theme for William H. Seward.[40] Trumbull lived in a state which excluded Negroes and he had defended their exclusion from Oregon, and Wade said later that the whites and blacks could not live harmoniously together, yet those two senators were assuring the North that the

37. *Appendix to Globe*, 34 Cong., 3 Sess., Dec. 9, 1856, 53.
38. *Ibid.*, July 2, 1856, 751.
39. *Globe*, 35 Cong., 1 Sess., Jan. 7, 1859, 265–266.
40. Seward, *Works*, Vol. IV, 225–250, 257–269.

Southern non-slaveholder had no interest in the institution of slavery.[41]

It was "slavery alone," said Horace Mann, which had arrested the progress of education and culture in the South.[42] The *Chicago Democratic Press* claimed that free schools were regarded in the South as a "nuisance," and Senator Israel Washburn, of Maine, after describing the Southern white laborer as "ragged, unhoused" and "untaught," declared that "The city of Portland, in my own State, has made more contributions to literature . . . than all the slaveholding states put together." [43]

On the basis of expressions uttered by some Southerners, it was frequently said in the North that the Southern slaveholder regarded slavery as the normal condition for all laboring men. It should be recalled that Senator Hammond in his "mud-sill" speech renounced slavery as a desideratum for whites, either by "law or necessity," and when Senator Doolittle, in 1860, claimed that Southerners widely championed the idea

41. Senator Brown, of Mississippi, answered, in the following language, the constantly repeated charge by Seward that the slaveholders constituted a privileged class which was oppressing the underprivileged non-slaveholding whites in the South: "If he expects, by appeals like these; to turn the hearts of the non-slaveholders of the South against slavery, he will miss his aim. They may have no pecuniary interest in slavery, but they have a social interest at stake that is worth more to them than all the wealth of all the Indies." He pointed out that, in his own state, the two races were about equal in number, and claimed that there would be a struggle for supremacy between them, if emancipation took place. See *Appendix to Globe*, 34 Cong., 3 Sess., Dec. 22, 1856, 94–95.

42. *Appendix to Globe*, 32 Cong., 1 Sess., August 23, 1852, 1080–1081.

43. *Chicago Democratic Press*, Nov. 10, 1856; *Appendix to Globe*, 34 Cong., 1 Sess., June 21, 1856, 635–637.

for both races, three Southern Senators denied the accusation.[44]

The personal character and traits of the slaveholder were assailed. When the Kansas-Nebraska Act was under consideration, the *New York Independent*, a religious journal, stated that it had "declared from the beginning that the South was untrustworthy; that there *could* be no honor among men" who defended an institution which was a "crime." That paper declared later that slavery demoralized "the manners and personal habits" of the slaveholders, as well as "their political ideas." [45] Joshua R. Giddings, in a speech full of invective, told the Southerners that they must know, and "the civilized world must know, that we do regard slaveholders far beneath the advocates of freedom, in their sense of moral obligations." He said that the North discarded the institution of slavery "solely on account of its barbarous nature." [46] Sumner, in eloquent language, described how slavery was destroying even the "Northern character," and how it was extracting from it all that there was of moral worth.[47]

The alleged brutal nature of the Southern slaveholder was emphasized considerably. The *New York Tribune*, commenting on the killing of an Irish waiter at Willard's Hotel in Washington by a Congressman Philip Herbert of California, attributed the deed to the

44. For such claims, see remarks of Israel Washburn, *Appendix to Globe*, 34 Cong., 1 Sess., June 21, 1856, 636, and of Senator James Doolittle in *ibid.*, 36 Cong., 1 Sess., Jan. 3, 1860, 98, 103. James Chesnut, Clement Clay and Albert Brown were Southern Senators who denied such a contention. For claim see also *New York Tribune*, Oct. 24, 1856.
45. *New York Independent*, March 23, 1854, June 26, 1856.
46. *Appendix to Globe*, 33 Cong., 1 Sess., May 16, 1854, 989.
47. *Ibid.*, Feb. 24, 1854, 269.

idea of "chivalry," and to the fact that it was easy for a "plantation Democrat" who killed Negroes "to kill an Irish waiter." The *Chicago Times* said that the "abolitionists" first thought Herbert was of Southern birth, but after finding out that he had come from New England, they laid the killing at the door of "his association with slaveholders." [48] The *Times* challenged the opposition press to relate some of the brutal actions in the North toward immigrants. The *Illinois State Journal* declared that, in Virginia and North Carolina, "the bowie knife and revolver" were "the only acknowledged code of ethics." [49]

In the Northern press, the most severe indictment of the South that came to the attention of the author was found in the *New York Times,* a paper conservative in some ways. "Southern gentlemen" once existed, but they were a thing of the past. The Southerner had "become a money-getter and a mammon-worshiper." The expansion of slavery had made that institution "a mighty gambling house of the most simply sordid nature." Culture and breeding had declined to the point where the South could not handle her simplest economic problems, nor secure a professor for her wealthiest university, even when a large salary was offered. This state of things had made "the tone of the public press and of the public men of the South . . . more and more vulgar, barbaric and indecent." "Vituperation" and "vile and foul" epithets were the order of the day. The North, however, had grown in resources, had made great cultural advance, and refinement of tone was characteristic of her press and public men. Almost

48. *New York Tribune,* May 9, June 4, 1856; *Chicago Times,* May 22, 1856.
49. *Illinois State Journal,* April 15, 1857.

a year after this comparison of the sections, that journal declared that the slaveholder had corrupted manners generally. His barbarism had crossed the Potomac, so that "We now-a-days in the sober North carry our pistols and knives, have our difficulties in the streets, butcher our men unawares in bar-rooms, and then fly to the police for refuge, just as our Southern confreres have been doing for half a century." [50]

Near personal encounters and violent language in both the House and Senate early in 1860 illustrate the fanatical extremes to which some of the actors in the sectional drama went. Owen Lovejoy, of Illinois, in the House in menacing fashion, assailed both slavery and slaveholders. Slaveholding he characterized as "more criminal" than "piracy" or "robbery," as "the sum of all villainy. Put every crime perpetrated among men into a moral crucible, and dissolve and combine them all, and the resulting amalgam is slaveholding." The South was drifting into "barbarism," a tendency checked only by some pure Christian women already in the slave states, and by the "Christian women" who had gone from the free states, and married in the slave states. Doctrines uttered by Southerners would be a "disgrace anywhere outside the five points of hell and the Democratic party." The slaveholders, he charged, paid their "debts by raising the mad-dog cry of abolition against the agents of your creditors." Roger Pryor, of Virginia, advancing toward Lovejoy as the latter approached the Democratic side, accused him of using "insulting language," an accusation which drew from John F. Potter, of Wisconsin, the statement that the opponents of Lovejoy had been using "violent and offensive language" for eight weeks. William Barksdale, of Missis-

50. *New York Times*, March 7, 1857, Jan. 23, 1858.

sippi, called the Illinois Representative "a black hearted scoundrel and nigger-stealing thief," and O. R. Singleton, also from Mississippi, referred to him as "a mean, despicable wretch." [51]

The *New York Tribune* felt that Lovejoy's speech was "calm and moderate" as compared to the abuse he and his associates had received for ten months, and that the "insults" heaped upon him by Southerners "outraged all the canons of propriety recognized among decent men." The *New York Times,* however, though condemning the Southerners for their "vulgarity," thought that Lovejoy was largely "responsible for the disgraceful scene." Lovejoy, the latter journal stated, was bitter over the murder of his brother, but after all that act was committed by non-slaveholders, most of whom were then dead. [52]

On June 4, 1860, Charles Sumner entertained the Senate with a speech which made the one entitled "The Crime Against Kansas" seem mild. His subject in 1860 was "The Barbarism of Slavery," and in it slavery was characterized as follows: "Barbarous in origin, barbarous in law, barbarous in all its pretensions, barbarous in the instruments it employs, barbarous in consequences, barbarous in spirit, barbarous wherever it shows itself, slavery must breed Barbarians, while it develops everywhere, alike in the individual and the society to which he belongs, the essential elements of Barbarism." So brutal was the South that "assassination" was "lifted to be one of the Fine Arts," and the slavery on which Southerners lived, "in all its fivefold

51. For Lovejoy's speech and the other proceedings see *Appendix to Globe,* 36 Cong., 1 Sess., April 5, 1860, 203–206.

52. *New York Tribune,* April 11, 1860, *New York Times,* April 16, 1860.

foulness, must become part of themselves, discoloring the very soul, blotting the character, and breaking forth in moral leprosy." [53]

Senator Chesnut, of South Carolina, was the only Southern Senator to reply to Sumner. He said that Southerners were not "inclined again to send forth the recipient of punishment howling through the world, yelping fresh cries of slander and malice." Chesnut however, did denounce the Massachusetts Senator in the following language: "In the heroic ages of the world men were deified for the possession and the exercise of some virtues—wisdom, truth, justice, magnanimity, courage. In Egypt, also, we know they deified beasts and reptiles; but even that bestial people worshipped their idols on account of some supposed virtue. It has been left for this day, for this country, for the abolitionists of Massachusetts to deify the incarnation of malice, mendacity and cowardice." [54] Unhealthy emotional attitudes were the inevitable product of such utterances as those to be found in the preceding pages.

53. Sumner, *Works*, Vol. IV, 127, 162–163, 177.
54. *Ibid.*, 237.

VIII

Sectional Divergence over Economic Factors

THERE are those who maintain that the fundamental cause of the break between the slave and free states was a clashing of economic interests, that the ideals of the agricultural South could not be harmoniously fused with those of the more diversified and complex economic life of the North. Conflicting cross-currents of an economic character did exist; but they were often intertwined with political and psychological factors in such a way that their significance in the sectional picture is not easy to gauge.

The successful business man was the ideal of the North in much the same way that the large planter was that of the South. Merchants, shippers, bankers and manufacturers constituted the upper crust of society, and often a man belonged to more than one of those classifications. Junius Morgan and Moses Taylor are good examples of merchants who were also bankers during the several decades that preceded the Civil War;[1] while Isaac Lawrence, one of many famous industrialists of that name, was shipowner, banker and merchant.[2] It has been said of the merchants that they

1. John Moody and George K. Turner, "Masters of Capital in America," in *McClure's Magazine*, Vol. XXXVI, 12, 73–75.
2. Walter Barrett, *The Old Merchants of New York City* (New York, 1863), 61–63.

were "the copy-book model of every school boy," [3] and "the bees that made the honey—the drones were the statesmen that made the noise." [4] Philip Hone, a prosperous merchant of New York and once mayor of the city, declared that there was "nothing in Paris or London" which could be compared to the "dry goods palace" that was operated by the noted financier, A. T. Stewart. [5]

The banker-merchants were often either interested directly in shipping enterprises, or indirectly as a result of financing them, and hence they constituted a factor in the agitation for shipping bounties in the 1850's. However, after England started to subsidize the Cunard Line of vessels in 1840, [6] there was a growing feeling in the United States that the latter should follow suit, if her own merchant marine were to keep pace with that of England. It was John Tyler, a Southerner, who as President in 1844 urged the policy of compensating our steamships for carrying the mails, [7] and his suggestion bore fruit less than three years after it was made when contracts were awarded, under acts of Congress, to E. K. Collins for transporting the mails between Liverpool and New York, and to A. G. Sloo, C. H. Aspinwall and others for such service between specified points on this continent. [8]

3. Moody and Turner, *op. cit.*, 4.
4. Barrett, *op. cit.*, 47.
5. *Philip Hone; Diary, 1828–1851*, Edited by Ellan Nevins, two volumes (New York, 1927) Vol. II, 772.
6. Marguerite M. McKee, *The Ship Subsidy Question in United States Politics*, in Smith College Studies in History, Vol. VIII (Northampton, Mass., 1922), 16.
7. See Message of John Tyler to Congress, December, 1844, *Appendix to Congressional Globe*, 28 Cong., 2 Sess., 20.
8. John R. Spears, *The Story of the American Merchant Ma-*

Beginning in 1852, heavy subsidies were given American steamship lines carrying the mails. The total appropriated for the purpose in that year was $1,940,250, and of this amount the Collins Line received $858,000 as compared with $385,000 previously.[9] The total for ocean mail service in 1855 was $3,574,458, but three years later that figure had been reduced to $1,460-750.[10] The following year (1859) Congress gave notice of the complete abrogation of mail contracts.[11]

One writer has suggested that the South was very largely responsible for the defeat of the ship subsidy policy, but another has pointed out that the responsibility rested mainly upon a very powerful group of unsubsidized ship-owners.[12] An examination of the Senate vote on the subsidy bills shows that the South was more strongly opposed than any section, but was by no means solidly so, and that there was considerable opposition in the West. Fifteen Senators from the eleven states ultimately to secede voted, in 1852, on the measure to increase the Collins subsidy. Of these, seven favored and eight opposed the bill. The majority of the Western senators also opposed, but the Northeast strongly favored, though the two Maine senators who represented

rine (New York, 1919), 264–265. The contracts were awarded in 1847.

9. Congressional Globe, 32 Cong., 1 Sess., August 28, 1852, 2442, August 23, 1852, 2306.

10. For 1855 appropriation see Appendix to Congressional Globe, 33 Cong., 1 Sess., 437, and for 1858, ibid., 35 Cong., 1 Sess., 605.

11. William W. Bates, American Navigation, The Political History of its Rise and Ruin, 347.

12. For first view see Winthrop L. Marvin, The American Merchant Marine (New York, 1902), 274–278, and for second, see Spears, op. cit., 291–292.

largely unsubsidized shippers were to be found with the opposition.[13] Twenty Southern senators voted on the bill to renew contracts in 1855. Fifteen were against and five favored. Seven other senators joined the fifteen, and two of these, Chase and Wade, were from Ohio.[14] The main arguments advanced in favor of subsidies were that they would enable the American merchant marine successfully to compete with that of England, and would give the nation ships that would be useful in time of war. It was claimed, on the other hand, that such steamers would not be useful in war, that the policy of subsidization was unfair to the independent shipowners, and that the many were being taxed for the benefit of a special, small group.[15] Since the special interest was in the North, it is not difficult to understand why Southerners stressed considerably the last argument.

Another Northeastern interest which was favored by bounties on the eve of the War between the States, and had been favored for years, was cod fishing. That aid was stimulated by the depressed condition of the industry, especially during the early years of the Republic, and by the plausible argument that those engaged in cod fishing received valuable training for the service of

13. *Globe,* 32 Cong., 1 Sess., May 19, 1852, 1393. The vote was 23 to 21.

14. *Appendix to Globe,* 33 Cong., 2 Sess., Feb. 28, 1855, 313. The vote was 26 to 22 in favor of renewing the contracts.

15. For arguments in favor, see remarks of William H. Seward and Judah P. Benjamin, and for those against, see remarks of Robert Toombs and Jefferson Davis, all in *Globe,* 35 Cong., 1 Sess., June 9, 1858, 2824–2836. See also, in opposition, views of Hunter in Simms, *Life of Hunter,* 95–96, and *Richmond Enquirer,* March 2, 1857. That journal declared that the subsidy system gave protection "to the North" which was "as objectionable as the worst tariff that ever disgraced our code books."

the navy.[16] It is estimated that individual fishermen, during the 1850's, received eighteen to twenty dollars per year, that the total annual bounty was approximately $350,000, and the total since aid started, $10,000,000.[17]

Though a minor matter of controversy, government aid to the fisheries did enter into the sectional controversy before 1860. Senator Clement C. Clay, of Alabama, made repeated and finally successful efforts to have the upper house repeal the bounty, and J. L. M. Curry, of the same state, introduced a similar measure in the House of Representatives in 1860. Clay replied to charges of sectionalism hurled at him by alleging that the principle he was assailing favored a distinctly sectional interest. Maine and Massachusetts, he claimed, received practically the entire bounty, and only New York received any outside of New England. Seward and William P. Fessenden, the latter from Maine, stressed the arguments that the cod fisheries needed aid to exist, and that they supplied a "nursery" for seamen for the navy.[18] A prominent Northern journal associated the opposition of the South to the fishing bounties with New England's opposition to slavery,[19] while Southern

16. Samuel S. Morison, *The Maritime History of Massachusetts, 1783–1860* (Boston and New York), 134–135, 310–311.

17. See remark of Representative Timothy Davis, of Massachusetts, in *Appendix to Congressional Globe*, 34 Cong., 3 Sess., Feb. 10, 1857, 218–222, and of Senator Clement C. Clay, of Alabama, in *Globe*, 34 Cong., 3 Sess., Jan. 20, 1857, 378–380.

18. For Clay's measure and debates over same, see *Globe*, 34 Cong., 3 Sess., Jan. 20, 1857, 378–380, and *ibid.*, 35 Cong., 1 Sess., May 11, 12, 1858, 2054–2055, 2079–2380, and 2239. For Curry's bill, see *ibid.*, 35 Cong., 1 Sess., Feb. 16, 1860, 808.

19. *New York Evening Post* quoted in *Mississippian* (Jackson, Miss.) May 19, 1858. *The New York Tribune*, Jan 23, declared that the South thought that only the "interests of negro slavery" were "worthy of the bounties of government."

journals were declaring that "it would be the excess of Christian forbearance" for the South "to consent to be burdened and taxed to equip their enemies," and that the North had shown a "contempt for Southern interests" not only in respect to slavery, but in all matters of economic policy.[20] In the vote on the Senate repeal bill referred to above, eighteen of the thirty votes in favor of repeal came from the eleven states soon to secede, and only two from those states opposed the measure. The West was divided, and the Northeast overwhelmingly opposed.[21] The bill did not pass the House, and it was not until the year after the war was over that Congress decided to abandon the policy of aid to the fisheries.[22]

The tariff had been a matter of controversy between the slave and free states during much of the period between 1816 and the middle of the century, though during most of the fifties the sectional attributes of that policy were not marked. However, by 1860 those attributes were very noticeable. Stimulated by the restrictive commercial policy of the Jefferson and Madison Administrations, many factories had sprung up in the New England and middle states by 1816, with the result that a protective tariff was enacted in that year to prevent the infant industries from being extinguished by England's policy of sending goods to the United States at low cost. The protection was increased, but over the bitter protest of t' e South, which was the great exporting but not the manufacturing section of

20. *Mississippian*, May 19, 1858; *Mobile Daily Register*, Jan. 14, 1859.

21. For vote, see *Globe*, 35 Cong., 1 Sess., May 19, 1858, 2239. There were twenty-five negative votes. Bell and Houston were Southern Senators opposing repeal.

22. Morison, *op. cit.*, 310–311.

the nation. South Carolina, more militant than her sister states which had the grievance also, nullified the tariff acts of 1828 and 1832, though, as the result of a compromise measure, actual nullification did not go into effect. The compromise prevailed until 1842, at which time a tariff act, construed by some as a protective and by others as a revenue bill, was passed. In 1846, the Polk Administration reduced the tariff, a step so strongly resisted that it was made possible in the Senate only by the casting vote of Vice-President Dallas. The admission of Texas as a state is here intertwined with the struggle over protection, for the measure of 1846, as opponents of it said at the time, could not have been passed without the votes of the Senators from Texas. The Walker Tariff, as it was called, was the last general measure until 1857, when Robert M. T. Hunter, of Virginia, Chairman of the Finance Committee of the Senate, prepared a bill which provided for a still further reduction of rates. There was a surplus in the Treasury at the time, so Hunter rather plausibly contended that a reduction in revenue would remove an incentive to spend and, by relieving the people of unnecessary taxation, stimulate business. The commercial elements of the East and many among the agrarian elements of the West did not favor a protective tariff in 1857. The vote on the measure shows that the South was almost a unit in favor of tariff reduction and the North was almost evenly divided.[23]

It is difficult to understand how there could have

23. For facts relative to tariff of 1857, see Simms, *Life of Hunter*, 103–106. The vote in the Senate was 33 to 12, and only Bell from the South was among the 12. The North and West gave 58 for and 70 against in the House, where only two Southern votes were negative.

been objection in the South to the revenue act of 1857. Yet the *Charleston Mercury*, articulate organ of the ultra South, denounced it as "far more unequal and unjust than the tariff it has superseded. Taxes are laid on everything the agriculturist uses and the manufacturer gets a large free list." That organ claimed that Charles Sumner regarded the act as the best for New England ever passed by Congress, and it contended that the tariff was a "species of agrarianism," involving the taking of a part "of the property of the consumer" and giving it "to the manufacturer." [24] On the other hand, the Republican *Boston Atlas*, once a Whig paper, declared that the former Whig principle of a protective tariff had passed for good, and that the act of 1857 settled the question in the "best manner possible." That manner it described as "The doctrine of incidental protection of manufacturing and commercial interests, by the addition of certain articles to the free list, and such distribution of the duties on other articles, as the conflict of interests would allow, without infringing upon the doctrine of a tariff strictly for revenue." [25]

The prediction of the *Atlas* that the tariff controversy was "settled" was not fulfilled. Two factors, one temporary and the other permanent, kept it from being so. The depression of 1857, due partly to wild speculation and to great haste in attempting to carry out various enterprises, affected adversely the manufacturing interests of the country, particularly the iron and woolen interests. The second of the factors was the rapid growth of manufactures. Iron production made unusual progress in Pennsylvania, Massachusetts, Ohio and New Jersey. The value of the woolen goods produced in

24. March 9, 1857, July 2, 1858.
25. March 13, 1857.

1860 was $80,000,000, and New England alone made more goods of that character than the whole country had in 1850. The proportion of population engaged in manufacturing in 1860 was one to eight in New England, one to fifteen in the middle states and one to eighty-two in the South. The net returns from manufacturing on the eve of the Civil War were $800,000,-000. In that phenomenal industrial development the name of Francis Lowell occupied the same place as that of Collins once did in connection with shipping and that of Stewart in the world of the merchants.[26]

In the late fifties the campaign for a higher tariff was making progress, though there was a reluctance on the part of some of the Republicans to press the matter. John W. Forney's *Philadelphia Press*, though Democratic, was assailing Buchanan and the Southern leaders for their "free-trade" proclivities, and the *New York Tribune* was pointing out the alleged advantages of protection and skilfully emphasizing the differences over that policy between the Democrats from the South and from Pennsylvania.[27] In the 1859–60 session of Congress, Justin S. Morrill of Vermont brought forward in the House a measure much to the liking of the iron interests, and to protectionists with other interests, be-

26. For growth of manufactures see Victor S. Clark, *History of Manufactures in the United States*, 2 volumes (New York, 1929 Edition), Vol. I, 504, 515, 558, 575, 580–582.

27. *The Philadelphia Press*, Jan. 21, 27, Feb. 3, 4, 12, 1859; *New York Tribune*, Jan. 25, 27, Feb. 15, 1859. At the same time a Southern journal was deploring the rise again of agitation for protection, and was contending that a temporary depression was no excuse, since the country was prosperous without protection before the depression. *Mississippian*, Feb. 1, 1859. The *Mobile Register*, Feb. 27, 1859, declared that the next Congress would fight the battle of protection, and that "that snake, which we thought killed, has been only scotched."

cause it raised the tariff rates generally to the point
they had reached in 1846. The bill passed the House by
a vote of 105 to 64, the sectional character of which is
well illustrated by the fact that the free states gave only
fourteen negative and the slave states only eight affirmative votes.[28] When the measure was being considered
in the senate, where it was finally postponed, great
pressure was exerted upon Hunter, Chairman of the
Finance Committee, by his Pennsylvania friends to use
his influence in securing favorable consideration for it.
He was told that many in the North cared little about
the question of slavery in the territories, but were an-
tagonistic to the South because of its opposition to protection. Should the bill pass, there was a feeling that it
would make a difference of 20,000 votes to the Democratic party in Pennsylvania, and would destroy a good
Republican campaign issue.[29] In the session of 1860–61,
Morrill's proposal passed the Senate, but only after a
dozen Southern senators had left their seats as a result
of the secession of their states.[30] Actually there was a
demand for a higher tariff in only certain localities in
the North; but the large free state vote for it may be
explained in terms of the political implications of a
presidential election year. Those implications will be
more fully suggested in a later chapter.

Bounties to shippers and to manufacturers were fundamentally of interest to the East, but there were eco-

28. Edward Stanwood, *American Tariff Controversies in the
Nineteenth Century*, 2 volumes (New York, 1903), Vol. II, 120–
121.
29. See letters from Pennsylvania Democrats to Hunter in
Hunter Correspondence cited in Simms, *Life of Hunter*, 108–109.
30. *Globe*, 36 Cong., 2 Sess., Feb. 14, 1861. The vote was
25 to 14.

nomic objectives in which the Northwest was particularly interested, and to which the South was generally opposed. The growing trade between the two free state sections during the fifteen years before 1861 seemed to make more necessary than ever improvements in rivers and harbors in the upper lake region, yet, due to Polk's vetoes, appropriations for such purposes, which had been approximately a half million dollars in each of the years 1844 and 1845, reached the vanishing point in 1848. They rose again, however, to the $2,000,000 mark in 1853, but under Pierce and Buchanan, the former particularly, were much reduced.[31]

Polk's vetoes led to considerable dissatisfaction in the Northwest with the Democratic party,[32] and no doubt help to explain the internal improvements plank in the Free Soil party platform in 1848. The Whigs, in somewhat guarded fashion, endorsed the same principle in 1852, while the Republicans took definite ground in favor in both 1856 and 1860. The Democrats opposed that policy in their platform in 1856.[33] Pierce's numerous vetoes of river and harbor bills, and the refusal of Congress to adopt Jefferson Davis' proposal that the states be permitted to lay tonnage duties,[34] placed the internal improvements question rather conspicuously in the political limelight in the presidential election year, 1856.

The reaction of the Southern press to Pierce's message of December 30, 1854, in which he took ground against federal internal improvements is fairly indicative of the

31. Emory R. Johnson, "River and Harbor Bills" in Vol. II of *Annals of the American Academy of Political and Social Science* (Phila., 1892), 782–812. See particularly 787–790.
32. Hubbart, *The Older Middle West*, 21–29.
33. Stanwood, *History of the Presidency*, 241, 252, 266, 273.
34. Nichols, *Franklin Pierce*, 299, 354–355.

sentiment of that section. It is true that the *Savannah Republican,* since the Savannah River needed improvements, could see in the message no sound constitutional arguments against improvements, yet the *North Carolina Standard* felt that the message was a "triumphant vindication" of a Democratic creed, and showed the "ruinous consequences" of such a system, and the *Richmond Enquirer* regarded the President's utterances as embracing principles which represented "a barrier to Federal encroachment" and "an impregnable bulwark of State rights." [35] The South generally was apprehensive that a free state majority in Congress would get the lion's share of appropriations, if they were made.

The Northwest spoke a different language. The *Detroit Free Press,* though a Democratic paper, felt that Pierce's vetoes of improvement bills were damaging the party, demanded that the Democratic nominee in 1856 make known his views, felt that the President had "deceived" the Northwest, and thanked "God" that his "term of office" was "drawing to a close." [36] The *Chicago Democratic Press,* a Republican paper, felt that, in the process of growth and development, the West had come to have such a need for river and harbor improvements, that it was not a party question. It represented the Chicago harbor as in an incredibly bad condition, and it denounced Douglas and Pierce for their hostility to

35. *Savannah Republican,* Jan. 10, 1855; *North Carolina Standard,* Jan. 10, 1855; *Richmond Enquirer,* Jan. 8, 1855. For further evidence of Southern hostility to internal improvements, see *Charleston Mercury,* April 6, 1857, and Ulrich B. Phillips, *The Life of Robert Toombs* (New York, 1913), 133–138.

36. Feb. 8, 1854, April 4, 1855, May 21, 1856. The journal pointed out, May 23, 1856, that the Michigan Democratic State Convention condemned Pierce's vetoes.

improvements, but more particularly directed its bitter invectives against the South, a section that was said to oppose the policy because the North was "outstripping" it in so many ways.[37]

If the system of land grants to aid railroads be regarded as a form of internal improvements, it should be emphasized that by the late 1850's only the states of the old South opposed that policy, though Eastern states had earlier. Florida, Alabama and Mississippi were as truly the recipients of such grants as Michigan, Wisconsin and Iowa. Indeed, when Douglas was attempting to secure a grant for the Illinois Central Railroad in the middle of the century, the passage of the measure was made possible by giving tracts of land to Alabama and Mississippi for the construction of a road from Mobile to the mouth of the Ohio.[38]

An economic objective of great interest to the farmers of the West and to the laborers of the East was free homesteads. The coming of vast numbers of immigrants during the fifteen years prior to 1860 gave additional momentum to the movement for free land. The Germans, many of whom settled in the West, were enthusiastic over the land bounty and opposed all efforts to restrict them in receiving it under the terms of various homestead bills proposed; the Irish, on the other hand, congregated mostly in the cities of the East, and hence did not have the same interest as the Germans in land policies. The increasing tide of immigration is shown by the fact that estimates place the number from 1790

37. Dec. 11, 1855, Dec. 22, 1856.
38. John B. Sanborn, *Congressional Grants of Land in Aid of Railways,* in Bulletin of the University of Wisconsin, No. 30, Vol. II (Madison, 1899), 27–35, 50, 53–54.

to 1800 at only 50,000, and from 1820 to 1830 at only 154,000; yet from 1840 to 1850, at 1,713,000, and from 1850 to 1860, at 2,378,000.[39]

The North-South sectional aspects of the homestead question were not clearly apparent until after 1852. In fact there was a great deal of opposition to such a principle in the East or Northeast until immigration made labor more plentiful and until a network of railroads tended to tie the Northwest and Northeast more closely together. While George Henry Evans, the great labor reformer, might declare that a man had a natural right to enough of the soil for subsistence, and Horace Greeley might proclaim the virtues of free lands as a means of preventing pauperism,[40] the factory owner was assured, through a steady incoming stream of foreigners, that other poorly paid laborers would take the place of those who went West.

The progress of the fight over free homesteads in Congress may be briefly summarized. A spectacular contest had been going on in that body over the principle in 1854 before the Kansas-Nebraska Act was passed. Hunter, in the Senate, proposed a graduation bill which the House would not accept. The Senate twice postponed bills in 1858, and in 1859 the casting vote of Vice-President Breckinridge killed the homestead measure. The next year, under the leadership of Galusha Grow, of Pennsylvania, in the House and Andrew Johnson, of Tennessee, in the Senate, the fight continued, but out of it came only a compromise measure, and that Buchanan vetoed. With few exceptions,

39. George M. Stephenson, *A History of American Immigration* (New York, 1926), 51–52, 99–101, 105–106.
40. George M. Stephenson, *The Political History of the Public Lands from 1840 to 1862*, 103, *et seq.*

votes from the slave states were against the free land proposal, and from the free states in favor of it.[41]

What is the explanation of the strong hostility of the South to free homesteads? It was alleged in that section that the public lands were pledged to secure the public debt, that, if they ceased to be a source of revenue, it would be necessary to raise the tariff, and that it was a dangerous agrarian policy to take what belonged to all and give it to some.[42] A more logical explanation of the Southern position is to be found, however, in the feeling, as the slavery controversy developed, that the free homesteads meant free soil. Such a principle, said one Southern journal, would "do more to spread free-soilism than any plan that could be devised," and another felt that its adoption would be an invitation to "foreign immigrants from all parts of the world" and to "every bankrupt in the United States" to exclude slaveholders from the West, if they chose to go.[43]

Northerners answered the above arguments with assertions that the customs duties could amply meet the debt obligations, that, if the proposal were agrarian in nature, it was "of that kind that levels up, and not that which levels down," that it would relieve the poor and destitute, whom the "proud," "pampered" and "aristocratic" slaveholders were trying to oppress, and that it

41. Benjamin Hibbard, *A History of the Public Land Policies* (New York, 1924), 375–380; Stephenson, *op. cit.*, 173, 185–187, 195–197, 208–212.

42. See remarks of William Smith, member of House from Virginia, and Judah P. Benjamin in Senate, in *Appendix to Globe,* 33 Cong., 1 Sess., Feb. 21, 1854, 241–243 and July 17, 1854, 1071–1074, respectively; also remarks of Thomas Clingman, Senator from North Carolina in *Globe,* 35 Cong., 1 Sess., May 19, 22, 1858, 2240, 2304.

43. *True Democrat,* Jan. 4, 1860; *Charleston Mercury,* March 19, 1859.

would achieve the same results as a Wilmot proviso.[44] After the failure of the homestead bill in 1860, the Republican press made much of the fact that its failure lay at the door of the slaveholding South, but that strategy can be more properly evaluated in a later chapter dealing with matters fundamentally political in nature.

Economic divergence North and South is not to be conceived of entirely in terms of differences over matters of national economic policy, for there was some sentiment in the South to the effect that the section was too dependent economically upon the more diversified industrial life of the North. The main currents of trade, it was said, passed through the latter section, and thus enabled its brokers, bankers and shippers to realize great profits at the expense of the South. That situation, coupled with the increasing tempo of the anti-slavery crusade, gave rise to a series of commercial conventions in the slaveholding states, beginning in the late 1830's and increasing in frequency in the 1850's. Other matters mentioned in those conventions will be discussed later, but suffice to say here that they agitated to some extent the questions of manufactures and a Southern trans-

44. See remarks of Representatives J. L. Dawson, of Pennsylvania, in *Appendix to Globe,* 33 Cong., 1 Sess., Feb. 14, 1854, 180–182, Galusha Grow in *ibid.,* Feb. 21, 1854, 240–243, William Windom in *Appendix to Globe,* 36 Cong., 1 Sess., March 14, 1860, 171, and S. C. Foster in *ibid.,* April 24, 1860, 245. The interest of the West in free homesteads is well reflected in the following sentiments of the *Detroit Free Press,* a Democratic paper: "It [the homestead bill] is a measure of more real beneficence, and of greater practical benefit to the human race, and is destined to accomplish a larger amount of good for the country, than any act of legislation of modern times. . . . it is the harbinger of hope and the way of deliverance of thousands and thousands of the sons of toil in the Old World." March 19, 1854.

continental railroad, but to a greater extent the matter of direct trade with Europe, particularly England.[45]

There was a considerable difference of opinion in the South in regard to the conventions as well as to the feasibility of their program of direct trade with Europe. Some thought the goal unattainable, others thought it desirable and attainable but condemned the conventions as "troublemakers" under the control of politicians, and still others felt that the periodical meetings were desirable because they were paving the way for political independence. An examination of a cross-section of the press, however, indicates that the critics were probably more numerous than the defenders.[46]

45. For a good account of the program of the conventions, see Herbert Wender, *Southern Commercial Conventions 1837–1859*, in Johns Hopkins University Studies in Historical and Political Science, series XLVII (Baltimore, 1930).

46. The *New Orleans Picayune* thought that, since the Southerners paid "profits to factors, storage and transportation," direct trade would be a desirable aim, but referred to the conventions as "a species of escape-valve for sectional patrotism," and gave assurance that the "Union is still cherished in the hearts" of the Southern people. Jan. 6, August 4, 1858, Jan. 8, 1859. The *North Carolina Standard* declared that the great body of Southern people was not responsible for the "views of a few politicians," that direct trade, through action, was uesirable, but that all Southern conventions had given more time "to abstract than to practical questions." Dec. 17, 1856. The *Mobile Daily Advertiser* denounced them as useless in accomplishing their purposes, and felt that they simply presented an opportunity for a parade of politicians. April 18, 1854, Jan. 11, 12, 19, 1855. In a series of articles in the *Augusta Constitutionalist*, Mark A. Cooper concluded that the South bought too much from the North, but that disunion was not a remedy. Slow and gradual diversification of economic life, he urged. Jan. 7, 10, 14, 19, 1860. The *Savannah Republican* did not even feel that direct trade was desirable, for, unlike the Northerners who had capital for trade operations, the Southerners would have to draw it from other pursuits. Jan. 5, 1857. On the other hand, the *Richmond*

The Republican press was caustic in its criticism of the commercial conventions. One journal felt that the South would never have the skilled labor to build ships or to work in factories until slavery was abolished, and labor made respectable for those not slaves.[47] The *New York Tribune* twitted the Charleston Convention of 1854 and the Knoxville one of 1857 about their violent harangues and resolutions, the South about its lack of capital and skilled labor, and its inability to cope with the free North, and said of the Charleston Convention that it swore "a new fealty to slavery, and poverty, and weakness and deterioration."[48] The *New York Times* charged that the conventions were political in nature, that they were for the purpose of inflaming the Southern mind against the North, that their members could talk, but had not the means to act, that, indeed, the gatherings had "become a chronic disease."[49] A Southern journal felt that the threat to Northern mercantile interests was the motive that prompted the criticism of

Enquirer praised the purposes of the conventions, which, if achieved, would tend to check Northern "insults" to the South, condemned their Southern critics as "the most dangerous enemies" to their section, and claimed that the meetings tended to strengthen "the union." Jan. 28, Dec. 11, 1856. The *Mobile Daily Register* characterized the Vicksburg Convention of 1859 "as the Southern Continental Congress," and declared that "in the Union, the South is to the North what its tail is to the comet—all that gives it glory and grandeur and forms the wonder and admiration of a gazing world, yet withal a mere appendage. Out of the Union, she becomes a fair heiress, having every nation on earth for her suitors." May 11, Nov. 15, 1859. The *Charleston Mercury* felt that, through the transit of its products, the South paid "numerous contributions" to those who were hostile to her, but that only political independence could change that transit and bring commercial independence. Jan. 14, Sept. 14, 1857.

47. *Chicago Press*, March 29, April 10, 27, 1854.
48. April 19, 1854, August 14, 1857.
49. Dec. 15, 1856, August 19, 1857, April 5, 1859.

the move toward Southern commercial independence.[50]

Railroads as a factor that produced closer economic ties between the grain and meat producing areas of the Northwest and the manufacturing centers of the East should not be overlooked as a factor that played some part in producing North-South sectionalism. It is said that, in 1847, there were only 660 miles of railroad in the five states comprising the Old Northwest, and not a line connected the lake waters with the Ohio; yet in 1860 there were, in those states, 9,362.69 miles,[51] and roads from Lakes Erie and Michigan touched the Mississippi at ten places and the Ohio at eight.[52]

Despite sectional divergence over economic matters, there were of course economic ties that tended toward unity. The cotton, sugar, molasses and citrus fruits of the South found a good and ready market in the North, and the manufactured goods, and to some extent the grain and meat supplies of the North, a very necessary one in the South. The planter in the South was interested in Northern credit, of which he had considerable in 1860, and hence many Northerners had a material interest in the South.

50. *Richmond Enquirer,* Dec. 16, 1856.
51. Frederic L. Paxson, "The Railroads of the Old Northwest," in Vol. XVII of *Transactions of the Wisconsin Academy of Sciences, Arts and Letters* (Madison, 1914), 243–275. See 249, 265–266.
52. Lippincott, *Internal Trade of the United States, 1700–1860,* 141.

IX

The Republican Triumph

THE presidential campaign and election of 1860 cannot be interpreted in their proper setting without a discussion of three other topics that have not yet been considered in their relation to sectionalism in the fifties. Those three are attempts at expansion southward, the movement to re-open the foreign slave trade and the John Brown raid.

The expansionist sentiment was to be found mostly in the South, 1850 to 1860, though it was not confined to that section, and there was considerable difference of opinion there in regard to efforts to acquire territory. Cuba was the area most likely to be acquired, but the Nicaraguan schemes of William Walker found some favor in the South. The attempts of Walker to make himself dictator in Nicaragua in 1856–57 have been interpreted as motivated by the desire to extend slavery, to further the interests of American capitalists and to bring a new state into the Union. Walker repudiated the latter idea, though he was willing to establish slavery under himself as dictator.[1] A New Orleans jury, in

1. William O. Scroggs, "William Walker's Designs on Cuba," *Mississippi Valley Historical Review*, Vol. I, 198–211. See especially 198–199.

1857, acquitted the would-be dictator of violating the neutrality laws of the United States,[2] and a prominent Southern journal contended that Walker, as the head of an army of a *de facto* government, was not a filibusterer, and should be accorded recognition as head of the government of Nicaragua.[3] On the other hand, a Southern journal called Walker's plans "piratical," [4] and the Knoxville Commercial Convention of 1857 voted down, 60 to 25, a resolution sympathizing with him and his efforts to establish slavery in the Central American country.[5]

The currents of opinion in regard to Cuba during the decade prior to 1861 are somewhat complex. That complexity arose from the fact that economic, racial, international and political factors were all intertwined with the Cuban question. As the result of unwarranted interference of Americans in the island, Spain had sometimes acted in severe fashion toward them. That action gave the excuse for the Ostend Manifesto, though the reasons for the policy suggested in that report are varied. In the Manifesto, Pierre Soulé, James Buchanan and John Y. Mason, United States ministers to Spain, England and France, respectively, suggested that the American Government try to purchase Cuba, but if Spain would not sell, we should then be justified in taking the island by force. However, it was no part of the program of the Pierce administration to pursue such a rash policy. John Slidell, of Louisiana, reported from the Committee on Foreign Relations of the Senate, in 1859, a

2. Smith, *Parties and Slavery*, 255–256.
3. *Augusta Daily Constitutionalist*, May 13, 1856.
4. *Arkansas True Democrat*, August 18, 1858.
5. See vote in *Savannah Republican*, August 20, 1857.

bill to appropriate $30,000,000 to be used by the President in negotiating a treaty with Spain for our acquisition of Cuba.

While the Ostend Manifesto and the Slidell bill may be taken as the focal points for the discussion of Cuban acquisition, Northern sentiment, especially Northern Republican sentiment, is not to be judged entirely by the reaction of the Republicans to those proposals. The Republican national platform of 1856 strongly condemned the Ostend Manifesto, but the platform of 1860 makes no mention of the Cuban question. The *New York Times* was concerned at reports that England was working with Spain to "Africanize" Cuba, a condition which it felt the whites of the United States could "never tolerate." That journal pointed out that the acquisition of the island would be to the advantage of all sections of the Union, since its possession would mean the extension of the slave labor system of the South, an increase in New England's commerce, and cheaper sugar and wider markets for the Northwest. The *Times,* however, opposed the Slidell bill as impracticable, and condemned the idea of giving $30,000,000 to Buchanan, which he might use for some other purpose than the acquisition of Cuba.[6]

However, there was considerable Republican opposition to the possible acquisition of Cuba on the ground that such a step would mean the further spread of slavery, and would represent an increase in the "slave power."[7] The debate over the Slidell bill became inter-

6. *New York Times,* Jan. 14, 1854, April 9, 1855, Jan. 18, 27, Feb. 21, 1859. The *Ohio State Journal,* though doubtful whether the North would ever be willing to admit Cuba as a slave state, was at one time willing to do so, though later bitterly opposed to the Slidell bill. Sept. 2, 1851, Jan. 31, 1859.

7. *New York Tribune,* Oct. 19, 1858, Jan. 13, 1859; remarks

twined with that over the homestead bill, and led Seward and Wade to charge that one group in the United States was interested in slaves for those who already had them or wanted to acquire them, and the other in "lands for the landless." [8] The Northern Democratic press, apparently unconcerned about slavery in Cuba, emphasized good order there and increased economic advantages for the United States as probable beneficent results of the island's acquisition.[9]

While there was considerable sentiment in the South in favor of the acquisition of Cuba, there were sharply conflicting currents of opinion in regard to such a policy. Those who favored it pointed out the economic advantages of such a step, and emphasized at length the danger that emancipation might take place, in which case hundreds of thousands of free Negroes would be a perpetual menace close to the institution of slavery.[10]

of H. E. Royce, Representative from Vermont, and of John P. Hale, *Appendix to Globe*, 35 Cong., 2 Sess., Feb. 15, 1859, 111–112, 163, respectively.

8. *Appendix to Globe*, 35 Cong., 2 Sess., Feb. 25, 1859, 1353, 1354.

9. *Boston Post*, Feb. 12, 1859; *Detroit Free Press*, March 16, 17, 1854; *Cincinnati Enquirer*, Feb. 11, 12, 15, 1859. It is interesting to note that the abolitionist, Gerrit Smith, favored acquiring Cuba because he thought that action would aid in the closing of the foreign slave trade there. Octavius Frothingham, *Gerrit Smith* (New York, 1879), 222–223.

10. Slidell, in his Committee Report, not only emphasized the economic advantages of annexation, but the necessity of checking the tendency toward Africanization. He pointed out that, by the Census of 1850, there were in the island 605,560 whites, 205,570 free colored and 436,100 slaves, and claimed that emancipation would soon come, perhaps as the result of the independence of Cuba, in which case he predicted "civil and servile" war. Senator S. R. Mallory, of Florida, in stressing the economic advantages of annexing Cuba, claimed that the matter should not be approached from a sectional angle. As to the claim that the South

The Southern opponents of the Cuban project assigned seemingly good reasons for their position. The *Richmond Enquirer* thought the "difficulties, perhaps insurmountable" in carrying out such a project. The security of slavery in Cuba was very doubtful, and, if secured, it would accelerate the already rapid movement of slaves from the border states southward. The *Mobile Advertiser* wanted the "clamor" about Cuba to cease, felt that the efforts to get her would lead to international complications, and that Cuba would ultimately be Africanized anyway. The *New Orleans True Delta* felt that annexation would ruin the sugar industry of New Orleans, and would either lead to the reopening of the African slave trade or the destruction of slavery in America. The suggestion was a "humbug" which was "ruinous" and "suicidal." [11]

The *New York Tribune*, in 1858, declared that the

wanted political advantages, he said that he had "long since surrendered" any such "delusive hope" as that of maintaining any "equilibrium" of political representation between the North and South. For Slidell's Report, see *Appendix to Globe*, 35 Cong., 2 Sess., Jan. 24, 1859, 90–95, and for Mallory's remarks, *ibid.*, Feb. 21, 1859, 294–295. The *New Orleans Picayune* feared complications with France and England, should we try to get Cuba, but it felt that an uncontrolled African population "almost within sight of three or four slave states" would be a menace to them, Jan. 26, 1859. The *Mobile Register* claimed annexation would be a boon to the South and West, in that it would free those sections from the "hampering commercial policy of the East." It regretted the "change" that had come "over the South" regarding annexation, and suggested that after all it was slave territory, in which England and France had a particular interest. Jan. 23, Feb. 1, 1859. The *Mississippian* felt that considerations demanding annexation had "increased both in number and in force." April 1, 1859.

11. *Richmond Enquirer*, Feb. 3, March 2, 1859; *Mobile Advertiser*, Jan. 25, 1855, Jan. 15, Feb. 11, 1859; *True Delta*, Jan. 29, 1859.

"purpose of re-opening the slave trade is seriously entertained by a strong and rapidly increasing party at
the South," [12] and another Republican newspaper accused "Virginia and the South" of giving "their sanction
to an open and flagrant violation of the Constitution
and laws of the land by an open and shameless revival
of the African slave trade." A religious paper declared
that "the South" would "go as a unit for the revivial
of the slave trade." [13] On the other hand, Northern
Democratic papers claimed that there was little sentiment in the South in favor of re-opening the trade. [14]

Southern opinion differed in regard to the matter.
Despite its legal prohibition, the foreign slave trade
had never been completely stopped, and was revived in
the fifties to a greater extent than usual. New York was
the main port from which went ships engaged in the
slave trade, and the South was of course the recipient
of slaves brought in. Attempts were made in different
parts of the South to bring in legally apprentices who
should serve for a period of years, but such attempts
were not successful. Howell Cobb, as Secretary of the
Treasury, refused to give clearance papers to E. Lafitte
and Company of Charleston, South Carolina, to import
apprentices, and, though a bill for such purposes passed
the Louisiana House in 1858, it failed in the Senate by
two votes. [15]

12. *New York Tribune*, Sept. 1, 1858.
13. *Worcester Palladium* of Nov. 30, 1859 and *New York Independent*, respectively, quoted in *Boston Post*, Dec. 8, 1859,
Dec. 29, 1856.
14. *Boston Post*, Dec. 8, 1859; *Detroit Free Press*, Dec. 9,
1856; *Chicago Times*, Dec. 6, 1856.
15. W. E. B. Du Bois, *The Suppression of the African Slave
Trade to the United States of America* (New York and London,
1896), 177–183.

Whether the South should lend its efforts in the direction of re-opening the foreign slave trade was the subject of considerable debate in the Southern commercial conventions during the fifties. Was it morally wrong or right to bring the slave from Africa to the South? What would be the effect of such a practice at that time upon world sentiment, which had steadily developed against the trade? Would such a policy be to the economic and political advantage of the slaveholding section, and what would be its effect upon the future of slavery? These were some of the questions raised, and answered in very different manner by various members of the conventions. Finally, at the Vicksburg Convention, in 1859, after such action had failed in previous conventions, a resolution was passed asking for the repeal of all laws, state or national, that stood in the way of re-opening the trade.[16]

While there was more sentiment in the states of the upper South against re-opening the foreign slave trade than in the lower, partly because the former sold slaves to a greater extent, one should not conclude that the majority sentiment of the cotton states was affirmative in the matter. John Forsyth's *Mobile Register* took an affirmative stand on the ground that more slaves meant more production and more political power; and that "civilized bondage" here was preferable to "barbarian bondage" in Africa. The *Mississippian* wanted removed anti-slave trade laws that were a "burning reproach" to the South, but granted that they could not be repealed in the Union. Re-opening the trade, it felt, would strengthen slavery in the border states. The *Charleston Mercury* had no objection to the trade, but deplored an

16. Wender, *Southern Commercial Conventions*, 177 *et seq.*, 197, *et seq.*, 211, *et seq.*, 230, *et seq.* The vote was 44 to 19, 234.

issue which was destroying harmony in the South.[17]

The *Augusta Constitutionalist* thought that re-opening the trade would affect adversely the public sentiment of the world, "divide and distract the South," and was "utterly impracticable" as long as the Union lasted. The *New Orleans Picayune* granted that most of the Negroes in Africa would live under better conditions in America, but felt that their importation would make the slavery problem here more difficult. That journal characterized the proposed Louisiana apprentice law as "repugnant" to the "sense of justice." The proposal to revive the African trade was denounced by the *Savannah Republican* as "a symptom of the political distemper with which South Carolina politicians have been afflicted for the past twenty years," and by the *Mobile Advertiser* as a policy which would "outrage the almost universal sentiment of enlightened Christendom," and as a "ridiculous hobby" inspired by "political stock-jobbers." [18] Finally, it should be pointed out that the Constitution of the Confederacy forbade the importation of slaves from abroad, if not from the states and territories of the United States.[19]

Abolitionism and Republicanism were not synonymous terms in the fifties, even if Toombs and many Southerners made them so; [20] yet abolition activities tended to give zeal and zest to the controversy over

17. *Mobile Register,* May 15, 1859; *Mississippian,* June 11, 1858, May 24, 1859; *Charleston Mercury,* Jan. 11, 1858, March 9, 1859.

18. *Augusta Constitutionalist,* March 4, May 16, 1858; *New Orleans Picayune,* March 5, 21, 1858; *Savannah Republican,* Dec. 6, 1856; *Mobile Advertiser,* July 18, 1854, May 14, 1859.

19. Du Bois, *op. cit.,* 189.

20. Toombs said that abolitionists, "better to conceal their purposes," called themselves "Republicans." *Appendix to Globe,* 36 Cong., 1 Sess., Jan. 24, 1860, 88.

other phases of the slavery question. Garrison burned
the Constitution publicly in the streets of Boston, and
Theodore Parker advised forcible resistance to the Fugitive Slave Law. Parker proclaimed the idea that Congress did have power over slavery in the states, and
warned the politicians that, if they did not keep step
fast enough with anti-slavery sentiment, they would be
supplanted by others who did.[21] Wendell Phillips denounced the South as "one great brothel, where half a
million women are flogged to prostitution, or worse still,
are degraded to believe it honorable." [22] Early in 1857,
the Abolitionists held a convention at Worcester, Massachusetts, and later in the year another at Cleveland,
Ohio. Disunion was the theme and aim of both conventions, and at the second the Union was called "a
crime and a curse." Garrison, Phillips, Parker Pillsbury
and Thomas Higginson were leading lights at Worcester, and Pillsbury and William Wells Brown at Cleveland. The Republican press, fearful that such radical
movements would be linked with its party, was quick to
denounce them.[23]

During the presidential election year, 1856, there had
been much talk in the South of slave insurrections.
There was supposed to be an insurrection planned, ex-

21. John Weiss, *Life and Correspondence of Theodore Parker*
(2 Vols., New York, 1864), Vol. II, 70, 91–95, 117–123, 157.
22. Wendell Phillips, *Speeches, Lectures and Letters* (Boston,
1884), speech before Massachusetts Anti-Slavery Society, Jan.
27, 1853, 108.
23. For account of Worcester Convention, see *Boston Atlas*,
Jan. 16, 1857, and for denunciation of proceedings, see *Atlas*,
Jan. 16, 30, 1857. For Cleveland Convention proceedings and
condemnation of same by Republican papers, see Edward O.
Purtee, *The Underground Railroad from Southwestern Ohio to
Lake Erie* (unpublished Doctoral Dissertation at Ohio State University, 1932), 159–162.

tending all the way from Delaware to Texas, to break on Christmas day of that year. Though much that was said was exaggerated rumor, there were more plots and individual slave crimes during the year than usual. Southerners attributed this state of unrest to Republican and abolition agitation, but their Northern opponents attributed it to the nature of the institution of slavery itself.[24] The climax of this period of abolition agitation was reached when John Brown, from a Maryland farm where he had been stationed for some time, led a small group of followers, October 16, 1859, to Harpers Ferry, Virginia, in an attempt to start a slave revolt and ultimately bring about emancipation. The raid had been planned at the home of Gerrit Smith in New York months before; and, in addition to Smith, Brown had had the co-operation of George Stearns, Thomas Higginson, F. B. Sanborn and others. Some of the participants in the early preliminaries went to Canada after the raid, and Smith himself went to the insane asylum at Utica.[25]

The reaction to the raid in the North was varied. The Democrats, in denouncing it, attributed it to the inflammatory feeling caused by the alleged radical utterances of Seward, Wade, Giddings and others.[26] If one may judge by the declaration in the Republican platform in 1860 condemning "lawless invasion" of a state "by armed force," and by the declarations of some of the Republican leaders, notably Seward, he might conclude that most of the Republicans condemned the raid.

24. Harvey Wish, "The Slave Insurrection Panic of 1856," *Journal of Southern History*, May, 1939, 206–222.
25. Frothingham, *Gerrit Smith*, 238–243.
26. *Cincinnati Enquirer*, Oct. 19, 20, 1859; *Boston Post*, Oct. 21, 29, 1859.

But not all did. The *Boston Atlas and Bee,* referring to Brown's execution, declared that "the prayers of millions of freemen are this hour ascending to Heaven in his behalf" and "the crown of martyrdom will be his." The *Boston Journal* stated that, after slavery was gone, what now seemed "just and proper" (Brown's execution) would "be regarded as a blot upon the escutcheon of the state." [27] The *New York Tribune* felt that peaceful methods should be used to bring about emancipation, but it would "not, by one reproachful word, disturb the bloody shrouds wherein John Brown and his compatriots are sleeping." [28] On the day that Brown was executed, numerous meetings of sympathy for him were held, bells were tolled in some places, a salute of one hundred guns was fired at Albany, and the Massachusetts Senate failed to adjourn by only three votes. Disorder and protest, however, were experienced at some of the meetings.[29] The abolitionists went to incredible extremes in their defense of Brown. In the words of Wendell Phillips, Virginia was "blacker than Algiers," and Brown had "twice as much right to hang Governor Wise" as the latter had to hang Brown. According to Parker, slaves had a natural right to kill their masters, and freemen to help them do so. He was convinced that, as people became more "intelligent and moral," attempts at insurrection would increase.[30]

In the South there was a tendency to link together

27. Quoted in *Boston Post,* Dec. 6, 1859.

28. *New York Tribune,* Oct. 19, 1859. Fite in his *Presidential Campaign of 1860,* 30–31, quotes a number of Republican papers that mildly sympathized with Brown and his cause.

29. For above accounts, see *New York Times,* Dec. 3, 1859; *New York Herald,* Dec. 3, 1859; *New York Evening Post,* Dec. 2, 3, 1859.

30. Phillips, *op. cit.,* 272; Weiss, *op. cit.,* 170–172.

Brown's raid, the insurrectionary ideas contained in Helper's *Impending Crisis* and the doctrine of an "irrepressible conflict" as proclaimed by Seward.[31] Several of the conspirators who aided Brown had escaped to Ohio and Iowa, and the Governors of those states, Dennison and Samuel Kirkwood, respectively, refused to surrender them when John Letcher, Governor of Virginia, requested their extradition. Kirkwood claimed that the papers Letcher sent were not properly made out, but there is reason to believe that he was trying to let the fugitive escape from Iowa before extraditing him.[32] The Southern press roundly denounced the Republican governors for their "unconstitutional" action in not returning the conspirators.[33] Some of the papers in the South emphasized the conservative reaction to the raid in the North, and claimed that the Northern radicals should learn from it that slavery was stable and not volcanic, as some of the radicals had alleged.[34] The developments late in 1859 led to much talk in the South of commercial discrimination against the North, and, as Professor Cole points out, after the Harpers Ferry incident one hundred and sixty students in a body left the medical school of the University of Pennsylvania and

31. *Augusta Constitutionalist*, Nov. 1, 29, Dec. 17, 1859; *Charleston Mercury*, Oct. 22, Dec. 6, 1859; *Richmond Enquirer*, Nov. 1, Dec. 7, 1859, Jan. 2, 1860.

32. Dan E. Clark, *Samuel J. Kirkwood* (Iowa City, 1917), 155–162. Kirkwood felt that the "unlawful" raid should be condemned, but claimed that the South was responsible for it as a result of its pro-slavery policy in Kansas, and expeditions to Cuba and Nicaragua. See *ibid.*, 148–149. The prisoner did flee from home before extradition could be effected.

33. *Mississippian*, March 6, June 15, 1860; *New Orleans Picayune*, March 23, 1860; *Richmond Enquirer*, March 6, 1860.

34. *Savannah Republican*, Oct. 19, 25, 1859; *New Orleans Picayune*, Oct. 25, Nov. 8, 1859.

the Jefferson Medical College, and transferred to the medical school at Richmond, Virginia.[35]

Before the stage is finally set for the presidential campaign and election of 1860, a word further must be said in regard to Douglas and the Republicans. Many of them had praised his stand in regard to the Lecompton Constitution, and there were signs, which did not, however, prove correct, that he and the Republicans might permanently join hands. After he won a very close fight for the United States Senate in Illinois, there were indications that the Republicans might swing to his squatter sovereignty doctrine. During the late months of 1858 and the early ones of 1859, the *New York Times* criticized Seward for his "extravagance" in claiming that the Democratic party, if not defeated, would establish slavery in all the states, and for his threats against slavery in the states where it existed. It predicted, however, that the Republicans would win in 1860, if the Democrats asked for congressional protection of slavery. At the same time, it praised Douglas and his pet principle of popular sovereignty, and claimed that the Republicans, in trying to keep alive the principle of congressional exclusion of slavery in the territories, were reviving "an issue as absolutely dead as that of the United States or a Protective Tariff" (sic).[36] Early in 1859, Eli Thayer, then a member of the House from Massachusetts, strongly defended popular sovereignty, said that the slavery question was settled in the

35. Arthur C. Cole, *The Irrepressible Conflict, 1850–1865* (New York, 1934), 51. *The New Orleans Picayune,* though opposing commercial restrictions against the North as impracticable, advised Southerners to remain at home for their education. Dec. 10, 1859.

36. *New York Times,* Oct. 28, Nov. 22, 1858, Jan. 10, Feb. 26, 1859.

territories, and denounced Republican politicians for predicting that slavery would "be established in Massachusetts and New Hampshire." He said that those same politicians, by their persistent cry that all was lost in Kansas, had been a greater obstacle to the free soil cause there than all other factors combined.[37]

This trend in the Republican party annoyed some of its leaders. The *New York Tribune* denied the contention of Douglas that the Republicans, in voting for the Crittenden-Montgomery bill, had accepted the principle of popular sovereignty. That journal claimed that they voted for it as a means of disposing of the Lecompton Constitution, which they were certain Kansas would reject.[38] Lincoln expressed great concern at the Republican trend toward that "insidious" doctrine of Douglas. It, with other discordant factors, would "tend to disrupt the national convention in 1860," it was in fact, the "chief danger" to the purpose of the Republican organization, and, if accepted, "it nationalizes slavery, and revives the African slave-trade inevitably."[39]

When the Republican national convention met in May, 1860, it was confronted with a long list of prospective nominees. Seward, in terms of long political service, was the outstanding man in the party, but two factors worked against his nomination. Some of his utterances concerning slavery made him appear radical, and he

37. *Appendix to Globe,* 35 Cong., 2 Sess., Feb. 24, 1859, 236–239.
38. *New York Tribune,* July 15, 1858.
39. Lincoln, *Works,* Vol. I, 535, 537–538, 540–541. These sentiments were expressed in letters and speeches in 1859. Lincoln's advice to Republicans not to discuss discordant factors in local conventions is in a letter to Schuyler Colfax, July 6, 1859, 535. The discordant elements which Lincoln mentioned were "personal liberty" laws, squatter sovereignty and immigration.

had favored state support for parochial schools in New York, a position not to the liking of the Know-Nothing group. Edward Bates, a conservative Republican from Missouri, Salmon P. Chase and Abraham Lincoln were among the possible choices. Lincoln, who showed considerable strength on the first ballot, and who had gained political prominence by his debates with Douglas, was nominated on the third ballot. Hannibal Hamlin, of Maine, was chosen as his running mate.

The Republican platform covered considerable ground. Very conspicuous were the planks in reference to economic policy and to immigration. River and harbor improvements, a protective tariff, free homesteads and a transcontinental railroad were endorsed. Opposition was expressed to state laws which impaired the rights of citizenship to immigrants as hitherto accorded. Changes in naturalization laws were opposed.[40] On slavery questions the platform represented an effort to satisfy conservative and radical anti-slavery groups. Joshua R. Giddings, seconded by George W. Curtis, succeeded in obtaining a plank endorsing the Declaration of Independence, which was said to be embodied in the Constitution, and to be "essential to the preservation of our Republican institutions." However, this plank was not deemed inconsistent with a declaration to the effect that each state had control over its domestic institu-

40. This "Dutch plank," which was strongly urged by Carl Schurz, was the outgrowth, in part, of a Massachusetts state law passed in 1859 which required persons of foreign birth who should become naturalized to delay two years before voting. The Democrats charged the Republicans with responsibility for the act. Some Eastern Republicans tried to disclaim responsibility for it, and Western Republicans criticized it. For the various positions, see *Boston Post*, May 9, 1859, Jan. 9, 1860 and *Ohio State Journal*, May 6, 1859.

tions. The provision on the territorial question and slavery was worded in such a way as to deny that any agency could legalize slavery in the territories, but positive action to prohibit it by Congress was conditioned by a "whenever such legislation is necessary" clause.[41] Attempts to re-open the foreign slave trade were condemned, and no reference was made to the fugitive slave question.

The Democratic national convention which met at Charleston, South Carolina, was a stormy one. For some time factors had been working toward a split in the Democratic party, and matters came to a climax in the convention over the question as to whether that body should endorse Federal protection for slavery in the territories, or adopt a policy which presumably left the matter of slavery to the people of the territories, contingent upon a Supreme Court decision as to their power over the troublesome question. If the former policy were adopted, said the Douglas Democrats, the party could carry no Northern states. The Southern states, said Southern Democrats, furnished sure electoral votes for the party, and hence their views should prevail. The Douglas policy was favored by the majority of the delegates, with the result that delegations

41. The plank read as follows: "Resolved, That the normal condition of the territory of the United States is that of freedom; that as our Republican fathers, when they had abolished slavery in all our national territory, ordained that no person should be deprived of life, liberty, or property without due process of law, it becomes our duty by legislation, whenever such legislation is necessary, to maintain this provision of the Constitution against all attempts to violate it; and we deny the authority of Congress, of a territorial legislature, or of any individual, to give legal existence to slavery in any territory of the United States." For entire platform, see Stanwood, *History of the Presidency from 1788 to 1897*, 291–294.

from eight Southern states withdrew from the convention.

Since no nomination was made at Charleston, a decision was made to assemble at Baltimore on June 18. The "bolters" decided to hold a convention at Richmond, but in the meantime prominent Southerners, such as Toombs, Hunter, Davis and James M. Mason, issued an "Address to the National Democracy," in which they urged the eight states whose delegates withdrew at Charleston to send delegates to Baltimore and not to Richmond. However, the "Address" emphasized the fact that the South had sure Democratic electoral votes, and warned that other states would "bolt" as some had at Charleston, unless concessions were made to the Southern position. The Douglas forces, which were in control at Baltimore, refused to seat many of the delegates sent by regular conventions in the cotton states, but instead gave most of the seats to contesting Douglas delegates, a policy which widened the rift in the Democratic party.[42] The Baltimore convention nominated Douglas and Senator Benjamin Fitzpatrick, of Alabama, but named Herschel V. Johnson, of Georgia, for Vice-President after Fitzpatrick had declined the nomination. Most of the Southern delegates withdrew from the convention, held another one and named John C. Breckinridge, of Kentucky, for President and Joseph Lane, of Oregon, for Vice-President. The dissenting delegates then joined the "bolters" at Richmond, where Breckinridge and Lane were also nominated.

Both Democratic platforms favored the acquisition

42. For above developments, see *Richmond Enquirer*, May 21, 23, June 20, 23, 25, 1860. The Buchanan administration was anti-Douglas, so among the Northern delegates there was some discord in the convention.

of Cuba, if it could be honorably acquired, condemned "personal liberty" laws in Northern states as "revolutionary" and "unconstitutional" and advocated a transcontinental railroad. On the question of slavery in the territories, the Douglas platform indicated a willingness to abide by a future decision of the Supreme Court on the powers of a territorial legislature over slavery, while the Southern Democratic platform demanded that all the departments of the Federal Government "if necessary," protect slavery in the territories, until those units became states, and could decide the matter for themselves.

However one views the origins and nature of the quarrel between Douglas and the Southern Democrats, the question may be raised as to whether the latter felt that they would, by pressing that quarrel to an issue and splitting the party, elect a Republican and thus precipitate secession. The answer is probably yes in the case of men like William L. Yancey and Robert B. Rhett, but no in the case of most Southern Democrats. Yancey, a great orator and ultra Southerner, and the moving spirit among the "seceders" from the Charleston convention, had written a letter in 1858 in which he expressed the view that neither a sectional nor a national party could save the South. He wanted the section to organize "Committees of Safety" to develop a strong Southern feeling, and he felt that they could, when the proper time came "precipitate the cotton states into a revolution." [43] There is reason for thinking, however, that many Southern Democrats believed that a split in the party would result in throwing the election into the

43. John W. Du Bose, *The Life and Times of William Lowndes Yancey* (Birmingham, 1892). See letter of Yancey to James Slaughter, of Georgia, June 15, 1858, 376.

House of Representatives, with salutary results for the Democrats.[44]

A fourth group, in 1860, chose as its candidates for President and Vice-President, respectively, John Bell and Edward Everett. That group, known as the Constitutional Union party, had as its platform the Constitution, the Union and the enforcement of the laws. Though the platform evaded mention of definite principles, it is significant that the presidential candidate of the party had voted against the Kansas-Nebraska Act, the Lecompton Constitution and the low tariff of 1857.

The campaign of 1860 was the climax to a long period of discussion of controversial questions, so it was natural that there should be reproduced during that campaign most of the arguments that had been hurled back and forth for a decade. Seward sallied forth into the West proclaiming the idea that the sectional controversy was essentially one between aristocracy and democracy, that the South had too long enjoyed great political power and that it was time to break that power.

44. Professor Dodd says that many Southerners felt that Douglas could carry the Northwest, which result would throw the election into the House. If the Democrats did not win there, they felt that they could choose a Vice-President in the Senate, who would become President. William E. Dodd, "The Fight for the Northwest," *American Historical Review*, Vol. XVI, 774–788. See 778–779. Laura A. White, *Robert Barnwell Rhett: Father of Secession* (New York and London, 1931), 163, holds that Yancey and Rhett wanted to split the Democratic party to accomplish secession, but that Davis and Slidell wanted to defeat Douglas and carry the election to the House, where they had a good chance to elect their favorite. The *Mississippian* thought that the South with small states had a much better chance of electing a Democrat in the House than in the electoral college. Feb. 9, 1860. For other contemporary expressions of belief that election might go to the House or ultimately the Senate, see *New Orleans Picayune*, May 6, 1860, *North Carolina Standard*, June 30, 1860.

Schurz denounced the allegedly broad, aggressive program of the slaveholders, and emphasized to the Westerners the Southern opposition to free lands. Yancey went North where he proclaimed the rights, as he interpreted them, of slaveholders under the Constitution, and pointed out the ways in which the institution of slavery was of economic benefit to the free states. Douglas lashed at Northern and Southern extremists, and said at Norfolk, Virginia, that he could not countenance secession, if the Republicans did win the election.[45] Lincoln said little, and Breckinridge professed loyalty to the Constitution and the Union. Davis, with the approval of Bell and Breckinridge, tried during the summer of 1860 to have Douglas withdraw, and all three unite upon another candidate. Douglas refused on the ground that such a policy would result in his followers supporting Lincoln.[46]

The Southern press showed generally a strong hostility to Republicans, but segments of it often used strong language in regard to other candidates and parties. The *Augusta Constitutionalist*, a Douglas paper, deplored the "disunion" tendencies of Southern Democrats, chided Bell for running on a meaningless platform, and for voting against the Kansas-Nebraska Act, called Lincoln "the father and author of the "irrepressible conflict;" and the Republican party a "disunion party." [47] The *Mobile Advertiser*, which favored Bell, felt that the

45. See Seward, *Works*, Vol. IV, 304, 346, 360–361, 372; Fite, *Presidential Campaign of 1860*, 301–329, 244–275, respectively, for speeches of Yancey at New York and Schurz at St. Louis; Milton, *Eve of Conflict*, 492–494, for utterances of Douglas.

46. William E. Dodd, *Jefferson Davis* (Philadelphia, 1907), 189; Fite, *op. cit.*, 224; Milton, *op. cit.*, 487.

47. *Augusta Constitutionalist*, May 6, 19, June 14, 1860.

fight in the Democratic party was between men, and
not over the principles professed, and, as for the Republicans, stated that Lincoln was getting a "shade
darker" each year. The *Savannah Republican* claimed
that all other parties were "sectionalized," and that Bell
and Everett were the "only national candidates." [48] The
True Democrat, a Breckinridge paper, strongly denied
that the man it was supporting was a disunionist, but
claimed that the Bell supporters by crying "disunion,"
and the Douglas supporters by advocating a "do-noth-
ing" policy were leading Northern Republicans to feel
that the South was not in earnest in resisting unconstitutional aggression. [49] The *Charleston Mercury* thundered against "Homestead, Tariff and Wilmot Proviso
bills" which were being "insolently rushed through the
House of Representatives," and stated that the Breckinridge party did look to independence rather than live
under the "simple despotism" of the Republicans. [50] The
Mississippian bitterly denounced Lincoln's "House-
Divided" speech, and declared that the Republican
ticket represented "all the meanness, the bigotry, and
the fanaticism of the Black Republican organization." [51]

The *New York Herald,* sympathetic with the Southern Democracy, claimed that the Republicans fully expected to abolish slavery, if they triumphed, and that
their campaign, particularly in the rural sections of the
North, drew its inspiration from Helper's *Impending
Crisis,* and from the radical speeches of Lovejoy and

48. *Mobile Advertiser,* May 12, 19, July 11, 1860; *Savannah
Republican,* July 25, 1860.

49. *Arkansas True Democrat,* August 25, Oct. 27, 1860.

50. *Charleston Mercury,* May 12, July 4, 1860. The "Wilmot
Proviso" reference was to a measure in the House which repealed
New Mexico's slave code.

51. *Mississippian,* May 29, July 13, 1860.

Sumner, all of which, it alleged, were widely circulated. The *Philadelphia Press* praised the conservatism of Douglas, condemned Southern Democrats as "disunionists," and bitterly denounced the *New York Herald* for trying to frighten the Southerners with dire predictions as to what would happen, if the Republicans won. It called the editor of the *Herald* a "vile" wretch, an "unscrupulous and remorseless" knave, who was "utterly debased, privately and publicly." [52] The *Detroit Free Press* likewise praised Douglas for his middle ground position, but unlike John Forney's *Philadelphia Press*, predicted secession in case of Lincoln's election, and declared that Lincoln was as much of an abolitionist as "Seward or Garrison." [53]

The Republican press followed several lines of strategy. The *New York Times* stated that the Republican opposition to slavery was only partly moral, that it was partly political, that the Republicans did wish to break the political power of the slaveholders, but not for any purpose of interfering with slavery. It predicted that the Republicans, if they won, would drop the slavery issue after the election, and would turn their attention to matters of domestic and foreign policy. No secession would follow, for the South was too dependent economically upon the North, and was also apprehensive of "insurrection" among the slaves.[54] The *New York Tribune*, reacting to reports of vicious treatment of anti-slavery men in the South, injected spice into the campaign when it declared that "men hanging on gibbets—regular or irregular" were frequently seen in the

52. *New York Herald,* April 25, June 2, Oct. 1, 17, 18, 24, 1860; *Philadelphia Press,* April 30, June 25, Oct. 4, 1860.
53. *Detroit Free Press,* June 2, 12, Nov. 4, 1860.
54. *New York Times,* May 30, July 17, August 3, 1860.

South, and that those who disturbed "civilization" there were "burned at the stake." That paper did state, however, that it was not the purpose of the Republican party to destroy slavery in the states.[55]

There was one decided advantage which the Republicans had in the campaign, and they availed themselves of it. There was no harmony among the Democrats in regard to an economic program, but the Republicans had a definite program. Even if Northerners generally did favor free homesteads by 1860, it could be emphasized, and was emphasized, that the majority of those Northerners in Congress were Republicans, and that the Southern wing of the Democratic party had done much to prevent the enactment of the homestead policy.[56] The Republican protective tariff policy was strong in Pennsylvania and New Jersey, and who, asked the *New York Tribune*, was responsible for its defeat except the Democrats?[57]

The results of the election show a wide discrepancy

55. *New York Tribune*, July 10, Sept. 21, 1860.

56. *New York Tribune*, Jan. 23, June 21, 25, 1860; *Illinois State Journal*, March 21, June 20, Oct. 3, 1860; *Ohio State Journal*, June 21, 26, 1860. Dodd, *op. cit.*, points out that a change of one vote in twenty-seven would have enabled Douglas to carry the states of Iowa and Illinois, and one in twenty, the entire Northwest. He thinks the homestead policy was a big factor in the Republican triumph in that section. While the Republican press was praising free homesteads, Southern papers were pointing out how such a policy strengthened "abolitionists," reduced revenues, acted as a "bribe" to undesirable aliens, and furthered unhealthy agrarian tendencies. See *True Democrat*, April 14, 1860, *New Orleans Picayune*, April 7, 1860.

57. *New York Tribune*, June 25, 1860. It is true that the *Philadelphia Press*, a Democratic paper, emphasized the fact that all Pennsylvania and New Jersey Democrats voted for the Morrill tariff in the House. June 6, 1860. That action, however, would hardly induce voters who thought the tariff fundamental to vote the *national* Democratic ticket.

between the electoral and the popular votes. Lincoln received 180 electoral votes, Douglas 12, Breckinridge 72 and Bell 39. The popular vote was Lincoln 1,866,452, Douglas 1,376,957, Breckinridge 849,781 and Bell 588,-879. Douglas had a powerful minority vote in the free states, and Lincoln did not receive a single popular vote in ten of the eleven states soon to secede. In fact, the Illinois Republican was outdistanced by his three opponents combined by nearly one million votes. Breckinridge received a bare majority of the votes in the slave states soon to secede, but a majority was cast against him in all the slaveholding states combined. The South was practically a unit in its opposition to the Republicans, but there was still much conservative opinion in the section.[58]

58. Stanwood, *History of the Presidency*, 297. South Carolina still chose electors by the legislature, so is not included in the analysis of the popular vote.

X

The Storm Breaks

An ATTEMPT has been made in the preceding pages to weave into the sectional pattern the various factors that contributed to hostile feeling between the North and the South. Students of the fifties do not by any means agree as to which factors should receive the greatest emphasis. Some have assigned the place of paramount importance to economic forces, others to political forces, others to the fanatical and vituperative reproaches which were hurled back and forth by extremists in each section, and still others to differences of constitutional construction. The writer appreciates the fact that all of these factors were, to some extent, intertwined; yet some seem entitled to more emphasis than others.

A minority, but apparently only a minority, in the South felt that there was too much economic dependence of its section upon the North, and that independence would remedy such a situation. The economic program of the Republicans, which no doubt helped to carry their party to victory, was generally opposed in the South. However, one is impressed with the small amount of space in the Southern press devoted to matters of economic policy as compared with that devoted to various phases of the slavery controversy. As for the tariff, it may be suggested that the North was far from being a unit in its favor in 1860, and that the demands for raising the duties were not drastic. In the South, Louisiana was protesting against the free trade ideas of South Carolina.[1]

The political factors in the sectional controversy were very marked. While the political leaders in the fifties may be accorded sincerity in their viewpoints on general phases of the slavery controversy, it is hard to escape the conclusion that some of them, inspired by political motives, exaggerated the dangers to their respective sections out of proportion to realities. Political factors are apparent in the Kansas controversy, the Dred Scott case, the split in the Democratic party and the failure to try compromise in 1860–61. Fanatical and unreasonable criticism by both Northern and Southern radicals did much to alienate the sections. Hunter expressed a feeling common to many Southerners when he declared that what Republicans said was almost more exasperating than what they did, for "nearly an entire generation of men in the nonslaveholding states must now have grown up in the constant habit of hearing such denunciation of slaveholders and slaveholding states as were calculated to infuse into their minds a spirit of hatred toward the South."[2] In the following

1. The *New Orleans True Delta* declared that the free trade ideas of South Carolina would, if enacted, "ruin" Louisiana. Nov. 20, 1860. Yet, as pointed out later, sectional differences over the tariff were accentuated when the Federal Government early in 1861 raised the tariff, and the Confederate Government soon after put into effect very low rates.

2. Simms, *Life of Hunter*, 167–168. The *Savannah Republican*, though absolving Southerners to too great an extent from blame for criticizing Northerners, expresses in the following language a feeling similar to that uttered by Hunter: "Have they [Southerners] written books and newspapers . . . to make you

quotation, Alexander H. Stephens, in somewhat exaggerated fashion, the author feels, gives his conception as to why there seemed to be an "Irrepressible Conflict": "The truth is I fear that if disunion should result, if by necessity it should come, we should be no better off in a new republic than we are in the present one. We should have the same or similar wrangling and confusion. Indeed if we were now to have a Southern convention to determine upon the true policy of the South either in the Union or out of it, I should expect to see just as much profitless discussion, disagreement, crimination and recrimination amongst the members of it from different states and from the same state, as we witness in the present House of Representatives between Democrats, Republicans and Americans. The troubles that now beset and environ us grow not out of the nature of our government or any real 'Irrepressible Conflict' between adverse interests. No such things; they grow out of the state of public opinion and the character of our public men north and south. There is a general degeneracy, confined not to one section or the other." [3]

There was a feeling in the South, not without reason, that a Northern majority was unwilling to accord the South, a minority section, the rights to which it was entitled under the Constitution. The "personal liberty" laws, in some cases at least, went a long way toward making a nullity the constitutional guarantees in regard

appear odious in the eyes of mankind? Have they reared up their children in the belief that you were a sinful and degraded race, far beneath them in all that constitutes a patriot, a citizen and a christian gentleman, and taught them to abhor and despise you?" Dec. 18, 1860.

3. *Correspondence of Toombs, Stephens and Cobb,* Stephens to J. Henly Smith, Jan. 22, 1860, 457–458.

to the return of fugitive slaves; and the apparent determination of the Republicans to exclude slavery from the territories, regardless of the Supreme Court decision to the contrary, seemed to suggest majority rule as the guiding constitutional principle of the Republicans.[4] As pointed out in the preceding chapter, after the John Brown raid Southern resentment was expressed because the Governor of Virginia was unable to get Republican governors in two states to honor requisition papers for the return of participants in the raid. Though the above developments and the "Irrepressible Conflict" and "House-Divided" utterances of Seward and Lincoln, respectively, gave plausibility to the Southern contention that the Republican party was "abolitionized" and meant to destroy slavery in the states, the writer does not feel that the party so intended, or that it could have in peace times accomplished such a purpose, had one existed. Evidence can be adduced to show that Lincoln was both conservative and radical in his slavery views, and that a portion of his party was radical.[5] But another portion of it was

4. As illustrative of the constantly expressed fear in the South that that minority section would be at the mercy of a Northern majority, see *Mobile Register*, May 13, 1859; *Augusta Constitutionalist*, Dec. 29, 1859; *Jefferson Davis, Constitutionalist*, Vol. IV, address to Senate, Dec. 10, 1860, 544–552.

5. Professor Arthur C. Cole concludes that, in the light of Lincoln's attitude before 1860, he would not have interfered with slavery in the states. See article in *American Historical Review*, Vol. XXXVI, July, 1931, 740–767, entitled "Lincoln's Election an Immediate Menace to Slavery in the States?" Professor J. G. de Roulhac Hamilton takes the view that many of the Republican leaders were radical, that Lincoln constantly became more so, and that the Republican party, in order to survive, had to be aggressive against slavery. See article in *American Historical Review*, Vol. XXXVII, July, 1932, 700–711, entitled "Lincoln's Election an Immediate Menace to Slavery in the States?" Lincoln

conservative, and, like the thousands of Northern Democrats, would never have countenanced positive action against slavery in the states. It is probable, however, that the verbal battle of the sections, no small factor in their estrangement, would have continued.

If the Republicans actually did not mean to prohibit slavery in the territories, it is unfortunate that they were so adamant in maintaining that they did. Yet, as Professor Randall has pointed out, Congress, in the winter of 1861, "when the Republicans and their allies had a slight majority in the lower house," organized the territories of Colorado, Dakota and Nevada without prohibition of slavery.[6] The fact that the policy of Congressional restriction of slavery in the territories was abandoned in practice suggests that there is at least some validity in the suggestion of Samuel S. Cox, of Ohio, that Republican policy was dictated by the desire for power.[7]

did write the following in a private letter to George Robertson, August 15, 1855: "So far as peaceful, voluntary emancipation is concerned, the condition of the Negro slave in America . . . is now as fixed and hopeless of change for the better as that of the lost souls of the finally impenitent. The Autocrat of all the Russias will resign his crown and proclaim his subjects free republicans sooner than will our American masters give up their slaves." *Works,* Vol. I, 215–216. Of course this utterance was only a prediction. Some of the Southern papers expressed concern that difficulties might arise as the result of Republican patronage in the South. See *Augusta Constitutionalist,* Nov. 16, 1860; *Mississippian,* Nov. 27, 1860.

6. J. G. Randall, *The Civil War and Reconstruction* (Boston and New York, 1937), 244.

7. Cox spoke, in part, as follows:
"Our southern friends do not know the Republicans as we do. They will be content with the tricks—and I trust allow us the honors. They will be as harmless in office as most men are. When General Wilson talks of grinding the slave power to powder, he never intends to use the powder, only to enjoy the power. . . .

The secession movement must now be followed, with attention to the factors that tended to enhance it and to check it. There is no doubt that, after Lincoln's election, sentiment in South Carolina was decidedly in favor of secession. On November 10, 1860, the Legisla-

The John Brown and Helper characteristics are convenient garments among them (Republicans), to be put on to proselyte the churches and the old women, and to be put off to placate wide-awakes and old Whigs. They do this for office. They do not think of its effect upon the South. It is a trick to be ignored when in office. . . .

"It is said that the reason why the South opposes the rule of Republicanism is, that their tenets are misrepresented at the South. I will not now show you what they profess at home. I hope they will fully avow, under the composing sweets of fat jobs and offices, their bad acts and worse avowals when out of office. And is there not reason for hope? Patience! Already they are willing to forego their congressional provisos against slavery. They have already proposed to drop intervention by Congress. They are willing to accept New Mexico as a slave state. Courage, gentlemen! I do not taunt, I applaud, this spirit of conciliation. The Republican party would enjoy its power. In this it is not peculiar, perhaps. It is a way men and parties have. . . . Mr. Lincoln in the White House may not be the rail-splitter out of it. Abraham, in faith, may offer up his 'irrepressible' offspring. He will be a conservative, with a total oblivion of the radical. The one will 'conflict' with the other; and the former will become all one thing without the other. I think he will disappoint the South as much as he will the abolition wing of his party. In their Sumner speeches and in their abolition platforms, it would seem as if the Republicans would hold the Union together by the running noose of John Brown gibbets; but when they approach the august presence of power, and undertake to rule thirty-one million people as already demonstrated here, they hold up the fasces of the Republic and wonder why we ever misunderstood or misrepresented their innocency!

"They see the African here in his relation to servitude. They know what he becomes in the North when free. They know that it is impossible to manumit him without injury irreparable to white and black. They will not sacrifice this Government of thirty-one million whites to do no good to three and a half million blacks." *Globe*, 36 Cong., 2 Sess., Jan. 14, 1861, 375.

ture of that state made provision for electing delegates to a convention which was to meet December 17, and that body passed the act of secession on December 20. The reasons assigned for the action included all the alleged aggressions of the North against Southern institutions, such as the "personal liberty" laws, hostile abolition sentiments and activities, the triumph of a party which denied the South equality in the territories and Lincoln's "House-Divided" speech. Economic factors, if not stressed primarily in the convention, nevertheless played a part in determining the action taken.[8] Since the South Carolina secessionists and most Southerners as well by 1860 contended that a state had a right, under the Constitution, to secede, a word must be said in regard to that doctrine. The sovereignty of the state was alleged as the basis of the right. That sovereignty, it was pointed out, was recognized by Great Britain when she made the Peace Treaty with the independent states in 1783, and was also recognized when the states made the Articles of Confederation. Even if the Constitution did not specifically recognize such sovereignty, nevertheless the states, in making the compact, reserved all powers not delegated, among which was their sovereignty. Should the compact be broken, as it was alleged to have been by the passage of the "personal liberty" laws, it was held to be no longer binding upon the states that suffered from

8. The *Charleston Mercury* had frequently denounced the economic policies of the Republicans (see Jan. 10, 13, 1860), and on Dec. 1, 1860, predicted that the whole program of free homesteads, internal improvements and a higher tariff would soon pass Congress. For complaints against the tariff and feeling of too much dependence on the North, see John G. Van Deusen, *Economic Bases of Disunion in South Carolina* (New York, 1928), 96–103, 328–330.

such laws. A state, according to the doctrine, might determine whether the Federal Government had exceeded its constitutional powers and determine "the measure and mode of redress." Much emphasis also was laid upon the declaration of Independence, which proclaimed the right of people to change their governments, if they became "subversive of the ends" for which they were created.

Whether the state sovereignty doctrine was sound or not, it was prior to 1860 frequently and vigorously asserted from time to time in all parts of the Union. The Legislatures of Connecticut and Massachusetts in 1812 and 1813 were resolving that those states were "free, sovereign and independent," and approximately twenty years later South Carolina and Georgia were asserting their sovereignty. Wisconsin followed suit in 1859. The Virginia and Kentucky Resolutions of 1798–99, which were endorsed by the Democratic party platforms in 1852 and 1856 and by some prominent Republicans in the fifties, were the basis of many of the assertions of the state sovereignty doctrine in later years.[9]

After the secession of South Carolina, the next state to take that step was Mississippi on January 9, 1861. The main question debated in the Convention of the latter state was whether slavery could better be saved

9. Professor Arthur Cole has pointed out that the Southern Whigs in the early fifties generally held that there was not a constitutional right of secession, though they did hold there was a right of revolution. They regarded the Federal Government as supreme in its sphere, and the Supreme Court as the arbiter in case of alleged infractions of the Constitution. See Arthur C. Cole, "The South and the Right of Secession in the early Fifties," *Mississippi Valley Historical Review*, Vol. I, No. 3, 1914, 377–399.

out of the Union or in it. Men with the greatest amount of slave property held that that property was more secure in the Union, but petty planters, lawyers and country politicians held otherwise.[10] What helped to keep at a high pitch the emotional feeling in both South Carolina and Mississippi during the secession movement were quotations in papers of those states of utterances by Northerners to the effect that the Southerners were blustering talkers who were afraid to secede.[11]

Acts of secession were passed by conventions in Florida on January 10, Alabama, January 11, Georgia, January 19, Louisiana, January 26 and Texas, February

10. Percy Lee Rainwater, *Mississippi Storm Center of Secession, 1856–1861* (Baton Rouge, 1938), 207, 219. Professor Rainwater describes the contest as follows: "The solid, conservative men of property who had composed the backbone of the old Whig party opposed disunion because they believed it would further endanger the perpetuity of slavery. Forming, on the other hand, the aggressive and cutting edge of the group which advocated the immediate secession of the state, were found, on the whole, the country editor, the provincial lawyer-politician, and the petty planter, these being the representatives of the group which made the Democratic party the dominant force in Mississippi politics." P. 221.

11. *Mississippian,* Dec. 11, 18, 1860. One of the typical utterances commented upon in the *Mississippian* (Dec. 11, 1860) and quoted at greater length in the *Charleston Mercury* (Dec. 20, 1860) was the following from the *Chicago Democrat:* "You have sworn that if we dared to elect such a man, you would dissolve the Union. We have elected him, and now we want you to try your little game of secession. Do it, if you dare. . . . The chivalry will eat dirt. They will back out. They never had any spunk, any how. . . . These knights of the sunny South are just such heroes (sic) as Sancho Panza was. They are wonderful hands at bragging and telling fantastical lies, but when it comes to action count them out." It may be suggested here that the *Augusta Constitutionalist,* a somewhat conservative Georgia paper, emphasized the alleged "incendiary" tone of the Republican press and orators as a strong Southern grievance. Nov. 17, 1860.

1. In Alabama there was a spirited contest between co-operationists and those who wished the state to act without concerted action among the Southern states. The co-operationists were strong in Northern Alabama, where there was some sentiment in favor of uniting that part of the state with Tennessee. When delegates were elected to the convention, those who favored straight-out secession won by a vote of approximately 35,693 to 28,181 for their opponents.[12] The fact that three states had already seceded when the Alabama Convention voted in favor of that action and that the Crittenden Compromise proposals were apparently doomed to failure undoubtedly enhanced the secession movement in Alabama. The way the movement gathered momentum is well illustrated in the attitude of the *Mobile Advertiser*. Immediately after Lincoln's election, though granting Southern grievances, it urged the Southern people to keep cool, because the Senate and probably the House were both hostile to Lincoln, and hence the situation would "be full of difficulty for him." It urged co-operation with the other Southern states as the only basis for secession, and even then the step should take place only after "careful" consideration and "long" deliberation. By December 23 it concluded that the "haughty" and "defiant" nature of the Republicans made the secession of Alabama only a question of time.[13]

There was a bitter struggle in Georgia over secession. Governor Joseph E. Brown, Howell Cobb, T. R. R.

12. Clarence P. Denman, *The Secession Movement in Alabama* (Montgomery, 1933), 97, 106, 115–116, 145. The ordinance of secession was passed by a vote of 61 to 39, though the straight-out secessionists were not that strong when delegates were elected.

13. *Mobile Advertiser*, Nov. 8, 20, 23, Dec. 23, 1860.

Cobb and Robert Toombs favored separation from the Union, though Toombs wavered in his policy from the time the Crittenden Compromise proposal was made until it was defeated in the Senate Committee of Thirteen. Alexander H. Stephens, Benjamin H. Hill and Herschel V. Johnson were the leading opponents of secession. Stephens felt that the Lincoln Administration could be checked in any hostile policy toward the South because the Republicans did not control the other departments of the Government. The diminutive Georgian also argued that his state should not secede unless the incoming Administration committed some overt act against her institutions. On December 19 the Georgia Legislature denounced the attitude and policy of the Republicans toward the South not only in respect to the slavery dispute, but in their desire to wield the taxing power of the Government to the advantage of the North. The Georgia Convention voted in favor of secession, 166–130.[14]

14. U. B. Phillips, *Georgia and State Rights* (Washington, 1902, from the Annual Report of the American Historical Association for 1901), 194 *et seq*. Phillips states that Georgians generally felt that there was a right of secession, but that the big slaveholders and progressive townspeople were largely responsible for the step. Pp. 209–210. Delegates to the Georgia convention who favored secession received an aggregate of 50,243 votes, those against, 37,123. See Pendleton, *Alexander H. Stephens*, 178. An argument advanced by T. R. R. Cobb for secession was that Georgia could make better terms out of the Union than in it. This was a position very similar to that taken by Timothy Pickering, of Massachusetts, during the period of New England discontent, 1800 to 1815. "To my ears there is no magic in the sound of Union," he said. If the objects of Union were "abandoned," or were "treacherously sacrificed by the Southern and Western States," then "let the Union be severed." However, Pickering explained that he believed New England, once separate, could make advantageous terms for a reunion with the other states. See views in letter to Edward Pennington, July 12,

When the Louisiana Convention met on January 26, the vote was overwhelmingly in favor of secession, though the popular vote in favor of secessionist delegates was only 20,448 against 17,296 for anti-secessionist delegates. The strong conservative sentiment in that state, overwhelmed as it was by the tide of events, is reflected in the press. The *New Orleans Picayune* wanted co-operation through a Southern convention, which it felt would lead the way for a general convention of all the states to attempt an adjustment of difficulties.[15] The *New Orleans True Delta* was unsparing in its criticism of Southern secessionists. It denounced the "disunion march of Rhett, Yulee, Jeff. Davis and Co.," called the secessionists "plotting, ambitious demagogues," and, though criticizing Northern politicians as responsible for Southern grievances, pointed to the large popular majority against Lincoln and the opposition of the Supreme Court and both Houses of Congress to his policy as proof that he could not harm the South.[16]

Despite the opposition of Sam Houston, Texas followed the secession tide on February 1, 1861 (on that date the Texas Convention passed an ordinance of secession later submitted to popular vote), and on

1812, in Adams, *Documents Relating to New England Federalism, 1800–1815*, 389.

15. *New Orleans Picayune*, Nov. 15, 30, Dec. 18, 1860. Dwight L. Dumond, in *The Secession Movement, 1860–1861* (New York, 1931), 121–123, distinguishes three groups of co-operationists in the South: those who favored immediate separation, but felt that there should be concerted action by the slave states, so as to give the idea of a United South; those who wanted a conference of Southern state representatives, to try to get guarantees from the North; and a third group who wanted co-operation to secure redress of grievances, but no secession until an overt act of aggression was committed by the new administration.

16. *New Orleans True Delta*, Nov. 18, 21, Dec. 13, 15, 1860.

February 4, 1861, there assembled at Montgomery
representatives from six Southern states for the purpose
of organizing a government. The provisional government then created of course later became permanent.
Jefferson Davis was chosen President and Alexander H.
Stephens Vice-President. Under the new government
slavery in the states of the Confederacy was guaranteed
against interference, and was to be protected in the
territories. The slave trade from abroad was prohibited.
Congress was forbidden to enact a protective tariff,
and, except in certain instances, to pass laws for internal improvements.

Whether a compromise on slavery questions, particularly the territorial question, would have checked
the secession movement after South Carolina severed
her connection with the Union is one of those unanswerable questions to which students of this period of
history have reacted in varied fashion. The main point
is that compromise was proposed, but was rejected as
a remedy for possible solution of sectional difficulties;
and the motives, or possible motives, for that rejection
should be noted. In each House of Congress, a committee was appointed to try to work out some plan of conciliation. In the lower House a Committee of Thirty-
three was appointed, but the Republicans in that group
were unwilling to grant that there was cause for unrest on the part of the Southerners, and hence any
need for new constitutional guarantees.[17] The Southern
Democrats claimed that they were discriminated
against in the appointment of members of the Committee, though they were sometimes criticized in their own
section for making such claims.[18]

17. Dumond, *op. cit.*, 192–193.
18. *True Delta*, Dec. 13, 1860. Professor Randall, in *The Civil*

In the Senate, early in December, 1860, there was appointed a Committee of Thirteen to devise plans of sectional adjustment. Included in its membership were such Senators as Wade, Seward, Douglas, Crittenden, Davis and Toombs. Toombs proposed an amendment to the Constitution providing protection for slave property on an equal basis with that afforded other property, except that each state had entire control over slavery in its limits. The proposal was defeated. Crittenden suggested a number of amendments to the Constitution, and a number of resolutions to be passed by Congress. He proposed amendments to the effect that slavery be prohibited in all territories North of the line of 36°30′, and be protected South of that line until the territory became a state; Congress should not abolish slavery in places under its jurisdiction situated in slave states, nor in the District of Columbia without compensation, not as long as slavery remained in Maryland and Virginia; Congress could not abolish the slave trade in the slave states; Congress should provide for payment for fugitive slaves who were rescued from the marshal, or, if he, by intimidation, were prevented from arresting them. The United States could then sue for damages the county in which the interference took place.

War and Reconstruction, 200–201, points out that the Committee was sympathetic toward the Southern view as regards the return of fugitive slaves and in guaranteeing slavery in the states from interference by Congress, but that its work was hampered by the uncompromising attitude of Southern secessionists. Dumond states that the Committee, appointed by a Republican speaker, was composed of sixteen Republicans, two supporters of Bell, only a small number of Douglas supporters from the North and an unusually large number of his supporters from the South. After two Southerners refused to serve, the Republican-controlled committee became a "graveyard" for every compromise proposal in the House. *The Secession Movement,* 156–157.

On the first of these propositions the vote was six for, seven against. The five Republicans were joined in the negative by Davis and Toombs. On all other propositions the vote was eight to five, the Republicans comprising the five negative votes in each case. Seward proposed for the Republicans that there should be an amendment to the fugitive slave law which would provide jury trial for fugitive slaves, and that Congress should request the state legislatures to review their "personal liberty" laws, and repeal or modify such as were contrary to the Constitution or laws passed in pursuance of that instrument. He then proposed the following amendment to the Constitution: "No amendment shall be made to the Constitution which will authorize or give to Congress the power to abolish or to interfere, within any State, with the domestic institutions thereof, including that of persons held to labor or service by the laws of said State." [19]

Where rests the responsibility for failure to adopt the Crittenden proposal as a means of settling the territorial dispute in relation to slavery? Mainly with the Republicans, it seems to the writer. Hunter, one of the Southern Democrats on the Committee of Thirteen, voted for the Crittenden proposal, and it appears that Davis and Toombs were both ready to do so, if the

19. *Reports of the Committees of the Senate of the United States for the Second Session of the Thirty-Sixth Congress.* (Report No. 288). "Journal of the Committee of Thirteen," 3–6. For Seward's proposal see 10–11. The amendment proposed by Seward in respect to slavery in the states was afterwards submitted to the states by Congress, though there was in that body considerable Republican opposition to it. The Republican vote in the House was 44 affirmative, 64 negative, in the Senate, 8 affirmative, 12 negative. *Detroit Free Press*, March 10, 1861. Some Republicans did not vote.

Republicans had been willing to vote accordingly.[20] It should be borne in mind that, at this time, slavery was not a matter of any practical significance in the territories. The proposed compromise, had it been accepted, would have made legally free the most considerable portion of the territory then in the United States, and therefore would have involved the surrender, in large part, of the legal rights which the Supreme Court had declared belonged to the South in all the territories.

What did the Republicans have to say in regard to the Crittenden proposal in relation to the territories? Lincoln, in letters to William Kellogg and E. B. Washburne, respectively, on December 11 and 13, 1860, opposed compromise on the ground that it "puts us under again, and leaves our work all to do over again." He wrote that it would demoralize the Republicans and their cause, that "the tug" had "to come, and better now than later," and that compromise would lead to filibustering expeditions southward.[21] Wade made a speech in the Senate December 17, 1860, in which he said that there was nothing to compromise, that it would be "humiliating and dishonorable" for Republi-

20. Dodd, *Jefferson Davis*, 195; Phillips, *Life of Toombs*, 206–210; Milton, *Eve of Conflict*, 525. While some evidence of an opposite nature could be presented, good evidence is at hand that Davis was a reluctant secessionist anyway. See Dodd, *op. cit.*, 205–207; Rainwater, *op. cit.*, 151–157. On Jan. 3, 1861, Crittenden suggested that his proposition by law be referred to the people of the United States for a vote. See *The Life of John J. Crittenden, with Selections from his Correspondence and Speeches*, edited by his daughter, Mrs. Chapman Coleman (2 Volumes, Philadelphia, 1871), Vol. II, 252. The Republicans were largely responsible for the defeat of that proposition.

21. Lincoln, *Works*, Vol. I, 657–658.

cans to compromise when they had "the verdict of the people" in their "pocket." He thought people "unworthy of free government, whenever it is denied in this Government that a majority fairly given shall rule." He warned the Southerners that they would be treated as "traitors," if they tried revolution and failed.[22] The *Illinois State Journal* stressed the façt that a majority had won in the election of 1860, attributed Southern discontent to the fact that the South had lost its political power, and claimed that Northern critics of the Republican policy were trying to make political capital "to use in future contests." [23]

The Republicans were greatly concerned that the acceptance of compromise proposals would weaken their party. Compromise, in the words of the *New York Tribune,* would "disband the Republican party," "would make shipwreck of our party." [24] The *New York Evening Post* deplored the tendency of a portion of the Republican press, including the *Albany Evening Journal,* to favor compromise, and of some of the Republicans to favor organization of the territories without providing for the prohibition of slavery. Such tendencies, it felt, would destroy Republican harmony in respect to the one great principle which held the party together.[25] Salmon P. Chase wrote to Lyman Trumbull that, if the Republican party would stick by its principles, it would control the Government for twenty or twenty-five years, and that "no disunion need create alarm—except the disunion of the Republican party." [26]

22. *Globe,* 36 Cong., 2 Sess., Dec. 17, 1860, 99–104.
23. *Illinois State Journal,* Dec. 12, 19, 26, 1860.
24. *New York Tribune,* Dec. 6, 1860, Jan. 8, 1861.
25. *New York Evening Post,* Jan. 2, 7, 1861.   —
26. *Trumbull Papers,* Chase to Trumbull **

In the private letters of Lyman Trumbull and Elihu
Washburne, one finds overwhelming evidence of this
fear that a policy of conciliation would ruin the Republican party.[27]

The Northern Democratic and border state press
pointed out in many ways why it regarded the Crittenden proposals with favor, and it criticized the Republicans severely for their refusal to accept them. Slavery,
it was emphasized, had run its course in the territories.
The compromise would mean the abandonment of a
Supreme Court decision which was decidedly favorable
to the South. Acceptance of the proposals would
strengthen conservative sentiment in the South, and
better enable the border states to work to advantage
in conciliating the states of the lower South. The Republicans had no right to place the Chicago platform
above the Union and the Constitution, and they did not
in 1860 constitute a majority, as was said, but only a
moderate-sized minority. Political ambition and party
considerations, it was charged, animated their non-
conciliatory course.[28]

27. See, for instance, in the *Trumbull Papers*, H. Barber to
Trumbull, Nov. 12, 1860; Thomas Richmond to Trumbull, Dec.
14, 1860; Wait Talcott to Trumbull, Dec. 16, 1860; Edward
Harte to Trumbull, Dec. 20, 1860. In *Washburne Papers*, see
Lane, Sanford and Company To Washburne, Dec. 4, 1860; W.
A. Baldwin to Washburne, Dec. 15, 1860; S. K. Raynter to
Washburne, Dec. 28, 1860. In some of these letters the point
is also emphasized that it would be morally wrong to compromise
on the question of slavery in the territories. Mary Scrugham, *The
Peaceable Americans of 1860–1861* (New York, 1921), elabo-
rates the above point of view. See especially, pp. 64–66.

28. For these various viewpoints, see *Boston Post*, Dec. 24, 27,
29, 1860, Jan. 11, 18, 23, 1861; *Detroit Free Press*, Dec. 4, 25,
1860, Jan. 1, Feb. 6, 1861; *Cincinnati Enquirer*, Dec. 20, 1860,
Jan. 9, Feb. 9, 1861; *New York Herald*, Dec. 19, 1860; *Louisville
Democrat*, Dec. 21, 23, 1860, Jan. 13, Feb. 9, 1861.

Down in the cotton belt the expression of opinion in two journals, one radical, the other conservative, indicates the reaction to the apparent failure of the Crittenden proposals. The *Mississippian* felt that the unhesitating rejection by the Republicans of a compromise, which "would have outraged the Constitution and degraded the South," confirmed Mississippi in her actions at the ballot box on December 20. The *New Orleans Picayune* felt that secession had been helped by Republican policy. "Mr. Crittenden of Kentucky . . . offers a plan of conciliation" and "it is received with scarcely the show of respect. . . . The master chiefs of the dominant section are dumb, or only speak so as to give new provocations to the excited and new discouragements to the moderate." [29]

What the effect of the acceptance of compromise would have been upon the cotton states is an unanswerable question. At least it may be suggested that anti-secessionists in states like Louisiana and Georgia constituted a powerful minority which, under favorable circumstances, might have been converted into a majority. The sentiment throughout the country was apparently decidedly favorable to compromise. It is admitted that many of the Republicans would have supported that policy, not to mention Northern Democrats and conservative Southerners. The business world leaned to conciliation, but the sentiment was by no means confined to that group.[30]

29. *Mississippian*, Dec. 28, 1860; *New Orleans Picayune*, Dec. 27, 1860.
30. Mayor Fernando Wood, of New York City, partly because of the commercial connection of that metropolis with the South, on January 7, 1861, sent a message to the city council urging secession of the city. The council authorized the distribution of the message in pamphlet form, but the pamphlets were not re-

The policy of James Buchanan in regard to the secession movement was developed at a time when plans for conciliation were much debated, if not perfected. Buchanan knew that conciliation was at an end if he used stern measures against South Carolina; and he felt, moreover, that the North was the aggressor in producing the situation that had developed. Those feelings, essential to an understanding of his secession policy, are emphasized in his message of December 3, 1860. In that message, Buchanan suggested three amendments to the Constitution, which were designed to give protection to that property in the territories and to make effective, as against the "personal liberty" laws, the fugitive slave law. He declared that secession was revolution, and that no state had a right to leave the Union, though there was no power to coerce a state. The Federal Government, he held, had sovereign authority where its power extended, and the Federal laws should be upheld, though it would be difficult to continue judicial processes in a state if the people there abandoned them. The framers of the Government, he said, "never intended to implant in its bosom the seeds of its own destruction, nor were they at its creation guilty of the absurdity of providing for its own dissolution." [31]

ceived enthusiastically. See Ed Alva S. Alexander, A Political History of the State of New York (3 Vols., New York, 1906) Vol. II, 348. For sentiment favorable to compromise among mechanics in Massachusetts, see Boston Post, Feb. 21, 1861, and for an account of the mass of petitions to Congress in favor, see Coleman, Life of Crittenden, Vol. II, 240–249, 281, 284.

31. George Ticknor Curtis, Life of James Buchanan (2 Volumes, New York, 1883), Vol. II, 337–350. It is interesting to note that some of the Republicans were taking anything but a firm attitude toward secession at the time Buchanan was confronted with that problem. The Ohio State Journal clearly and

During December, 1860, Buchanan found himself in a controversy with the South Carolinians over the status of the forts in Charleston harbor. He refused to turn them over to the South Carolina authorities, but he did have an understanding with the South Carolina delegation in Congress to let the military situation remain as it was until an agreement should be reached in regard to the forts.[32] When Major Robert Anderson, who felt that discretionary authority permitted the step, removed on December 26, 1860, from Moultrie to Fort Sumter, he took action which provoked strong resentment against Buchanan on the part of the Southerners, who claimed that the President had not kept his agreement with them.[33] Buchanan, on the basis of general orders that had been given to Anderson with which the President was unfamiliar, but which seemed to leave it to Anderson's discretion as to whether to move from Moultrie, upheld the commander's action when the Southerners insisted that he be sent back from Sumter to Moultrie.[34] An attempt to reinforce Sumter by send-

unmistakably took the position that a state had a right to leave the Union, and that to coerce it back by the power of the Federal Government would "entirely change the nature of Federal authority." Shortly after taking this position, that journal reversed it, and said that its previous editorial had been "misunderstood." Nov. 13, 28, 1860. On Nov. 17, 1860, the New York Times thought it unjust and inexpedient "to hold the states together by force," and on Dec. 18, 1860, it denounced the idea of peaceable secession. It is well known that the New York Tribune (Nov. 9, 1860) set forth an elaborate argument in favor of self-government for the South, and hence peaceable secession, but on March 7, 1861, advocated retaking of the forts already in Confederate hands.

32. Samuel Wylie Crawford, The Genesis of the Civil War: the Story of Sumter, 1860–1861 (New York, 1887), 37–39.

33. Crawford, op. cit., 140–149.

34. Philip G. Auchampaugh, James Buchanan and His Cabinet

ing *The Star of the West* with food provisions and military equipment was thwarted when the secessionists fired upon the vessel.

One more unsuccessful attempt to compromise the sectional difficulties was made before Buchanan went out of office.[35] This was at the Convention which met in Washington on February 4, 1861, pursuant to a call of the Virginia Legislature. John Tyler presided, and other distinguished representatives from some of the twenty-one states represented were Reverdy Johnson, Frederick Frelenghuysen, William C. Rives, Salmon P. Chase, James W. Grimes, Stephen Logan and Thomas Ewing.[36] The Convention, voting by states, did recommend some amendments to the Constitution, though their recommendations received scant consideration in Congress. One amendment proposed was an extension of the Missouri Compromise line to the Pacific, with provision for judicial decisions to determine the status of slavery in the territory south of the line. Another provided for payment for fugitive slaves, where the marshal was prevented from arresting them, or in case they were seized by mobs after the arrest. However, coupled with this proposal was one to the effect that "Congress shall provide by law for securing to the citizens of each State the privileges and immunities of citizens of the several States, "a clause which apparently was aimed at preventing detention of free Negroes taken from ships in Southern ports. The vote was nine

on the Eve of Secession (Duluth, Minnesota, 1926), 96–97, 157–160, 165.

35. Border state attempts in behalf of a national convention will be referred to later.

36. L. E. Chittenden, *A Report of the Debates and Proceedings in the Secret Sessions of the Confederate Convention Held at Washington, in February, 1861*, 18, 453.

to eight on the first proposition and twelve to seven on the second. The New England states, Rhode Island excepted, were generally hostile to whatever was proposed in the Convention, and North Carolina and Virginia opposed both of the above suggestions.[37]

Not only were some of the Northern states unrepresented at the Conference, but there was lack of anything like a spirit of harmony among the delegates present. Before their sessions closed they found themselves angrily debating the right of secession.[38] Representatives from Massachusetts and New York, apprehensive that the Republicans were becoming too compromise-minded, requested Zachariah Chandler, Senator from Michigan, to ask the governor of that unrepresented state to send delegates to help save their party. "Ohio, Indiana and Rhode Island are caving in," wrote Chandler, "and there is danger of Illinois; and now they beg us, for God's sake, to come to their rescue, and save the Republican party from rupture. I hope you will send *stiff-backed* men or none. The whole thing was gotten up against my judgment and advice, and will end in thin smoke." He added that "Some of the manufacturing states think that a fight would be awful. Without a little blood-letting this Union will not, in my estimation, be worth a rush." [39]

Under the unusual conditions existing on March 4, 1861, the country naturally awaited with interest and anxiety what Lincoln would say in his inaugural address. The address, as was to be expected, was devoted largely to a discussion of phases of the slavery con-

37. *Ibid.*, 440–447.
38. *Ibid.*, 396, *et seq.*
39. *Ibid.*, 468–469. This letter is quoted also in the *Cincinnati Enquirer*, March 1, 1861.

troversy and to the President's idea of the nature of the Union. He renewed his pledge not to interfere with slavery in the states. In regard to slavery in the territories, he stated that the Constitution did not say whether Congress could prohibit it there or not, so suggested that a majority "held in restraint by constitutional checks and limitations" should decide such a doubtful matter. What the Supreme Court said was entitled to respect on the part of other departments of the Government, and was obligatory upon parties to a suit, but "At the same time, the candid citizen must confess that if the policy of the Government, upon vital questions affecting the whole people, is to be irrevocably fixed by decisions of the Supreme Court, the instant they are made, in ordinary litigation between parties in personal actions, the people will have ceased to be their own rulers, having to that extent practically resigned their government into the hands of that eminent tribunal."

Lincoln held that the fugitive slave law, while upon the statute books, should be enforced, but felt that there should be, under such a law, safeguards for free men. He coupled with the latter suggestion one to the effect that Congress should pass a law for the enforcement of that clause in the Constitution providing that "The citizen of each state shall be entitled to all privileges and immunities of citizens of the several states."

The President held that no state could lawfully get out of the Union, and hence the acts of secession were void. He claimed that the Union antedated the states, that it had its beginning in 1774. He promised to "hold, occupy and possess the property and places belonging to the government," and to enforce the laws of the Union, yet if the hostility in any community were so great as to prevent competent people in the community from holding Federal offices, he would refrain from putting obnoxious strangers there, and would forego for the time the legal right of using such offices. No violence, he promised, would be used, unless the Southerners themselves became the "aggressors." [40]

Lincoln's inaugural address was praised, criticized and interpreted in various ways by the press of the country. The *New York Tribune* stated that Lincoln

40. Lincoln, *Works*, Vol. II, 1–7. Though Lincoln expressed a conviction that existing law ought to be enforced, he would evidently, had times been normal, have worked for a modification of the fugitive slave law. Further light is thrown on Lincoln's ideas concerning the fugitive slave controversy in two letters which he wrote before his inauguration. To William Kellogg, December 11, 1860, he expressed the opinion that "the fugitive-slave clause of the Constitution ought to be enforced—to put it in its mildest form, ought not to be resisted." To John A. Gilmer, he wrote, December 15, 1860, that he had never read any of the "personal liberty" laws, but would be glad of their repeal, if they were in conflict with the fugitive slave law. However, neither as a private citizen or as President would he be justified in recommending "repeal of a statute of Vermont or South Carolina." Lincoln, *Works*, Vol. I, 657–658, 658–659. Apart from Lincoln's policy, it may be suggested that most Republicans voted for, or refrained from voting against, a resolution introduced in Congress, in December, 1860, by Garnett B. Adrain, a Representative from New Jersey, recommending repeal of all statutes, including personal liberty bills, enacted by State Legislatures and in conflict with or in violation of the Constitution and the laws of Congress pursuant thereto. The resolution passed December 17 by a vote of 153 to 14. *Globe*, 36 Cong., 2 Sess., Dec. 17, 1860, 108. The passage of this resolution seems to suggest that the fugitive slave controversy might have been adjusted, yet the question has to be raised as to what authority was going to decide whether the "personal liberty" bills were constitutional or not. If the states themselves, perhaps not much was to be expected as a result of the resolution. It should be said, however, that several Northern states repealed or modified their "personal liberty" laws.

rightly held that the decision on the territorial question and slavery rested with the people and not with the Supreme Court. The *Cincinnati Enquirer* took Lincoln to task for speaking "with great fluency" of the majority, when, as it stated, he represented only a minority, having had nearly one million popular majority against him in the election of 1860. The *Richmond Enquirer* declared that the inaugural was a "declaration of war," but the *Louisville Democrat* claimed that the address did not indicate a "disposition for coercion." [41]

What were some of the currents at work as Lincoln proceeded to develop his policy in regard to secession? The revenue situation, for one thing, presented some rather baffling aspects. The Morrill Tariff, which had been passed by the Federal Congress, increased the rates at about the same time that the Confederate Congress was putting into effect a very low tariff. The disparity between the tariffs, it was pointed out, would harm the North in regard to trade, and therefore it was wise to reduce the rates of the Morrill Tariff. However, some who favored that step were insistent that needed revenues be collected at Southern ports, or that the ports be blockaded so as to force ships to come to Northern ports. The revenue difficulties, said some, showed the wisdom of compromise as a means of reunion.[42]

41. *New York Tribune*, March 6, 1861; *Cincinnati Enquirer*, March 6, 1861; *Richmond Enquirer*, March 5, 1861; *Louisville Democrat*, March 6, 1861.

42. The confused situation is shown by the following newspaper opinions: "If no remedy is applied, the corner stone of the future greatness of the Southern Confederacy will be laid in the ruins of the financial, agricultural, manufacturing and commercial interests of the non-slaveholding states. Revenue, we bid fair soon to have none." "The trade of the Southern states, and of the cotton states especially, is of more importance to New York, and

While the Northeast was fearful of losing its trade to the South, of losing revenue and of heavier taxation in case the Confederacy existed permanently, the Northwest was concerned primarily lest an independent South control the mouth of the Mississippi to the disadvantage of Northwestern trade. That fear was expressed by Democrats and by Republicans, nor was it eased by Southern assurances that their fears were unfounded.[43]

indirectly to Boston and Philadelphia also, than the whole trade of the West put together." *New York Herald*, March 20, 2, 1861.. That journal favored compromise. "If neither of these things be done [closing of Southern ports or collecting revenue], our revenue laws are substantially repealed; the sources which supply our treasury will be dried up; we shall have no money to carry on the government; the nation will become bankrupt before the next crop of corn is ripe." *New York Evening Post*, March 12, 1861. See also Feb. 16, March 26, 1861. That journal also wanted the Morrill Tariff reduced, and favored no conciliation of the South. The *New York Times* felt that "the Rebel states of the Union" would be crippling the "loyal," unless the revenues were collected, and wanted to know what New York could "care for a Union which compels her to pay duties on imported goods, and permits those who reject its authority to import them duty free?" March 13, April 12, 1861. That journal also wished to have the Morrill Tariff reduced. The *New York Tribune* advised enforcement of the laws, but no "weak concessions to rebels and traitors" by repealing the Morrill Tariff. March 14, April 3, 1861. The *Philadelphia Press* hoped through conciliation to bring about reunion, but Pennsylvania, it stated, after gaining a higher tariff after years of struggle, would not see that advantage "rudely snatched away." April 1, 1861. All the revenue difficulties would have been avoided, said the *Boston Post* and the *Detroit Free Press*, had compromise prevailed. *Boston Post*, March 28, 1861, *Detroit Free Press*, March 15, 23, 1861.

43. See remarks of Representatives John McClernand, of Illinois, and Samuel Cox, of Ohio, *Globe*, 36 Cong., 2 Sess., Jan. 14, 1861, 369–371, 375; E. M. Coulter, "Effects of Secession upon the Commerce of the Mississippi Valley," *Mississippi Valley Historical Review*, Vol. III, No. 3, 1918, 275–300, especially

But the main current at work as Lincoln developed his policy was the tendency toward a split in his party. Should the administration follow a conciliatory policy, symbolic of which would be the abandonment of Fort Sumter, hold the border states in the Union thereby, and perhaps through them reconstruct the Union, or should it follow a stern policy toward the seceded states? As the Southern States seceded, most of the forts had been taken over by the respective state authorities. Fort Sumter in South Carolina, Pickens and one or two other forts in Florida, however, remained in the hands of the Federal authorities. At a Cabinet meeting on March 15, 1861, Lincoln asked the members of the group the following question: "Assuming it is possible now to provision Fort Sumter, under all the circumstances is it wise to attempt it?" Five of the seven members gave a negative answer, Montgomery Blair gave an affirmative one, and Chase an affirmative one, in case the action did not produce war.[44] Fort Pickens was still to be held as symbolic of the national authority. If Fort Sumter were surrendered, that action could be construed as one dictated by military necessity, or as one calculated to conciliate the South.

Meantime a great deal of discussion was going on outside of administrative circles in regard to Fort Sumter as well as in regard to the matter of conciliating the South. The *New York Times*, before Lincoln's inauguration, had advocated the passage of a law by Congress permitting New Mexico to form a state constitution with or without slavery, advancing as a reason the fact that the controversy over compromise was harming the

278–279; *New Orleans Picayune*, Dec. 19, 25, 1860; *Mobile Advertiser*, Dec. 23, 1860.

44. Lincoln, *Works*, Vol. II, 11–22.

Republican party. That journal later advocated the abandonment of Fort Sumter, on the ground that holding it would precipitate war and would alienate the border states.[45] The *New York Tribune* denounced the suggestion of the *Times* in regard to New Mexico, contended that such a policy would destroy the Republican party, condemned Seward for his conciliation tendencies, and claimed that the "hideous front of compromise" would be raised with the likelihood of success, if Fort Sumter were abandoned.[46] The criticism of Seward was prompted by the fact that the Secretary of State felt that conciliation of the border states would aid them in transmitting their Union feelings to the Confederacy, or failing thus to preserve the Union, that object might be accomplished by a constitutional convention.[47]

In March there was a strong feeling that Sumter would be evacuated. Not only was Seward, through Justice John Campbell, assuring the Confederate commissioners that it would be evacuated, but newspapers were stating the same thing with almost a tone of certainty.[48] But the order did not come, and the Democratic press charged that the delay was due to the political situation in the Republican party, or to the fear of the effect of a positive policy upon the forthcoming spring elections.[49] The *New York Herald* in

45. *New York Times,* Feb. 22, March 12, 1861.

46. *New York Tribune,* Feb. 25, March 8, 12, 1861.

47. Bancroft, *Life of Seward,* Vol. II, 97–103.

48. *New York Tribune,* March 11, 1861, spoke of its evacuation as "imminent," and *Cincinnati Enquirer,* of March 14, 1861, as practically a "certainty."

49. *Detroit Free Press,* March 20, April 3, 1861; *New York Herald,* March 25, April 2, 1861. Now that some of the elections were over, these journals predicted that the policy would be known.

March predicted big Democratic gains in forthcoming elections in Rhode Island and Connecticut in April, and its predictions were verified.[50] Between April 1 and 3, the Democrats won a state election in Rhode Island, defeated two Republican congressmen in Connecticut, and carried city elections in Cincinnati, Brooklyn and St. Louis.[51]

The final phase of the Sumter drama must now be narrated. Early in April Lincoln decided to send a relief expedition to Fort Sumter. In pursuance of a promise which he had made to Governor Francis Pickens, of South Carolina, he dictated to the Governor a message on April 6, and the message was received on April 8 It was a notification to the effect that Fort Sumter would be supplied "with provisions only;" but that no effort would be made to reinforce it with men and arms, unless there was resistance or the fort was attacked, or until further notice. Events now moved rapidly. The Southerners had reason for thinking that the fort would be evacuated, and hence the determination to reinforce it with provisions and the added threat of something more to follow aroused them to intense feelings. After a brief hesitancy, for they had been reluctant to be responsible for the first shot, the Confederate authorities ordered the fort reduced on the morning of April 12.

It is the opinion of Professor Charles W. Ramsdell, based on careful evidence, that Lincoln, unwilling to compromise sectional issues and finding his administration and his party in a precarious situation, deliberately maneuvered the Southerners into firing the first shot, so that they might seem to the North to be

50. *Boston Post*, April 6, 1861; April 2, 6, 1861.
51. *Boston Post*, April 6, 1861; April 2, 6, 1861.

the "aggressors." By that action he would cement the discordant elements in his own party when the political tide was running against it, and would bring many Democrats to the support of a war for the Union. According to Ramsdell, when Lincoln sent Ward Lamon to Charleston, the purpose of the visit was to discover the feeling there toward a relief expedition, which feeling was found to be very hostile. However, Lamon left Governor Pickens under the impression that the fort was to be evacuated, and that he was there to prepare the way for that step. When food supplies were sent to the garrison, Northern people thought only that food was being sent "to hungry men," but Lincoln was certain that, by his expedition and the "threat" in his note, he would provoke hostilities on the part of the South. Ramsdell presents evidence from the *Diary* of Orville Browning to the effect that Lincoln told Browning that "the plan succeeded. They attacked Sumter—it fell, and thus did more service than it otherwise could." [52] A popular impression of Lamon's

52. Charles W. Ramsdell, "Lincoln and Fort Sumter," *Journal of Southern History*, Vol. II, August, 1937, 259–288.

John S. Tilley, in a well documented work, *Lincoln Takes Command* (Chapel Hill, 1941), does much to relieve the South of the charge of aggression in firing the first shot of the war. He points out that both Governor Pickens and Major Anderson were given the impression by Lamon that Sumter would be evacuated, and were therefore surprised when there was notification that the fort would be provisioned. "Provisioning," he emphasizes, involved the sending of a naval and military expedition to Charleston harbor. This expedition had been planned with great secrecy, and the Southern authorities secured their first definite information of it through the interception of Federal mails from Sumter several days before the firing commenced. A transport, an armed cutter and a warship were off Charleston harbor the first day of the bombardment of Sumter. Other ships with military supplies and reinforcements were on the way. See especially 149, *et seq.*

mission to Charleston is registered in the declaration of
the *Philadelphia Press* that "the evacuation of Fort
Sumter has doubtless been decided upon," and that
Lamon had been sent to Charleston to confirm statements which had been made as to scanty supplies, and
to make arrangements for the removal of the troops.[53]
The *New York Evening Post,* though convinced that
the majority of the Northern people were ready to
stand behind the Administration when it made known
its intention to provision Sumter, nevertheless admitted
its belief that "Three weeks ago the belief that Mr.
Lincoln intended to pursue a 'conciliatory' policy met
with the approval of a great part—perhaps a majority
—of northern men." [54]

Differences of opinion as to the best method of sav-
ing the Union, political factors and economic factors,
all have to be considered in connection with the evolu-
tion of a policy toward Fort Sumter. The firing on the
fort produced an intensely emotional feeling in the
North, and carried many of the conciliators to the
support of the Administration. The case of Douglas well
illustrates that feeling when he declared that "There
can be but two parties, the party of patriots, and the
party of traitors. We belong to the first." [55] Some of
the Democratic papers, however, though indicating
their support of the Union cause, still bitterly criticized the Republicans for alleged responsibility for
what had occurred.[56]

53. *Philadelphia Press,* March 26, 1861.
54. *New York Evening Post,* April 8, 1861.
55. Milton, *Eve of Conflict,* 561.
56. *Cincinnati Enquirer,* April 13, 1861. The *Detroit Free
Press* expressed its attitude as follows: "While we condemn the
wretched fanaticism and folly and wickedness which have produced the national calamities, and lament and deplore the

The Fort Sumter episode and Lincoln's call on April 15, 1861, for seventy-five thousand troops to suppress the secession movement had marked effects on the border slave states. With four of those states—Kentucky, Missouri, Maryland and Delaware—which did not leave the Union, it is not necessary to deal in detail. Sentiment in the first three was sharply divided, and Kentucky and Missouri were both represented in the Confederate Congress. The general sentiment in the four border states that did secede—Virginia, North Carolina, Tennessee and Arkansas—as well as in the others, was that the South did have grievances, but not sufficient to justify secession, and that some compromise plan should be devised to settle the North-South controversy.

The attitude of the *North Carolina Standard* was that of many in the border states. It emphasized the fact that the other two departments of the Federal Government were hostile to the Lincoln Administration, and that there was a powerful minority opposed to him in the free states. Should the Federal Government take away any of the constitutional rights of the South, then that section should resist the policy. It suggested that the legislatures of the states take steps toward the calling of a national convention to suggest amendments to the Constitution, and predicted that "The great deep of the popular heart would be touched and roused, and the rising billows, under the guiding hand of the great Ruler of men and nations, would bear the old ship of

fratricidal conflict, it is nevertheless our duty to support the government in a contest for its own preservation, notwithstanding the contest was precipitated, needlessly and criminally, by the men who administer it." April 13, 1861.

state, with new timbers and canvas." [57] Senator Thomas
Clingman, of North Carolina, felt that Lincoln was
elected because he was "a dangerous man," and that the
"abolition" tide was constantly increasing in the North,
yet North Carolina, he asserted, was willing to wait to
see whether the Republicans had guarantees to offer
which were compatible with her honor and safety.[58]

The *Louisville Democrat* criticized the unyielding attitude of the Republicans and the rashness of the secessionists, and suggested that, if New England and the
cotton states would not take steps for conciliation, then
the Mississippi Valley, "the great heart of the Union,"
should do so. That journal favored a Southern convention, a border state convention or a national convention.[59] Arkansas, in a convention meeting March 4,
voted down a proposition to refer the matter of secession to the voters, but did provide for a vote August 5
on the question of secession or co-operation with the
border slave states. The convention indicated a willingness to send delegates to a border state convention to
be held at Frankfort, May 21.[60] In Tennessee, early in
February, the proposition to call a convention was defeated by a vote of 68,282 to 59,449, but in the election,
at the same time, of delegates to the prospective con-

57. *North Carolina Standard*, Nov. 29, Dec. 1, 29, 1860.
58. *Globe*, 36 Cong., 2 Sess., Dec. 4, 1860, 3–5.
59. *Louisville Democrat*, Dec. 21, 1860, Jan. 1, 15, 22, Feb.
7, 1861. At the same time that the House of Representatives defeated the Crittenden territorial compromise, 113 to 80, it defeated a proposal to call a national convention, 109 to 74. *New
York Tribune*, Feb. 28, 1861.
60. David Y. Thomas, *Arkansas in War and Reconstruction,
1861–1874* (Little Rock, 1926), 57, 70–71.

vention, the anti-secessionists won by a vote of 91,803 to 24,749.[61]

Virginia had her ultras, but was, on the whole, conservative prior to the April policy of Lincoln. Edmund Ruffin was a good example of an ultra, and the *Richmond Enquirer*, with occasional lapses, showed a strong leaning toward the secessionists of the lower South.[62] Many in Virginia strongly condemned South Carolina for seceding, but even most who thought her course unwise were opposed to the policy of coercing a state, and did feel that the South had grievances.[63] The Virginia Legislature provided for the calling of a convention which met on February 13, and which, on April 4, showed its anti-secession character by defeating, 88 to 45, a motion to refer a secession ordinance to the people in May. The conservatives in the convention during most of March received assurances from Seward that no attempt would be made to hold Fort Sumter, and the convention sent such men as John B. Baldwin, William Ballard Preston, Alexander H. H. Stuart and George Randolph to interview Lincoln in regard to his Fort Sumter policy and attitude toward coercion.[64] During the early part of 1861, North Carolina likewise showed conservative tendencies. On January 29 the Legislature of that state referred to the people the mat-

61. James W. Patton, *Unionism and Reconstruction in Tennessee, 1860–1869* (Chapel Hill, 1934), 12.
62. The *Richmond Enquirer*, Dec. 24, 1860, suggested that the Northern states might still stop the secession movement by offering terms of adjustment to South Carolina, but for ultra leanings see issues of Dec. 25, 1860, Jan. 17, 23, March 28, 1861.
63. Henry T. Shanks, *The Secession Movement in Virginia, 1847–1861* (Richmond, 1934), 133–134, 144–145.
64. *Ibid.*, 160, 181–182, 190–193, 195–197.

ter of calling a convention to consider Federal affairs. Soon thereafter that proposition, which was much more strongly supported by secessionists than by anti-secessionists, was defeated by a vote of 47,323 to 46,672.[65] The rest of the story can now be briefly told. The sentiment in the four border states of Tennessee, Arkansas, Virginia and North Carolina was for compromise but against coercion, and since the policy with which those states were confronted was not compromise but coercion, it is not difficult to understand how they were swept out of the Union. On May 6 the Tennessee Legislature submitted a secession ordinance to be voted on June 8, at which time it was adopted by a vote of 108,399 to 47,233.[66] On May 7 the Arkansas convention reassembled and voted overwhelmingly in favor of secession.[67] In North Carolina secession tendencies had been enhanced by the failure of Congress to adopt the proposals of the Washington Peace Conference, and by the dissatisfaction of even many of the Unionists with Lincoln's inaugural address. The Fort Sumter policy and the President's call for troops led to the summoning of a convention which on May 20 unanimously voted to sever the bonds with the Union, though a fair-sized minority considered the act of separation as revolution instead of inherent in the sovereignty of the state.[68] On April 17 the Virginia convention, 88 to

65. For developments in North Carolina from the election of Lincoln to the time of the defeat of the call for a convention, see Joseph Carlyle Sitterson, *The Secession Movement in North Carolina* (Chapel Hill, 1939), 177–223.
66. Patton, *op. cit.*, 21.
67. Thomas, *op. cit.*, 81–82.
68. Sitterson, *op. cit.*, 225–249.

45, adopted a secession ordinance, and provided for a popular vote on it May 23.[69] It was carried by a large majority. With that state went Robert E. Lee, who loved the Union and might have had command of the Union armies, but was unwilling to draw his sword save in defense of Virginia.[70]

69. Shanks, *op. cit.*, 204.
70. For an excellent and full account of Lee's mingled feelings on the eve of the great struggle, and of his offer of the command of Union armies, see Douglas S. Freeman, *R. E. Lee, A Biography* (4 volumes, New York and London, 1934), Vol. I, 412, *et seq.*, 435–437, 633–637.

BIBLIOGRAPHY

BIOGRAPHIES, CORRESPONDENCE, WORKS AND PAPERS

BIRNEY, JAMES G. Birney, William, *James G. Birney and His Times.* New York, 1890.

BROWN, ALBERT GALLATIN. Ranck, James B., *Albert Gallatin Brown, Radical Southern Nationalist.* New York and London, 1937.

BROWN, JOHN. Villard, Oswald G., *John Brown, 1800–1859; A Biography Fifty Years After.* Boston and New York, 1910.

BUCHANAN, JAMES. Auchampaugh, Philip, *James Buchanan and His Cabinet on the Eve of Secession.* Lancaster, Pa., 1926.

———. Curtis, George Ticknor, *Life of James Buchanan.* 2 vols., New York, 1883.

———. Moore, John Bassett, ed., *The Works of James Buchanan.* 12 vols., Philadelphia and London, 1910.

CALHOUN, JOHN C. Hunt, Gaillard, *Life of John C. Calhoun.* Philadelphia, 1908.

———. Meigs, William M., *The Life of John C. Calhoun.* 2 vols., New York, 1917.

CHANNING, WILLIAM E. Channing, George, ed., *The Works of William E. Channing.* 6 vols., Boston, 1846. Vol. II especially helpful.

CHASE, SALMON P. *Diary and Correspondence of Salmon P. Chase,* in Annual Report of the American Historical Association, Vol. II. Washington, 1902.

———. Hart, Albert Bushnell, *Salmon Portland Chase.* Boston and New York, 1899.

———. Shuckers, J. W., *Life and Public Services of Salmon Portland Chase.* New York, 1874.

250   BIBLIOGRAPHY

CLAY, HENRY. Schurz, Carl, *Life of Henry Clay.* 2 vols., New York, 1887.

———. Van Deusen, Glyndon G., *Life of Henry Clay.* Boston, 1937.

CRITTENDEN, JOHN J. Coleman, Mrs. Chapman, ed., *The Life of John J. Crittenden, with Selections from His Correspondence and Speeches.* 2 vols., Philadelphia, 1871.

CURTIS, BENJAMIN R. Curtis, Benjamin R., ed., *A Memoir of Benjamin Robbins Curtis, with some of His Professional and Miscellaneous Writings.* 2 vols., Boston, 1889.

DAVIS, JEFFERSON. Dodd, William E., *Jefferson Davis.* Philadelphia, 1907.

———. McElroy, Robert, *Jefferson Davis, the Real and the Unreal.* 2 vols., New York and London, 1937.

———. Rowland, Dunbar, ed., *Jefferson Davis, Constitutionalist. His Letters, Papers and Speeches.* 10 vols., Jackson, Miss., 1923.

DOUGLAS, STEPHEN A. Johnson, Allen, *Life of Stephen A. Douglas.* New York, 1908.

———. Milton, George Fort, *The Eve of Conflict: Stephen A. Douglas and the Needless War.* Boston and New York, 1934.

———. Sparks, Edwin E., ed., *The Lincoln-Douglas Debates of 1858.* Springfield, Ill., 1908.

FREMONT, JOHN C. Nevins, Allan, *Fremont, Pathfinder of the West.* New York and London, 1939.

GARRISON, WILLIAM LLOYD. *William Lloyd Garrison, 1805–1879. The story of his life told by his children.* Boston and New York, 1894.

GILMER, FRANCIS WALKER. Davis, Richard B., *Francis Walker Gilmer: Life and Learning in Jefferson's Virginia.* Richmond, 1939.

HUNTER, ROBERT M. T. Simms, Henry H., *Life of Robert M. T. Hunter: A Study in Sectionalism and Secession.* Richmond, 1935.

———. Ambler, C. H., ed., *Correspondence of Robert M. T.*

Hunter, 1826–1876, Annual Report of American Historical Association, Vol. II, Washington, 1916.

HAMMOND, JAMES H. Merritt, Elizabeth, *James Henry Hammond, 1807–1864.* Baltimore, 1923.

JEFFERSON, THOMAS. Randall, Henry S., *The Life of Thomas Jefferson.* 3 vols., New York, 1858.

JOHNSON, HERSCHEL V. Flippin, Percy S., *Herschel V. Johnson of Georgia, State Rights Unionist.* Richmond, 1931.

KING, RUFUS. King, Edward, ed., *The Life and Correspondence of Rufus King, Comprising His Letters, Private and Official, His Public Documents and His Speeches.* 6 vols., New York, 1894. Only volume VI useful for this study.

KIRKWOOD, SAMUEL. J. Clark, Don Elbert, *Samuel J. Kirkwood.* Iowa City, 1917.

LEE, ROBERT E. Bruce, Philip A., *Life of Robert E. Lee.* Philadelphia, 1907.

———. Freeman, Douglas, *R. E. Lee, A Biography.* 4 vols., New York and London, 1934. Volume I useful for this study.

LINCOLN, ABRAHAM. Beveridge, Albert J., *Abraham Lincoln, 1809–1858.* 2 vols., New York, 1928.

———. Charnwood, Lord, *Abraham Lincoln.* New York, 1917.

———. Morse, John T., Jr., *Abraham Lincoln.* 2 vols., Boston and New York, 1894.

———. Nicolay, John G., and Hay, John, eds., *Abraham Lincoln: Complete Works, Comprising His Speeches, Letters, State Papers, and Miscellaneous Writings.* 2 vols., New York, 1920.

———. *Lincoln-Douglas Debates.* See Douglas.

MCLEAN, JOHN. Weisenburger, Francis P., *The Life of St. John McLean: A Politician on the United States Supreme Court.* Columbus, 1937.

PARKER, THEODORE. Commager, Henry Steele, *Theodore Parker.* Boston, 1936.

———. Weiss, John, *Life and Correspondence of Theodore Parker.* 2 vols., New York, 1864.

PHILLIPS, WENDELL. Austin, George Lowell, *The Life and Times of Wendell Phillips*. Boston, 1901.

———. Phillips, Wendell, *Speeches, Lectures and Letters*. Boston, 1884.

PIERCE, FRANKLIN. Nichols, Roy F., *Franklin Pierce: Young Hickory of the Granite Hills*. Philadelphia, 1931.

QUITMAN, JOHN A. Claiborne, J. F. H., *Life and Correspondence of John A. Quitman*. 2 vols., New York, 1860.

RHETT, ROBERT BARNWELL. White, Laura A., *Robert Barnwell Rhett, Father of Secession*. New York and London, 1931.

RUFFIN, EDMUND. Craven, Avery, *Edmund Ruffin, Southerner: A Study in Secession*. New York and London, 1932.

SEWARD, WILLIAM H. Bancroft, Frederic, *The Life of William H. Seward*. 2 vols., New York and London, 1900.

———. Baker, George E., ed., *Works of William H. Seward*. 5 vols., Boston and New York, 1887.

SHERMAN, WILLIAM T. Howe, M. A. De Wolfe, ed., *Home Letters of General Sherman*. New York, 1909.

SMITH, GERRIT. Frothingham, Octavius B., *Gerrit Smith*. New York, 1879.

STEPHENS, ALEXANDER H. Pendleton, Louis, *Alexander H. Stephens*. Philadelphia, 1908.

———. Phillips, U. B., ed., *The Correspondence of Robert Toombs, Alexander H. Stephens and Howell Cobb*. Annual Report of the American Historical Association for the year 1911. Vol. II, Washington, 1913.

SUMNER, CHARLES. *Charles Sumner. His Complete Works*. 20 vols. Statesman edition, Boston, 1900. Volumes V and VI especially useful for this study.

TANEY, ROGER B. Swisher, Carl Brent, *Roger B. Taney*. New York, 1935.

———. Tyler, Samuel, *Memoir of Roger B. Taney*. Baltimore, 1922.

TAYLOR, JOHN. Simms, Henry H., *Life of John Taylor: The Story of a Brilliant Leader in the Early Virginia State Rights School*. Richmond, 1932.

TOOMBS, ROBERT. Phillips, U. B., *The Life of Robert Toombs.* New York, 1913. For *Toombs Correspondence,* see Stephens.

TRUMBULL, LYMAN. *Trumbull Papers,* Library of Congress.

TYLER, JOHN. Chitwood, Oliver Perry, *John Tyler: Champion of the Old South.* New York and London, 1939.

——. Tyler, Lyon G., *Letters and Times of the Tylers.* 3 vols., Richmond, 1884.

WADE, BENJAMIN F. Riddle, A. G., *The Life of Benjamin F. Wade.* Cleveland, 1886.

WASHBURNE, ELIHU. *Washburne Papers,* Library of Congress.

WEBSTER, DANIEL. Adams, Samuel Hopkins, *The Godlike Daniel.* New York, 1930.

——. Fuess, Claude M., *Daniel Webster.* 2 vols., New York, 1930.

WELD, THEODORE DWIGHT. Barnes, Gilbert H., and Dumond, Dwight L., eds., *Letters of Theodore Dwight Weld, Angelina Grimke and Sarah Grimke, 1822–1844.* 2 vols., New York, 1934.

WILMOT, DAVID. Going, Charles B., *David Wilmot, Free-Soiler.* New York, 1924.

YANCEY, WILLIAM L. DuBose, John Witherspoon, *The Life and Times of William Lowndes Yancey.* Birmingham, 1892.

NEWSPAPERS AND PERIODICALS [1]

African Repository, 1826–1892. Of 67 volumes only four used. Washington.

American Farmer. Volumes II, VI, VIII and X used. Baltimore.

Anti-Slavery Magazine, 1835–1837. 2 vols., New York.

Anti-Slavery Record, 1835–1837. 3 vols., New York.

Augusta Constitutionalist, 1856, 1858–1860. Augusta, Ga.

Boston Atlas, 1854–1857. Boston.

1. This list does not include newspapers sometimes cited, but only as quoted from other papers.

Boston Courier, 1859. Boston.

Boston Post, 1852–1861. Boston.

Charleston Mercury, 1857–1860. Charleston, S. C.

Chicago Press, 1854–1856. Chicago.

Chicago Times, 1856, 1858, 1860. This paper went under the name *Times and Herald* in 1860. Chicago.

Cincinnati Enquirer, 1854, 1856–1861. Cincinnati.

De Bow, J. D. B., ed., *The Commercial Review of the South and West*. 31 vols., New Orleans, 1848–1853.

————, *The Industrial Resources, etc., of the Southern and Western States*. 3 vols., New Orleans, 1852–53.

Detroit Free Press, 1854–1856, 1860–1861. Detroit.

Huntsville Democrat, 1853. Huntsville, Ala.

Illinois State Journal, 1857, 1860–1861. Springfield, Illinois.

Lawrence Herald of Freedom, 1855–1857. Lawrence, Kansas. Incomplete.

Leavenworth Journal, 1857. Leavenworth, Kansas.

Leavenworth Weekly Herald, 1854–1857. Leavenworth, Kansas. Incomplete.

Lecompton National Democrat, 1857. Lecompton, Kansas. Incomplete.

Louisville Democrat, 1860–1861. Louisville.

Mississippian, 1858–1860. Jackson, Miss.

Missouri Republican, 1858. St. Louis.

Mobile Advertiser, 1851–1860. Mobile.

Mobile Register, 1857, 1859. Mobile.

National Enquirer, 1836–1838. 3 vols., Philadelphia.

New Orleans Picayune, 1852, 1853, 1856–1860. New Orleans.

New Orleans True Delta, 1859–1861. New Orleans.

New York Evening Post, 1859–1861. New York.

New York Herald, 1859–1861. New York.

New York Independent, 1854, 1856. New York. A religious Journal.

New York Times, 1854–1861. New York.

New York Tribune, 1852–1861. New York.

North Carolina Standard, 1855–1858, 1860. Raleigh.

Ohio State Journal, 1851, 1852, 1854, 1859–1861, Columbus, Ohio.

Philadelphia Press, 1859–1861. Philadelphia.

Richmond Enquirer, 1852–1861. Richmond, Va.

Savannah Republican, 1851–1860. Savannah.

Southern Advocate, 1851–1852. Huntsville, Alabama. Incomplete.

Southern Sovereign, 1855–1857. Atchison, Kansas. Incomplete.

True Democrat, 1852–1860. Little Rock, Arkansas.

OTHER SOURCES

Adams, Alice, *The Neglected Period of Anti-Slavery in America, 1808–1831.* Boston and London, 1908.

Adams, Henry, *Documents Relating to New England Federalism, 1800–1815.* Boston, 1877.

Adams, Nehemiah, *A Southside View of Slavery.* Boston, 1854.

Alexander, De Alva Stanwood, *A Political History of the State of New York.* 3 vols., New York, 1906. Volume II used.

Ambler, Charles H., *Sectionalism in Virginia from 1776 to 1861.* Chicago, 1910.

American Annual Cyclopoedia of the Year 1861. New York.

Annual Report of the American Anti-Slavery Society; with the Speeches Delivered at the Meeting. Third Report. New York, 1836.

Ballagh, J. C., *History of Slavery in Virginia.* Baltimore, 1902.

Bancroft, Frederic, *Slave-Trading in the Old South.* Baltimore, 1931.

Barker, Eugene C., "Notes on the Colonization of Texas," *Mississippi Valley Historical Review,* X, 141–152 (1923).

———, "The Influence of Slavery on the Colonization of Texas," *Mississippi Valley Historical Review,* XI, 3–36 (1925).

Barnes, Gilbert, H., *The Anti-Slavery Impulse*. New York and London, 1933.

Barrett, Walter, *The Old Merchants of New York City*. New York, 1863.

Bassett, J. S., *Anti-Slavery Leaders of North Carolina*. Baltimore, 1898.

———, *Slavery in the State of North Carolina*. Baltimore, 1899.

Bates, William W., *American Navigation. The Political History of its Rise and Ruin*. Boston and New York, 1902.

Bruce, Kathleen, *Virginia Iron Manufacture in the Slave Era*. New York and London, 1931.

Buck, Paul, "The Poor Whites in the Ante-Bellum South," *American Historical Review*, XXXI, 41–55 (1925).

Burgess, John W., *The Middle Period*. New York, 1897.

Cairnes, J. E., *The Slave Power. Its Character, Career and Probable Designs*. London and Cambridge, 1863.

Carey, Charles H., *History of Oregon*. Chicago and Portland, 1922.

Carpenter, Jesse T., *The South as a Conscious Minority*. New York, 1930.

Catterall, Helen T., ed., with additions by James J. Hayden, *Judicial Cases Concerning American Slavery and the Negro*. 5 vols., Washington, 1936.

Chadwick, F. E., *Causes of the Civil War*. New York and London, 1906.

Chittenden, L. E., *A Report of the Debates and Proceedings in the Secret Sessions of the Conference Convention Held at Washington in February, 1861*. New York, 1864.

Clark, Victor S., *History of Manufactures in the United States*. 2 vols., New York, 1929.

Cole, Arthur C., "Lincoln's Election an Immediate Menace to Slavery in the States?", *American Historical Review*. XXXVI, 740–767 (1931).

———, "The South and the Right of Secession in the Early Fifties," *Mississippi Valley Historical Review*, I, 377–399 (1914).

———, *The Irrepressible Conflict, 1850–1865*. New York, 1934.

———, *The Whig Party in the South*. Washington, 1913.

Corwin, Edward S., "The Dred Scott Decision in the Light of Contemporary Legal Doctrines," *American Historical Review*, XVII, 52–69 (1911).

Cotterill, R. S., "The Beginnings of Railroads in the Southwest," *Mississippi Valley Historical Review*, VIII, 318–326 (1922).

———, *The Old South*. Glendale, California. 1936.

Coulter, E. Merton, "A Century of a Georgia Plantation," *Mississippi Valley Historical Review*, XVI, 334–346 (1929).

———, "Effects of Secession upon the Commerce of the Mississippi Valley," III, 275–300 (1916).

———, *A Short History of Georgia*. Chapel Hill, 1933.

Craik, Elmer LeRoy, *Southern Interest in Territorial Kansas, 1854–1858*. Reprinted from collections of Kansas Historical Society, vol. XV (1916).

Craven, Avery, *Soil Exhaustion as a Factor in the History of Virginia and Maryland, 1606–1860*. Urbana 1926.

———, "Coming of the War Between the States: An Interpretation," *Journal of Southern History*, II, 303–322 (1936).

Crawford, Samuel W., *The Genesis of the Civil War: The Story of Sumter, 1860–1861*. New York, 1887.

Davidson, Philip, "Industrialism in the Ante-Bellum South," *South Atlantic Quarterly*, XXVII, 405–425 (1928).

Davis, Jefferson, *Rise and Fall of the Confederate Government*. 2 vols., New York, 1881.

Denman, Charles Phillips, *The Secession Movement in Alabama*. Montgomery, 1933.

Dodd, William E., "The Fight for the Northwest," *American Historical Review*, XVI, 774–778 (1911).

———, *The Cotton Kingdom*. New Haven, 1919.

DuBois, W. E. B., *The Suppression of the African Slave Trade*. New York and London, 1896.

258   BIBLIOGRAPHY

Dumond, Dwight L., *The Secession Movement, 1860–1861.*
New York, 1931.

Eaton, Clement, "The Freedom of the Press in the Upper
South," *Mississippi Valley Historical Review,* XVIII, 479–
499 (1931).

———, "A Dangerous Pamphlet in the Old South," *Journal
of Southern History,* II, 323–334 (1936).

Fite, Emerson D., *Presidential Campaign of 1860.* New
York, 1911.

Fitzhugh, George, *Sociology for the South, or the Failure of
Free Society.* Richmond, 1854.

Flanders, Ralph B., *Plantation Slavery in Georgia.* Chapel
Hill, 1933.

Fleming, Walter L., "The Buford Expedition to Kansas,"
American Historical Review, VI, 38–48 (1900).

Fox, Early Lee, *The American Colonization Society, 1817–
1840.* Baltimore, 1919.

Gaines, F. P., *The Southern Plantation: A Study in the Development and the Accuracy of a Tradition.* New York,
1924.

Garrison, George P., *Texas: A Contest of Civilizations.* Boston and New York, 1903.

———, *Westward Extension, 1841–1850.* New York and
London, 1906.

Gates, Seth M., "Southern Investments in Northern Lands
before the Civil War," *Journal of Southern History,* V,
155–185 (1939).

Gray, Lewis Cecil, *History of Agriculture in the Southern
United States to 1860.* 2 vols., Washington, 1933.

Green, Fletcher M., *Constitutional Development in the
South Atlantic States, 1776–1860.* Chapel Hill, 1930.

Hall, Captain Basil, *Travels in North America in the Years
1827 and 1828.* 3 vols. Edinburgh, 1829 and 1830.

Hamilton, J. G. de Roulhac, "Lincoln's Election an Immediate Menace to Slavery in the States?," *American Historical
Review,* XXXVII, 700–711 (1932).

Harlow, Ralph V., "The Rise and Fall of the Kansas Aid Movement," *American Historical Review*, XLI, 1–25 (1935).

Harper, Hammond, Simms and Dew, *Pro-Slavery Argument*. Charleston, 1853.

Harrington, Fred Harvey, "The First Northern Victory," *Journal of Southern History*, V, 186–205 (1939).

Harris, N. Dwight, *The History of Negro Servitude in Illinois and of the Slavery Agitation in that State, 1719–1864*. Chicago, 1904.

Hart, Albert Bushnell, *Slavery and Abolition, 1831–1841*. New York and London, 1906.

Hawk, Emory Q., *Economic History of the South*. New York, 1934.

Helper, Hinton R., *The Impending Crisis of the South: How to Meet It*. New York, 1857.

Hendrick, Burton J., *Statesmen of the Lost Cause*. New York, 1939.

Hesseltine, William B., *A History of the South, 1607–1936*, New York, 1936.

Hibbard, Benjamin, *A History of the Public Land Policies*. New York, 1924.

Hodder, Frank H., "Some Aspects of the English Bill for the Admission of Kansas," *American Historical Association Report*, 201–210 (1906).

——, "The Authorship of the Compromise of 1850," *Mississippi Valley Historical Review*, XXII, 525–536 (1936).

——, "The Railroad Background of the Kansas-Nebraska Act," *Mississippi Valley Historical Review*, XII, 3–22 (1925).

——, "Some Phases of the Dred Scott Case," *Mississippi Valley Historical Review*, XVI, 3–22 (1929).

Hosmer, William, *The Higher Law in its Relations to Civil Government: With Particular Reference to Slavery and the Fugitive Slave Law*. Auburn, 1852.

Hubbart, Henry Clyde, *The Older Middle West, 1840–1880*. New York and London, 1936.

Hundley, D. R., *Social Relations in our Southern States.* New York, 1860.

Hurd, John C., *The Law of Freedom and Bondage in the United States.* 2 vols., New York, 1862.

Jenkins, William S., *Pro-Slavery Thought in the Old South.* Chapel Hill, 1935.

Johnson, Emory R., "River and Harbor Bills," *Annals of the American Academy of Political and Social Science.* Volume II, Philadelphia, 1892.

Johnson, Guion G., *Ante-Bellum North Carolina, A Social History.* Chapel Hill, 1937.

Johnson, Thomas C., *Scientific Interests in the Old South.* New York and London, 1936.

Kansas. *Transactions of the Kansas State Historical Society, Embracing the Third and Fourth Biennial Reports, 1883–1885.* Volume III, Topeka, 1886.

Knight, Edgar W., *The Influence of Reconstruction on Education in the South.* New York, 1913.

——, *Public Education in the South.* Boston and New York, 1922.

Lippincott, Isaac, *Internal Trade in the United States, 1700–1860.* St. Louis, 1916.

Lloyd, Arthur Y., *The Slavery Controversy, 1831–1860.* Chapel Hill, 1939.

Lundy, Benjamin, *The War in Texas.* Philadelphia, 1836.

Malin, James C., "The Pro-Slavery Background of the Kansas Struggle," *Mississippi Valley Historical Review,* X, 285–305 (1923).

Martin, Asa Earl, *The Anti-Slavery Movement in Kentucky prior to 1850.* Louisville, 1918.

Martineau, Harriet, *Society in America.* 2 vols., New York and London, 1937.

McCormac, E. I., "Justice Campbell and the Dred Scott Decision," *Mississippi Valley Historical Review,* XIX, 565–571 (1932).

McKee, Marguerite M., *The Ship Subsidy Question in United States Politics.* Northampton, Mass., 1922.

McKee, Thomas H., *The National Convention and Plat-forms of All Political Parties, 1789 to 1905*. Baltimore, 1906.

McTyeire, Holland N., *A History of Methodism*. Nashville, 1884 and 1924.

Mellon, Matthew T., *Early American Views on Negro Slavery*. Boston, 1934.

Mitchell, Broadus, *The Industrial Revolution in the South*. Baltimore, 1930.

Moore, Albert B., *History of Alabama and her People*. 3 vols., Chicago and New York. Volume I useful for this study.

Morison, Samuel Eliot, *The Maritime History of Massachusetts, 1783–1860*. Boston and New York, 1921.

Munford, B. B., *Virginia's Attitude Toward Slavery and Secession*. Richmond, 1909.

Murray, Hon. Amelia M., *Letters from the United States, Cuba and Canada*, 2 vols., London, 1856.

Nevins, Allan, ed., *The Diary of Philip Hone, 1828–1851*. 2 vols., New York, 1927.

——, *American Social History as Recorded by British Travellers*. New York, 1923.

Newman, Albert H., *History of the Baptist Churches in the United States*. New York, 1915.

Olmsted, Frederick L., *A Journey in the Back Country in the Winter of 1853–54*. 2 vols., New York and London, 1860 and 1907.

——, *A Journey in the Seaboard Slave States*. 2 vols., New York and London, 1856 and 1907.

Owsley, Frank L., "Origins of the American Civil War," *Southern Review*, V, 609–626 (1940).

——, and Harriet C., "The Economic Basis of Society in the Late Ante-Bellum South," *Journal of Southern History*, VI, 24–45 (1940).

Patton, James W., *Unionism and Reconstruction in Tennessee, 1860–1869*. Chapel Hill, 1934.

Paxson, Frederic L., "The Railroads of the Old Northwest,"

Transactions of the Wisconsin Academy of Sciences, Arts and Letters. Volume XVII, Madison, 1914.

Phillips, U. B., *American Negro Slavery.* New York, 1918.

———, *Life and Labor in the Old South.* Boston, 1930.

———, *Georgia and State Rights.* Washington, 1902.

———, "The Central Theme of Southern History," *American Historical Review,* XXXIV, 30–43 (1929).

Purtee, Edward O., *The Underground Railroad from Southwestern Ohio to Lake Erie.* Unpublished doctoral dissertation, Columbus, Ohio, 1932.

Quillin, Frank U., *The Color Line in Ohio.* Ann Arbor, 1913.

Rainwater, Percy Lee, *Mississippi Storm Center of Secession, 1856–1861.* Baton Rouge, 1938.

Ramsdell, Charles W., "The Natural Limits of Slavery Expansion," *Mississippi Valley Historical Review,* XVI, 151–171 (1929).

———, "The Changing Interpretation of the Civil War," *Journal of Southern History,* III, 1–25 (1937).

———, "Lincoln and Fort Sumter," *Journal of Southern History,* III, 259–288 (1937).

Randall, J. G., "The Civil War Restudied," *Journal of Southern History,* VI, 439–457 (1940).

———, *The Civil War and Reconstruction.* Boston and New York, 1937.

Ray, P. Orman, *The Repeal of the Missouri Compromise.* Cleveland, 1909.

Rhodes, James Ford, *History of the United States from the Compromise of 1850.* New York, 1893–1907. Of the total of 9 volumes, only the early ones were useful in connection with this study.

Robert, Joseph C., *The Tobacco Kingdom: Plantation, Market, and Factory in Virginia and North Carolina, 1800–1860.* Durham, 1938.

———, *The Road from Monticello: A Study of the Virginia Slavery Debate of 1832.* Durham, 1941.

Russel, Robert R., "The Pacific Railway Issue in Politics

Prior to the Civil War," *Mississippi Valley Historical Review*, XII, 187–201 (1925).

———, *Economic Aspects of Southern Sectionalism, 1840–1861*. Urbana, 1924.

Russell, John H., *The Free Negro in Virginia, 1619–1865*. Baltimore, 1913.

Sanborn, John B., *Congressional Grants of Land in Aid of Railways*, University of Wisconsin Bulletin, Vol. II, Madison, 1899.

Savage, William S., *The Controversy over the Distribution of Abolition Literature, 1830–1860*. Washington, 1938.

Scroggs, William O., "William Walker's Designs on Cuba," *Mississippi Valley Historical Review*, I, 198–211 (1914).

Scrugham, Mary, *The Peaceable Americans of 1860–1861*. New York, 1921.

Sellers, James L., "Republicanism and State Rights in Wisconsin," *Mississippi Valley Historical Review*, XVII, 213–229 (1930).

Shanks, Henry T., *The Secession Movement in Virginia, 1847–1861*. Richmond, 1934.

Shryock, Richard H., *Georgia and the Union in 1850*. Durham, 1926.

Siebert, Wilbur H., *The Underground Railroad from Slavery to Freedom*. New York, 1898.

Sitterson, Joseph Carlyle, *The Secession Movement in North Carolina*. Chapel Hill, 1939.

Smedes, Susan D., *A Southern Planter*. A life of Thomas S. Dabney, who was a social, not a political, product of the old South. New York, 1900.

Smith, J. Russell, *The Ocean Carrier*. New York and London, 1908.

Smith, Theodore C., *Parties and Slavery, 1850–1859*. New York and London, 1906.

Spears, John R., *The Story of the American Merchant Marine*. New York, 1919.

Spring, Leverett W., *Kansas: The Prelude to the War for the Union*. Boston, 1885.

264 BIBLIOGRAPHY

Stanwood, Edward, *History of the Presidency from 1788 to 1897.* Revised by Charles G. Bolton. Boston and New York. 1924.

——, *American Tariff Controversies in the Nineteenth Century.* 2 vols., New York, 1903.

Stenberg, Richard R., "The Motivation of the Wilmot Proviso," *Mississippi Valley Historical Review,* XVIII, 535–541 (1931).

Stephens, Alexander H., *A Constitutional View of the Late War between the States.* Philadelphia and Chicago, 1870.

Stephenson, George M., *The Political History of the Public Lands from 1840 to 1862.* Boston, 1917.

——, *A History of American Immigration.* New York, 1926.

Stephenson, Wendell H., *Isaac Franklin: Slave Trader and Planter of the Old South.* University, Louisiana, 1938.

Stirling, James, *Letters from the Slave States.* London, 1857.

Sydnor, Charles S., "The Free Negro in Mississippi before the Civil War," *American Historical Review,* XXXII, 769–788 (1927).

——, *Slavery in Mississippi.* New York and London, 1933.

Thomas, David Y., *Arkansas in War and Reconstruction, 1861–1874.* Little Rock, 1926.

Thompson, Slason, *A Short History of American Railways.* New York and London, 1925.

Tilley, John Shipley, *Lincoln Takes Command.* Chapel Hill, 1941.

Turner, Edward R., *The Negro in Pennsylvania, 1639–1861.* Washington, 1911.

United States, *Congressional Globe, 1847–1861.*

——, *Eighth Census, 1860.*

——, *House and Senate Documents.* 34th Congress, 1st Sess., House Report No. 200, *Howard Report.* 36th Congress, 1st Sess., House Report No. 648, *Covade Report.* 36th Congress, 2nd Sess., Senate Report No. 288. *Journal of Committee of Thirteen.*

——, *Reports of Cases Argued and Adjudged in the*

Supreme Court of the United States. Report No. 60, vol. XIX, Washington, 1857.

Van Deusen, John G., *Economic Bases of Disunion in South Carolina.* New York, 1928.

Weld, Theodore, *American Slavery as it is: Testimony of a Thousand Witnesses.* New York, 1839.

Wender, Herbert, *Southern Commercial Conventions, 1837–1859.* Baltimore, 1930.

Whitfield, Theodore M., *Slavery Agitation in Virginia, 1829–1832.* Baltimore, 1930.

Williams, George W., *History of the Negro Race in America from 1619 to 1880.* 2 vols., New York and London, 1885.

Wish, Harvey, "The Slave Insurrection Panic of 1856," *Journal of Southern History,* V, 206–222 (1939).

Woodson, Carter G., *The Negro in Our History.* Washington, 1932.

Index

Dabney, Thomas S., as intellectual product, 28

Davis, Jefferson, on fugitive slave law of 1850, 54; opposes Compromise of 1850, 56; interviews Pierce on Kansas-Nebraska Act, 60; railroad aims of, 64; resolutions of and debates with Douglas on slavery in the territories, 115–117; on political character of anti-slavery crusade, 141; on Republican policy toward slavery in the states, 149; on possible extension of slavery into free states, 153n; opposes shipping subsidies, 172n; attitude of toward Douglas Democrats in 1860, 204; policy during campaign of 1860, 207; chosen President of Confederacy, 224; on compromise in 1860, 225, 226; mentioned, 179

Dayton, William L., Republican candidate for Vice-President in 1856, 88

De Bow, J. D. B., on non-slaveholding whites and slavery, 19; advocates use of slave labor in manufacturing, 23, 24; as famous editor, 29

Democratic Party, in election of 1848, 49; in election of 1852, 56–57; effect upon of Kansas-Nebraska Act, 86; in election of 1856, 88–92; opposes internal improvements in 1856, 179; split of in 1860, 203–206; in campaign and election of 1860, 206–211; victories of in 1861, 241

Dennison, William, Governor, refuses to surrender participants in John Brown Raid, 199

Detroit Free Press, on Sumner-Brooks affair, 82; on Jefferson's slavery policy, 126; on Negro

policy, 134; favors internal improvements, 180; on free homesteads, 180n; on acquisition of Cuba, 191; on re-opening of foreign slave trade, 193; on presidential contest of 1860, 209; on compromise, 1860–61, 229, 238n; on Fort Sumter policy, 240; alleges Republican responsibility for war, 243, 243n, 244n

Dew, Thomas R., argument mentioned, 4; defends slavery, 16–18

Dix, John A., on race question in territories, 135

Dixon, Archibald, for repeal of Missouri Compromise, 59; on slave as property, 101

Donelson, Andrew J., candidate for Vice-President in 1856, 88

Doolittle, James, defends state rights in Wisconsin, 122; lauds Jefferson's views, 126; on Negro problem, 132, 133; claims South favors slavery for both races, 163, 164; mentioned, 155n

Douglas, Stephen A., favors compromise of 1850, 50, 54; champions Kansas-Nebraska Act, 58–60, 61 *et seq.;* sponsors measure to settle Kansas question, 84, 85, 86; breaks with Buchanan over Lecompton proceedings, 98; debates with Lincoln concerning Supreme Court, 111–114; Freeport Doctrine of, 113, 114; debates with Davis status of slavery in territories, 115, 116, 117; condemns "higher law" doctrine, 119; debates race question with Lincoln, 131, 132; chides Republicans on Negro exclusion in Kansas, 136; favors admission of Oregon, 137;

secures land grants for railroads, 181; Republican support of for President, 200, 201; nominated for President in 1860, 203, 204, 205; policy in campaign of 1860, 207, 208, 209, 210, 211; for compromise in 1860, 225, 226; supports Lincoln's policy after the firing on Fort Sumter, 243; mentioned, 56, 81, 151, 202

Dred Scott case, background of and Supreme Court decision in, 102–109; reactions to in the press, Lincoln-Douglas and Davis-Douglas debates, 109–118; mentioned, 149, 150, 151n

"Dutch plank," explained, 202n

Education and culture, character of in South, 25, 26, 27–29; South compared with other sections in respect to, 29–30; Northern tendencies in respect to stimulate abolition movement, 37, 38; character of in South criticized by Northerners, 92, 163, 165, 166; character of in North criticized by Southerners, 160, 161

Elections, presidential, of 1848, 48–49; of 1852, 56–57; of 1856, 88–92; of 1860, 201–211

Emerson, John, in Dred Scott case, 102

Emerson, Ralph Waldo, as abolitionist, 38

Emigrant aid societies, purposes of and agitation over, 72–77

English, William H., Kansas proposal, 98–99

Evans, George H., favors free homesteads, 182

Everett, Edward, candidate for Vice-President in 1860, 206

Ewing, Thomas, at Washington Peace Convention, 233

Fessenden, William P., opposes admission of Oregon, 136, 137; favors fishing bounties, 173

Fillmore, Millard, attempts to enforce fugitive slave law of 1850, 54; candidate for Whig nomination for President in 1852, 56, 57; as know-nothing candidate for President in 1856, 89, 90, 91, 92

Finney, Charles, as abolitionist, 38

Fitzhugh, George, defends slavery, 16–18; radical nature of on slavery question, 153; books published by, 155

Fitzpatrick, Benjamin, declines nomination for Vice-President in 1860, 204

Flenniken, Robert, Free-soil candidate in Kansas for delegate to Congress, 74

Foote, Henry S., favors Compromise of 1850, 56

Forney, John W., assails Buchanan's law tariff stand, 177; in campaign of 1860, 209

Forsyth, John, favors foreign slave trade, 194

Fort Pickens, reason for holding, 239

Fort Sumter, attitude of Buchanan toward, 232, 233; controversy over Lincoln's policy toward, 239–243; effect of Lincoln's policy toward on border states, 244, 246

Free Democratic Party, in election of 1852, 57

Free homesteads, economic and sectional aspects of controversy over, 181–184; failure to pass measure for in Congress, 182; intertwined with Cuban question, 191; in campaign of 1860, 202, 207, 208, 210

INDEX

Hammond, James, defends slavery, 16–18; criticizes Northern social system, 159; mentioned, 163

Harper, William, argument mentioned, 4; defends slavery, 16–18, 19

Harpers Ferry Raid, 197 et seq.

Hayne, Paul H., mentioned, 29

Helper, Hinton R., *Impending Crisis* of and controversy over, 155–158; mentioned, 199, 208

Henderson, John, mentioned, 46

Herbert, Philip, controversy over killing by, 164, 165

Higginson, Thomas, at Worcester Convention, 196; helps plot John Brown Raid, 197

"Higher law" doctrine, controversy over, 118–119

Hill, Benjamin H., opposes secession, 222

Hone, Philip, on merchants, 170

Hosmer, William, publishes book on *Higher Law,* 119

Houston, Sam, opposes Kansas-Nebraska Act, 67; opposes repeal of fishing bounties, 174n; opposes secession, 223

Hundley, David R., on labor in the South, 4, 5

Hunter, Robert M. T., on Compromise of 1850, 56; interviews Pierce on Kansas-Nebraska Act, 60; believes slavery extension impossible, 68; on meaning of Kansas-Nebraska Act, 70; on "higher law," 119; sponsors tariff of 1857, 175; proposes public land measure, 182; attitude of toward Douglas Democrats in 1860, 204; on hatred of North toward South, 213; favors compromise in 1860, 226

Illinois, character of farms in, 5, 6; hostility in to Negro, 128, 129

Immigration, hostility of Know-Nothings to, 89; increasing tide of, 181, 182; effect of upon sectional issues, 181, 182, 183; Republican policy toward in 1860, 201n, 202

Indiana, character of farms in, 5, 6; hostility in to Negro, 129

Internal improvements, party platform planks concerning, 179; sectional attitudes toward, 179–181; endorsed by Republicans in 1860, 202

Iowa, hostility in to Negro, 129

Iverson, Alfred, claims Republican party abolitionized, 148

Jackson, Andrew, on abolition literature, 42

Jefferson, Thomas, on race question, 18, 19; slavery views of, 31, 32, 125, 126, 127

Johnson, Andrew, favors free homesteads, 182

Johnson, Herschel V., candidate for Vice-President in 1860, 204; opposes secession, 222

Johnson, Reverdy, at Washington Peace Convention, 233

Jones, Sam, participates in Kansas quarrels, 80

Julian, George W., candidate for Vice-President in 1852, 57

Kansas, activities of emigrant aid societies and Missourians in, 72–77; political developments in, 77–79; physical violence in, 79–80; affairs of in Congress, 80–86; as factor in election of 1856, 88, 91; attitude of Buchanan toward, 92–99; admitted to Union in 1861, 99; free Negroes excluded by free-soil element in, 136; small number of slaves in, 146, 147

Preston, William B., interviews Lincoln on Fort Sumter policy, 246

Prigg vs. Pennsylvania, case of, 50

Pryor, Roger, quarrel of with Lovejoy, 166

Pugh, George, claims Davis accepted Freeport Doctrine, 115, 115n; compares free Negro with slave, 134

Quitman, John A., opposes Compromise of 1850, 56

Railroads, growth of in South, 22, 23; aims for transcontinental as factor in producing Kansas-Nebraska Act, 63–65; land grants to, 181; implications of growth of Northeast to Northwest, 182, 187; both major parties favor transcontinental in 1860, 202, 205

Randolph, George, interviews Lincoln concerning Fort Sumter policy, 246

Reeder, Andrew H., as Governor of Kansas Territory, 74, 77, 78; support of by free-soilers, 78, 79; elected U. S. Senator under Topeka Constitution, 83

Republican Party, origins of, 86; in election of 1856, 88, 90–92; controversy over abolition sentiments of, 148, 149, 195, 215, 215n; endorses internal improvements in 1856 and 1860, 179; national convention of in 1860, 201–203; in campaign and election of 1860, 206–211; attitude of toward compromise in 1860–61, 227, 228, 229, 239, 240; defeats of in 1861, 241

Rhett, Robert B., opposes fugitive slave law of 1850, 54;

favors secession of South Carolina in 1850, 55; attitude of toward split in Democratic party, 205; denounced for secession sentiments, 223

Richardson, William A., candidate for Speaker in 1855–56, 87

Richmond Enquirer, on Kansas-Nebraska Act, 68; on Lecompton Constitution, 96n; lauds Dred Scott decision, 111; on status of slavery in territories, 117, 118; attacks Wisconsin's stand against the Supreme Court, 123; on spread of slavery, 153n; on Helper's Impending Crisis, 158; assails Northern social system, 160; opposes shipping bounties, 172n; opposes internal improvements, 180; favors Southern commercial conventions, 186n; on acquisition of Cuba, 192; on John Brown Raid, 199; on Lincoln's inaugural address, 237; on secession, 246, 246n

Ritchie, Thomas, on Compromise of 1850, 56

Rives, William C., at Washington Peace Convention, 233

Robertson, George, mentioned, 216

Robinson, Charles, free-soil leader in Kansas, 78, 80

Rockwell, Julius, on race question, 135

Ruffin, Edmund, as agricultural reformer, 21; as omnivorous reader, 28; as Southern ultra, 246

Sanborn, F. B., conspirator in John Brown Raid, 197

Sandidge, John, on admission of Oregon, 137

Sanford, J. F., in Dred Scott case, 103

Savannah Republican, on South Carolina's policy in 1850, 55; on Kansas-Nebraska Act, 67; condemns both Sumner and Brooks, 83; on Speakership contest of 1855, 87n; favors internal improvements, 180; opposes Southern commercial conventions, 185n; on re-opening of foreign slave trade, 195; on presidential contest of 1860, 208; on Northern hatred of South, 213n

Schurz, Carl, defends state rights in Wisconsin, 123; in campaign of 1860, 207

Scott, Winfield, candidate for President in 1852, 56, 57

Secession, main reasons for, 212–216, 218–219; in South Carolina, 217–219; in Mississippi, 219, 220; in Florida, 220; in Alabama, 220, 221; in Georgia, 220, 221, 222; in Louisiana, 220, 223; in Texas, 220, 223; attitude of Southern Whigs toward, 219n; possible effects of failure of compromise upon, 221, 229, 230, 244, 247; attitude of Buchanan toward, 231; attitude of portion of Northern press toward, 231n; attitude of Lincoln toward, 235, 236; attitude of North Carolina toward, 244, 245, 247; attitude of Arkansas toward, 244, 245, 247; attitude of Tennessee toward, 244, 245, 246, 247; attitude of Virginia toward, 244, 246, 247, 248

Seward, William H., opposes Compromise of 1850, 53; denounces Kansas-Nebraska Act, 62; claims Dred Scott decision the result of conspiracy, 111, 114; advocates "higher law" doctrine, 53, 118; on Negro as inconsequential factor in sectional controversy, 133; on Negro exclusion in Kansas, 136; radical utterances of concerning slavery, 151, 152; on political power of slaveholders, 162; favors shipping subsidies, 172n; favors fishing bounties, 173; on Cuban question, 191; blamed for John Brown Raid, 197, 199; criticism of as radical, 200; failure of to secure presidential nomination in 1860, 201, 202; in campaign of 1860, 206; utterances of as factor in secession, 215; opposes Crittenden Compromise in 1860, but proposes amendment to Constitution touching slavery, 225, 226; conciliation policy of, 240; assures Southerners of evacuation of Fort Sumter, 240, 246; mentioned, 54, 57, 88, 144, 150

Shannon, Wilson, Governor of Kansas Territory, 92

Sheahan, James W., on Kansas-Nebraska Act, 64–65

Sherman, John, in Speakership contest of 1859, 157

Sherman, William T., on slavery and political character of controversy concerning, 145; criticizes brother for endorsing *Impending Crisis,* 157

Shields, James, on slave as property, 100

Shipping bounties, attitude of Government toward, 170–171; attitude of sections toward, 171–172

Simms, William Gilmore, defends slavery, 16–18; as writer, 29

Singleton, O. R., quarrel with Lovejoy, 167